THE WHICH? GUIDE TO DIVORCE

THE WHICH? GUIDE TO DIVORCE

HELEN GARLICK

Consumers' Association

Which? Books are commissioned and researched by
The Association for Consumer Research
and published by Consumers' Association,
2 Marylebone Road, London NW1 4DF
Distributed by The Penguin Group:
Penguin Books Ltd, 27 Wrights Lane, London W8 5TZ

Based on *Divorce: Legal Procedures and Financial Facts* (Consumers'
Association); text completely revised and new material written
by Helen Garlick

Index by Marie Lorimer
Typographic design by Paul Saunders
Cover illustrations by courtesy of Bubbles Photo Library/Loisjoy
Thurston; Michelle Smith and The Image Bank/Patrick Doherty

First edition August 1992
Second edition August 1994
Copyright © 1992 and 1994 Consumers' Association Limited

British Library Cataloguing-in-Publication Data
A catalogue record for this book is available from the British Library

ISBN 0 85202 522 X

Typeset by Paston Press Ltd, Loddon, Norfolk
Printed and bound by Firmin-Didot (France) Groupe Herissey
N° d'impression: 27673

CONTENTS

About the author

Helen Garlick was the matrimonial partner of a firm of solicitors in Camden Town, London until 1988 when she chose to devote more time to writing and training. She is the author of several books, writes regularly in the press and appears on television and radio talking about legal/family issues. She is a lecturer at the Oxford Institute of Legal Practice. Helen is married and has two children.

Acknowledgements

The Which? Guide to Divorce has been a team effort: my warmest thanks are due to all those who contributed towards it. I am grateful in particular to Imogen Clout, the team at the National Council for One Parent Families, Hilary Halpin (Director of the Divorce Conciliation and Advisory Service) and Zelda West-Meads of RELATE. David Nichols wrote the section on Scotland and Mary Connolly advised on the section on Northern Ireland.

Helen Garlick

INTRODUCTION

More than one in three marriages end in divorce. Experts argue over what factors are most likely to lead to marriage breakdown: second or subsequent marriages, marriages begun when one or both partners were very young, marriages under stress because of money worries and marriages between those in very stressful jobs have all been identified as vulnerable.

But the one factor that all separating or divorcing couples have in common is that where there was previously one household to maintain there will now be two. *The Which? Guide to Divorce* focuses on helping couples to minimise the costs of the divorce process itself in order to free up as much money as possible for the family. Cut out the bickering and the vindictiveness, and don't use your solicitor as an expensive emotional prop, are the key messages here.

The implementation of the Child Support Act 1991, and the Child Support Agency it established in 1993, have fundamentally altered the way in which people experience the legal and practical processes of divorce. The Agency was set up with the laudable aim of improving the system for payment of child maintenance, a system which was no longer doing its job. Sadly, the result has been a lost opportunity. The switch to a formula-based child maintenance system could have been kept simple – say, by opting for a percentage of income to be paid to the children. But its byzantine complexity not only makes it very difficult to grasp but extremely unwieldy to administer and the backlog of work now faced by the Agency threatens to overwhelm it. The delays in processing claims mean that those who most need financial support – children being looked after by lone parents – are losing out.

The Agency is facing a barrage of criticism, much of it justified, some of it not. It set out to ensure that absent parents should pay a fair and decent level of maintenance for their children, but this basic principle is being overlooked in the clamour. There is still time for an overhaul to bring the system into line with the original vision. Tinkering with a flawed mechanism is not the answer.

Other flaws in the system also await reform. Divorce continues to be fault-based, which means that facts have to be engineered to prove that one spouse caused the breakdown of the marriage, unless both partners are prepared to wait for at least two years before getting divorced.

Recommendations for a change to a one-year wait, to allow both spouses time to reflect on whether they really want a divorce as well as to make considered plans for the future, may well have been sidelined. It is to be hoped that the same does not happen to recent sensible proposals for dividing up pensions on divorce.

On a more optimistic note, the changes brought into the system by the Children Act 1989 have considerably improved it. Parents are now encouraged to make their own arrangements for their children following divorce or separation, rather than looking to the court to do this for them. Where conflicts do arise, simpler and more specific court orders can be sought in order to resolve them; moreover, couples do not have to wait until a divorce comes through before applying for one. Grandparents (and other family members) can make court applications to see their grandchildren, and, most importantly, children's voices are better heard within the system, as it ensures that their wishes and feelings are taken into account along with a range of other factors affecting their welfare.

Divorce is never easy, but this Guide endeavours to help you through the maze. Good luck.

CHAPTER 1

THE COSTS OF DIVORCE

> **LEGAL HEALTH WARNING**
> This could be the most important chapter of the book for you:
> please do not be tempted to skip it

IT IS all too easy to 'forget' about the question of costs until your divorce and financial problems are resolved, but then the total sum of costs that has built up can come as an unexpected shock and can severely limit your and your spouse's ability to adapt to your future lives apart.

The issue of costs can create severe problems in divorce where one or other party is determined to mount an expensive legal campaign against the other. Whenever there is a legally fought dispute over the children, or over spousal maintenance or property, both sides will generally have to instruct solicitors (and perhaps barristers too). There will therefore be two bills to pay at the end of the case. It is sometimes possible to get an order for costs made against a spouse who 'loses' a case, but the courts are usually reluctant to do so. In any event, whoever 'wins' or 'loses' and whoever gets an order for costs against whom, the two sets of legal fees will still have to be paid out of the same source – the couple's joint assets. The more the lawyers get, the less the family will be able to share between them. This is especially true in a recession, when the assets and the individuals' earning power may be considerably restricted.

This does not mean that it is necessary to cave in to a spouse who is demanding too much. A good solicitor (see Chapter 3 on where to get legal help) will be able to negotiate strongly on your behalf and can in most cases work out a reasonable settlement with your spouse's solicitor without the added expenses of a full-blown court battle. Using the Child Support Agency to work out the amount of child support and collect it from your ex-partner will cut down on legal costs, although fees are charged by the Agency (see the end of this chapter and Chapter 5). You may be able to work out agreements yourself together with your spouse in order to cut down even further on legal costs (see the next chapter on Financial planning for divorce). But gaining a good understanding of the system of legal costs is also crucial.

In the following pages you will find an explanation of how legal aid works, how costs in the proceedings are worked out and how solicitors charge. We also explode the myth about legal aid meaning *free* legal help: this is only rarely the case.

Legal advice and assistance and legal aid

At your first interview with the solicitor, it is worth asking if you qualify for legal advice and assistance and/or for legal aid. The solicitor should tell you about this even if you do not ask. Whether you are eligible will depend on your circumstances.

What is commonly referred to as 'legal aid' in matrimonial cases is two different things. The first is 'legal advice and assistance' where the solicitor can advise you and deal with correspondence for you but is unable to appear in court on your behalf. This is commonly known as the 'green form scheme' because of the colour of the application form. 'Assistance by way of representation' (ABWOR) is effectively an extension of the green form scheme to cover representation in, for example, the magistrates' court, on an application for spousal maintenance or residence/contact outside divorce proceedings.

Secondly, there is full-blown civil legal aid, for which you can apply to cover representation in ancillary matters – for example, disputes about the children or financial proceedings.

Whether you qualify for any form of legal advice and assistance depends on your financial circumstances and, in the case of full-blown legal aid, on the merits of your case. The limits for financial eligibility for legal advice and legal aid are reviewed by the government each year.

The Legal Aid Act 1988 made some amendments to the way the legal aid system is administered. The Act provided for the setting up of a new Legal Aid Board, which took over the old Legal Aid administrative structure in April 1989. The Legal Aid Board is separate from the Law Society, which until 1989 used to administer legal aid.

You may find that not all solicitors are willing to take on legal aid cases because their remuneration for these is lower than for private work. Your local Citizens Advice Bureau should be able to give you names of solicitors willing to take on legal aid work.

The green form scheme

The basic idea behind the legal advice and assistance scheme, known as the green form scheme, is to give the opportunity of obtaining legal advice to people who would not otherwise be able to afford it.

The scheme entitles you to up to three hours of the solicitor's time in a matrimonial case (but only if a petition is drafted), and two hours in all other cases. The solicitor's hourly rate for preparing a case under the green form scheme is fixed at £43.25 per hour (in London £45.75). (This hourly rate, reviewed annually by the government, has been frozen for the last couple of years.) If your income (less certain allowances) is under £70 per week you should qualify for getting green form advice as long as your capital is under certain limits. If you receive income support, family credit or disability working allowance you will automatically qualify on income but you also have to come within capital limits.

Work the solicitor may do under the green form advice and assistance scheme relevant to money and divorce includes:

- general advice on whether there are grounds for divorce or judicial separation
- advice on questions of domicile; proving the validity of a foreign marriage
- advice on the procedure for getting a divorce

- drafting the petition and documents to accompany it
- advising on defending a divorce and the implication of doing so
- help with an application for full legal aid
- advice on obtaining an injunction
- registration of a charge on the matrimonial home
- advice about who will look after the children, about 'parental responsibility', 'residence and contact orders', and other orders under the Children Act 1989
- advice about spousal maintenance, and arrangements concerning the family home
- correspondence or discussions with solicitors acting for the other spouse to try to negotiate a settlement.

However, as the Child Support Agency now normally deals with child maintenance, green form advice is not usually available for child support unless the problem concerns a question of law.

The green form scheme is appropriate for simple undefended divorces or for negotiating straightforward settlements. When the initial time limit is used up, the solicitor can apply to the Legal Aid Board to exceed the limit (although you will have to wait for the extension to be granted before actually being able to get further legal advice). One request for an extension is usually granted without too much difficulty if the solicitor can show that the extra work proposed is merited.

You are entitled to only one green form covering all matters 'arising from proceedings or judicial separation' – the divorce itself, spousal maintenance, issues concerning children and injunctions. This means that you are not entitled to two hours of the solicitor's time for each separate matter connected with divorce. If, however, there are other matters arising from the matrimonial situation but not part of the divorce, these can form the subject of a separate green form application and entitle you to up to a further two hours' time.

A separate green form could cover, for instance, correspondence with a building society, hire purchase and finance companies and public utilities over problems about payments of bills, instalments or other debts following the breakdown of a marriage.

Eligibility for the green form scheme

The solicitor carries out the assessment of your financial means while you are there, basing the calculations on the figures provided by you: your savings and other capital, your gross weekly income, your own outgoings and those of any dependants. The solicitor enters these details on the green form and can tell you straightaway, by use of a 'key card', whether you are eligible for the legal advice scheme. The figures given here came into effect in April 1994: the amounts are uprated annually, so check with your solicitor (or the Legal Aid Board's leaflet *Legal Aid: A Practical Guide to Legal Aid* available free from the Legal Aid Board, 85 Grays Inn Road, London WC1X 8AA) (tel: 071–813 1000).

Capital

Your disposable capital (such as shares, savings and so on) must not exceed £1,000 (or £1,335 if you have one dependant, £1,535 if two dependants, for example). The value of the family home and its contents, personal clothing and tools of a trade are not counted as part of disposable capital.

Anyone receiving income support, family credit or disability working allowance automatically qualifies on income but must also come within the capital limits. (Note that the capital limits are £2,000 higher for ABWOR – see earlier in the chapter – so that an applicant with no dependants can have £3,000 savings, for example.)

Income

The disposable income limit is £70 in the last seven days. Disposable income is your weekly income after deduction of tax and National Insurance contributions and after deducting an allowance for any dependants, namely:

£26.00 for a spouse or partner
£15.65 for a child under 11
£23.00 for a child aged 11 to 15
£27.50 for a child aged 16 or 17
£36.15 for a dependant aged 18 or over (for example, a disabled son or daughter).

The income of the spouse or partner is not included where he or she has a contrary interest in the case at issue, as would be the case when a divorce was contemplated. This means that the non-working wife of even a very wealthy man may be eligible for the green form scheme.

Before April 1993, those on low incomes which were slightly above the basic limit were eligible for green form advice on the basis that they paid a contribution assessed on the amount of their income. But in April 1993 the numbers of those eligible for legal aid were dramatically cut. One of the cuts meant that green forms with a contribution were abolished, so nowadays green form advice is available only to those on low incomes. If your income is higher than the basic limits, you will have to pay your solicitor's fees privately (some solicitors may be willing to be paid in monthly instalments).

If you do qualify for advice under the green form scheme it is well worth seeking it from a solicitor who undertakes legal aid work. Not only will your legal advice be free but you will also be exempt from court fees. (The same applies to those on legal aid.)

If you are eligible, you have to sign the green form confirming that the information given is correct and that you accept the terms.

The solicitor has a charge (similar to the 'statutory charge' in civil legal aid cases – see page 20) on money or property 'recovered or preserved' subject to certain exemptions (including maintenance, the client's main or only home and £2,500 recovered in matrimonial cases). This means that if your costs are not recovered from the other side they must be met by you out of unexempted money or property recovered or preserved. In certain limited circumstances, the solicitor's charge may be waived but this requires the authority of the Legal Aid Board.

The legal aid scheme

Where there is likely to be any contest, or a hearing in court, the green form scheme will not be adequate but you can apply for a legal aid certificate. Civil legal aid is available for applications in a divorce court relating to any spousal maintenance orders, property orders, lump sum orders and arrangements for children. (An application is a request to a court for that court to make a particular order.)

Legal aid is not generally available for an undefended divorce; nor is it available for preliminary appeals against Child Support Agency assessments (see further Chapter 5).

If a legal aid certificate is issued to you, this means that the services of a solicitor (and of a barrister, where appropriate) will be paid for initially by the legal aid fund. You may have to pay a contribution (usually by instalments), but otherwise no initial payment will be required. Later, however, if assets are recovered or preserved for you within the legal proceedings and the 'statutory charge' applies (see later), your legal costs will be deducted from those assets before being paid to you. So beware the myth that legal aid is free: this is by no means always true.

Applying for legal aid

Your solicitor will supply the application forms for legal aid and may assist you to complete them under the green form scheme. You will need to complete an application form (and an emergency application form if appropriate) and a statement of your financial circumstances.

The forms are sent to the local Legal Aid Board office for consideration of the legal merits of your case and then to the legal aid assessment office of the Benefits Agency (formerly Department of Social Security) to assess what contribution (if any) is required. There are different financial means forms to be completed depending on whether you are or are not receiving income support or are living outside England and Wales. If you are in work confirmation of your income must be provided.

Eligibility for legal aid

As with the green form scheme, the criteria are disposable income and the amount of disposable capital, but the limits are higher. The general rule is that if either is above its limit, you will not be eligible for legal aid. In a matrimonial dispute your spouse's income or capital are ignored when disposable income and disposable capital are calculated.

The figures given below came into effect in April 1994. Each year these figures are updated: check with your solicitor (or the Legal Aid Board's leaflet *Legal Aid: A Practical Guide to Legal Aid*).

Income

Disposable income is your annual income net of tax and National Insurance contributions, but including child benefit and any maintenance received under a court order or agreement from your spouse. From this will be deducted:

- expenses incurred in connection with employment (fares to work, trade union membership dues, child-minding costs)
- rent or mortgage payments
- council tax
- insurance commitments
- maintenance paid to your spouse from whom you are living apart
- allowance for dependants: if you and your spouse are living together, £1,356 is deducted from annual income for her/him and £816 to £1,885 for each dependant, according to age
- allowances may also be made for some other items including outstanding debts.

A contribution towards your legal costs will be required unless your disposable income is less than £2,382 a year. The most you can be asked to pay by way of contribution is one quarter of the amount (25p in every £1) by which your disposable income is above £2,382 and under £7,060 a year.

Capital

For disposable capital, the following are ignored:

- the value of the house you live in
- the value of any other property or money that is 'in dispute' between you and your spouse (for example if your spouse is laying claim to some shares that you own)
- furniture, personal clothing, tools of a trade and, usually, a car.

Apart from this, virtually everything that is capable of being valued in money terms will count as disposable capital: not merely cash or deposits or shares but, for example, sums that could be borrowed on the security of insurance policies. Also counted in are jewellery (other than engagement and wedding rings), antiques and other valuables. There are, however, extra capital items that are exempted for pensioners assessed on a sliding scale.

Where the capital assets come to between £3,000 and £6,750, you will have to contribute a lump sum equal to the capital above £3,000. This means a maximum of £3,750. This payment is additional to any contribution that has to be made because of your income. There are higher limits for 'capital disregards' for pensioners on particularly low incomes. For example, a pensioner whose income is between £1,571 and £1,870 per year (excluding interest) will be entitled to have £10,000 of capital disregarded.

Waiting for the decision

A disadvantage of applying for legal aid is that you may have to wait for some weeks before knowing whether a legal aid certificate will be issued. The only exception to this is where an emergency certificate is issued, for example to cover injunction proceedings. Your solicitor may apply for emergency legal aid either in writing, or over the telephone, thus getting a much quicker response, but the Legal Aid Board's area officer may refuse to grant emergency legal aid over the telephone except in the most extreme cases. Emergency written applications should be dealt with by return of post.

A legal aid certificate does not normally cover work done before the date the certificate is issued. By that time the limit of the green form is likely to have been reached, and the Legal Aid Board is unlikely to allow further extensions on a green form except in relation to the divorce itself. This means that your case will come to a halt once an application for legal aid has been made, unless you can pay the solicitor yourself.

On being granted legal aid

If the decision is that your case is approved on legal merits and that you are eligible without a contribution, the legal aid certificate confirming that legal aid has been granted will be sent to your solicitor, with a copy to you.

If a contribution is required, you will be sent an offer setting out details of the amount of contribution required and how you will be expected to pay it. Contributions based on income are

Disposable income and contributions

If less than £2,382 a year	'Free' legal aid i.e. no contribution (provided capital also within 'free' limit)
If between £2,382 and £7,060	Contribution: 1/36 of excess over £2,382 per month
£7,060	Upper limit for legal aid for matrimonial cases

Disposable capital and contributions

If less than £3,000	'Free' legal aid i.e. no contribution (provided income also within 'free' limit)
If between £3,000 and £6,750	Contribution: £1 for £1 on excess over £3,000
£6,750	Upper capital limit for legal aid

ongoing and payable at the rate of 1/36 of the excess over £2,382 for the life of the legal aid certificate. Any capital sum contribution will have to be paid there and then. If you feel there has been some error in calculating your own financial circumstances, you can ask for a detailed breakdown of your assessment. If it is incorrect, you can ask to be reassessed. Once you accept the offer, a legal aid certificate will be issued and there need be no further delay. However, if you do not accept the offer, you will not yet be legally aided so the solicitor will not yet be able to act for you.

The legal aid certificate will not be issued until after you have accepted the offer and have made the first monthly contribution. You will also be obliged to make any lump sum payment required of you.

It is important to keep up monthly payments and to carry out the conditions of the legal aid certificate (such as informing the legal aid office of any changes in your financial situation, perhaps brought about because of maintenance payments).

Normally no work done by the solicitor before the legal aid certificate was issued is covered. The solicitor is entitled to charge you for any pre-certificate work and you will have to pay (unless the work was carried out under the green form scheme).

Revocation or withdrawal of your certificate

If it is found that you have in some way misled the Legal Aid Board about your financial position, your legal aid certificate will be revoked. This means that it is treated as though it never existed. Your solicitor will then be entitled to seek to recover from you the full amount of costs he or she would have charged on a private basis rather than the reduced fees under the legal aid certificate.

If you fail to respond to correspondence with the Board, or fail to meet your monthly repayments, your certificate can be discharged (ended) although (unlike the situation where a certificate is revoked) this does not make you liable for the full costs assessed on a private client basis.

There is a further penalty in the Legal Aid Act 1988: if any person intentionally fails to comply with regulations about information to be furnished by him or her, or in the furnishing of such information knowingly makes any false statement or false representation, he or she will be liable to a fine, or imprisonment for up to three months.

If your income or capital changes

If your yearly disposable income increases by more than £750 or decreases by more than £300 following the assessment, you must inform the Board's area office. You will then be reassessed and your contribution may be adjusted or the certificate discharged, so that you become responsible for your legal costs from then on (but not retrospectively).

As far as disposable capital is concerned, you must report increases of £750 or more. You may be called upon to pay another lump sum contribution and/or the certificate may be taken away. If in doubt report any financial changes to the Legal Aid Board.

Legal fees for someone on legal aid

A person granted legal aid ceases to become personally responsible for his or her own legal fees. A solicitor for a legally aided person is not able to bill the client direct for work within the limits of the legal aid certificate. From the solicitor's point of view the financial limits on legal aid work mean that he or she may not be paid to attend court on your behalf if there is a barrister acting, and so a solicitor's clerk may be sent instead. Practically speaking, the personal attendance of your solicitor at this stage would make little difference. A client is unable to insist on the solicitor's personal attendance in such circumstances, even by offering to pay him or her additional costs: such an extra payment is not allowed where you hold a legal aid certificate.

The statutory charge

Solicitors should hand to all applicants for legal aid the last page of the application form explaining how the scheme works and should also personally explain to a particular applicant how the statutory charge may affect him or her.

The statutory charge is intended to recoup some of the taxpayer's money which finances the legal aid fund.

Sometimes the legal aid fund has to pay out more than it collects by way of contribution from the legally aided person. Even if a costs order has been made it may not meet the legal aid bill in full, so in order to recover what the Legal Aid Board will have to pay out the Board has a first call on any money or property recovered or preserved either under an order or by an agreed compromise.

This applies to all proceedings for which legal aid is granted, not just those relating to the property recovered or preserved. For example, if a legal aid certificate covered the divorce, a residence application, an injunction and an application for a transfer of property order, the legal fees for all those proceedings would be part of the charge on the property transferred.

'Property' could be a lump sum payment, the value of the house (or a share of it) and any other asset that was transferred or handed over or has been kept. In matrimonial proceedings, the first £2,500 of any property gained or preserved is exempt from the statutory charge, and the charge does not apply to any maintenance payments made.

Property is held to have been recovered or preserved in the proceedings even if the case is settled halfway through without an order having been made, or if an order is made based on agreement.

Only if the property was genuinely never in dispute would there be no risk of the statutory charge applying in the end. For example, if you had come to a final agreement before the application for legal aid was made, or if, in correspondence, it had been conceded that the other party always had the property rather than that it was now being transferred, this would be evidence that there was no element of dispute. Ideally, if it could be achieved in time, you could send an agreed statement with the application for legal aid, so that the Legal Aid Board would know from the start that no property would be gained or preserved in the proceedings.

Postponement

Where the property is being transferred to a legally aided spouse rather than sold, and is to be used as a home for the assisted person (or his or her dependants) that spouse does not have to pay the statutory charge there and then. Instead, the charge is put on the house but is not enforced until the house is sold (provided the conditions below are satisfied).

The fund's postponement of enforcing the charge is relevant also when property has been 'preserved'. For example, if the house belongs to the wife and the husband's application for a share in it does not succeed, the wife has preserved her ownership of the house and the statutory charge will be enforced – but only when she comes to sell the house.

When the house is being sold so that another house or flat can be bought with the proceeds of sale or where, under any court order or by agreement, other money is to be used to purchase a home, the Legal Aid Board can agree to put the charge on the new home, provided that:

- the property or money is specifically expressed, in the court order or agreement, to be used as a home or to purchase a home for the legally aided person or his or her dependants

- the Legal Aid Board is satisfied that the net value of the new home will cover the amount of the charge and the legally aided person agrees in writing that a legal charge can be registered against the new property and that interest will be paid on the outstanding amount.

Interest on the charge
Whenever payment of the statutory charge to the Legal Aid Board is postponed, simple interest at the rate of (at present) 8 per cent per year (simple interest) is payable from the date of registration of the legal charge until the date the sum secured by the charge is paid off. This means that if you do not pay your statutory charge when it arises, you will have to pay interest until it is eventually settled. In times of rising house prices, the increase in value of your home should offset the interest accruing, but you should be aware, particularly if house prices remain stagnant or even fall, of your liability to repay the statutory charge with the accrued interest. If you do not agree to pay the interest, the charge cannot be postponed and must be enforced immediately.

No charge
In some cases, the statutory charge will not apply. Here is an example.

Husband and wife and two children live in a council house. The husband walks out on the wife and pays her no maintenance. The wife, who does not work, claims income support. The husband admits adultery, and asks for a divorce. The wife goes to a solicitor for advice under the green form scheme (no contribution is required from her because she is on income support) for help with her divorce petition and also advice on transferring the tenancy wholly to her.

The husband becomes violent towards the wife and the children, and she has to apply for an injunction. He seeks a residence order and causes difficulty over agreeing about contact (see Chapter 8).

For all of these matters, the wife gets legal aid (no contribution required).

Irrespective of how many hundreds of pounds are run up in legal fees on her behalf, she will never have to pay a penny to the legal aid fund because no property on which any value can be placed has been 'recovered or preserved'. The local authority tenancy has no value in this context.

The husband applies for legal aid to defend the transfer of property application and the injunction and to apply for a residence order. He gets a legal aid certificate subject to a contribution.

Win or lose, however, he will not be required to pay anything more towards his own legal costs.

The net result is that the legal aid fund ends up paying virtually the whole of both parties' costs.

Running up legal aid costs

High legal costs can be run up over what may in essence be quite trivial disputes. Solicitors' duty to the legal aid fund requires them to report to the Legal Aid Board if they consider that the client is acting unreasonably – for example, by refusing to accept a reasonable offer of settlement.

Even if you are on legal aid, it is still important to ask your solicitor to keep you posted on the costs of the case, particularly where the house or a lump sum is being negotiated for, and to explain to you what the statutory charge entails.

How the statutory charge gets paid

In legally aided cases, any lump sum payment ordered by the court has to be paid to the solicitor: only he or she can give a receipt for it. He or she has to pay it all into the legal aid fund; the recipient has to wait until the legal aid fund has settled up the costs before being paid the balance. But if a solicitor's undertaking is given that the cost of the case will not be more than a given amount, he or she can pay just that amount into the fund and the rest direct to the recipient (subject to authorisation from the Legal Aid Board to do so) if the money is not to be used for the purchase of a new home.

If the money is being released for a home purchase and payment of the statutory charge is being deferred, once the Legal Aid Board has agreed to defer payment of the charge, your solicitor can use the funds for the new property purchase.

Legal advice and/or legal aid

	'Green form' scheme (legal advice and assistance)	Legal aid scheme
Who is financially eligible?	Anyone with disposable income of not more than £70 per week and with disposable capital of not more than £1,000 (with extra allowances for dependants)*	Anyone with disposable income of not more than £7,060 per annum and with disposable capital of not more than £6,750
What does it cover?	Advice, and help with documents up to 2 hours of solicitor's time (or 3 hours if a petition is drafted) except (usually) matters related to child support	All legal work required, including representation in court by a solicitor and, if necessary, barrister
How long does it go on?	Until the limit is reached (but extension can be applied for)	Until case concluded

* For ABWOR, the capital allowance increases to £3,000 plus allowances

How do I apply?	By giving information to solicitor about income and savings; he or she completes 'green form' if you are eligible	By completing application forms given by solicitor to send to local Legal Aid Board area office with your personal details, grounds for case, and details of your income, expenses and capital
How long does a decision take?	Solicitor decides there and then	Weeks while assessment is being made; solicitor cannot do legal aid work until certificate is issued (emergency certificate granted in urgent cases)
What does it cost me?	'Free' if disposable income under £70; where property (other than home) or lump sum is over £2,500 recovered or preserved, solicitor's charge is taken from it	If disposable income between £2,382 and £7,060 per annum, contribution payable by monthly instalments and if disposable capital between £3,000 and £6,750, capital contribution payable when offer of legal aid is accepted. On recovery or preservation of property over £2,500 when statutory charge arises, legal costs of case taken from property recovered or preserved

Costs in the proceedings

Irrespective of whether or not you obtain a Legal Aid certificate, but particularly if you have to pay the solicitor yourself, it is important to explore whether you may be able to get some of your legal costs paid by your spouse or whether you are laying yourself open to an order for costs being made against you. The issue of costs is complex and, remember, whether the costs are paid by you or your spouse, ultimately they will considerably reduce the amount of money available in the 'pot' for later division.

How solicitors charge

Solicitors basically charge by the hour, so that every interview, every telephone call, every letter and indeed every time the solicitor opens your file, means additional expense to you, the client. Most solicitors charge out their time in units of five or six minutes. Short letters or telephone calls count as one unit each. Work that takes longer will be rounded up to the nearest unit.

Ask what the solicitor's hourly charging (or 'charge-out') rate is, preferably before making an appointment. If you are seeing a solicitor under the low-priced interview scheme (see page 66), you can ask him or her what the usual charging rate would be. Remember that the charges apply not only to the time spent with you but also to writing letters, talking to witnesses or to the other spouse's solicitor, and attending court. Check whether the rate includes a percentage mark-up for 'care and attention' or whether that is additional. Ask the solicitor to let you know whenever the charging rate is reviewed and changed. Value Added Tax ($17\frac{1}{2}$ per cent) is payable on fees and on some out-of-pocket expenses, like travel. A care and attention mark-up can be 25–60 per cent or even more and is likely to be charged in a particularly complex case, for example, or where action has to be taken at great speed.

There will be additional costs (often called disbursements) such as court fees, fees of any barristers engaged and, if there are major areas of dispute over the value of items of property, valuer's fees as well. In complex cases involving a business, your solicitor may also advise you that an accountant should be instructed to prepare a report on the business.

In many cases you may be asked to pay a sum of at least £200 on account of your future costs. Some solicitors deliver interim bills on account at various stages, which you will have to pay. Although this will increase your outgoings, interim billing is a good practice as it gives you a clear idea of where you stand, and paying as the case proceeds avoids having to find a large amount at the end.

A solicitor's hourly charging rate can be anything from £50 upwards (plus VAT) in a provincial firm; in London it may be from £80 to £120 an hour plus VAT, and, in really upmarket firms, charging rates of over £185 an hour plus VAT are not uncommon. So, using your solicitor as an emotional prop rather than as a legal adviser can turn out to be an extremely expensive luxury.

You are entitled to query your solicitor's bill and to ask for a fully itemised account, and disbursements. If still dissatisfied, you are entitled to have the bill 'taxed' (see below). Normally, you should do this within one month of the date on the bill.

A solicitor is not entitled to sue for his or her bill on a con-·tentious matter unless a month's notice has been given to the client with a reminder of the client's right to have the bill taxed.

Taxation of costs

Taxation is the process whereby the district judge at the county court considers the solicitor's bill and decides whether the charges are fair and reasonable in the circumstance of the particular case.

For taxation, the bill has to be drawn up in a specially detailed form, in chronological order of the steps taken. If there is a court appointment for taxation, the solicitor can also charge for attendance at court on taxation to determine the fee to be paid. There is a court fee for taxation of costs, currently five pence per pound or part of a pound of the final taxed costs.

The Solicitors' Complaints Bureau (address on page 68) produces a free leaflet about querying your bill called *Complaints about Solicitors' Charges*.

Reducing the chances of paying your spouse's costs

You can reduce your potential liability for paying your spouse's costs by making a reasonable offer to settle the financial questions. (This 'Calderbank letter' is discussed on page 185.) If the offer that you make is fair, and your spouse chooses not to accept that offer and proceeds to a full financial hearing, he or she places himself or herself in a much riskier situation. If the court ultimately makes an order which is similar or less generous than the offer that you made, your spouse may be ordered to pay not only his or her own costs but a contribution to yours as a penalty for stubbornly increasing costs without merit.

Costs awarded

If you want your spouse to pay at least a part of your legal costs, you must make a request 'for costs' at each stage of the proceedings, whenever orders are sought.

In a divorce, there is usually not just one set of proceedings: apart from the obtaining of the divorce decree, there may be matters of litigation on spousal maintenance, property adjustment or application, under the Children Act, all of which run up costs. On applications on any of these proceedings, or any 'interlocutory' (i.e. interim) hearings, costs will usually be 're-served' by the district judge to be dealt with on the final hearing or outcome of your case. At an interim hearing, a party will be ordered to pay the costs only if that party is in some way at fault then. At the conclusion of any final hearing, you can or should ask the district judge or judge to make an order for costs and he or she decides there and then whether to make such an order.

If you are asking the court to make an order by consent (that is, in terms agreed by you and your spouse), one of the agreed terms can be in respect of costs.

The court will bear in mind, at a financial hearing, the effect of any order for costs and will be conscious, for example, that such an order will still leave the recipient with a part of the overall bill to meet. Sometimes, the amount of the wife's share in any property is increased to take account of her liability for her own costs instead of an order for costs being made against the husband.

Where an order for costs is made in favour of a party who is legally aided against the other spouse who is paying privately, new rules apply if the legal aid certificate was issued after 25

February 1994. The rules say that the legally aided party's solicitors can claim legal fees worked out on private rates against the party ordered to pay the costs and can get back these higher fees from him or her. The legally aided spouse will not be affected either way (i.e. will not benefit or lose out) but his or her solicitors will be able to charge extra fees. (The rule changes were brought in to try to stem the numbers of solicitors stopping doing legal aid because of the low hourly legal aid rates.)

If someone on legal aid is ordered to pay the other party's costs (this happens infrequently), the legal aid certificate does not cover this: the person is likely to have to pay out of his or her own pocket. The court must determine the amount that is reasonable for the legally aided person to pay and will usually say that an order for costs cannot be enforced without the court's permission. It may limit the amount of such costs to the equivalent of the person's legal aid contributions and make the costs payable by instalments over twelve months.

The costs may be awarded by the court on a standard basis or (the higher level) an idemnity basis.

Unless otherwise specified an order for costs usually means standard costs. This means that you will recover from the person ordered to pay the costs usually between 60 and 80 per cent of your own bill. The term 'indemnity costs' is used to mean that your bill for legal costs (whether you are legally aided or not) will be met in full. When an order for costs is made and a figure cannot be agreed, the bill will be taxed. The bill should be sent for taxation within three months of the date of the order for costs.

Costs in different types of proceedings

The issue of costs is fairly complex and you can expect a different approach to the question of costs depending on the type of proceedings. Set out below are some practical examples.

For the divorce

The petitioner can ask for costs (although this is not usual where the petition is on the basis of two years' separation with consent). If an order for costs is made, the petitioner's solicitor has his or her charges assessed by reference to scales laid down by the Matrimonial Causes (Costs) Rules 1988 (for costs incurred before 14 October 1991). For costs incurred since that date, the Matrimonial Causes (Costs) Rules 1991 have been amended by the Family Proceedings Costs Rules 1991 and the Legal Aid in Family Proceedings (Remuneration) Regulations 1991. (Unfortunately, the whole area of costs is rather complex and confusing – not least now because of the various sets of rules that apply.

For example, a wife goes to see a solicitor to obtain a simple divorce based on her husband's adultery. She has to settle up with her own solicitor. She obtains an order for costs, assessed on the appropriate scale, at £175. But she has insisted on 'five star' service, requiring the solicitor to come personally to her house, spending many hours discussing the matter, and speaking to him many times on the telephone to find out how the case has been progressing, and her solicitor's bill comes to £800. She has to pay the £625 difference herself.

A similar situation could arise where the wife, instead of consulting local solicitors, instructs expensive upmarket solicitors to conduct the divorce for her. Again, this is a luxury for which she herself must pay.

For an injunction

Injunction proceedings can run up very substantial costs. The successful applicant should obtain an order for costs against the respondent. But, in many cases, this may not be worth the paper it is written on, either because the respondent disappears or because he has no funds.

For residence, contact and other orders

Considerable costs can be run up in disputes over orders under the Children Act, such as for residence or contact with the children. The fact that one parent obtains an order stating that the children would reside with him or her instead of the other does not necessarily mean that that parent has 'won' in the same sense as would be the case in, for example, a claim for damages for personal injuries, so both parties may be left to bear their own costs. The court is likely to order one party to pay the other's costs only if that one's behaviour during the proceedings has been in some way quite unreasonable, causing unnecessary delays and expense.

Financial matters

The fact that the wife obtains an order for spousal maintenance or an order relating to the matrimonial home does not necessarily mean that she will be awarded costs, but the impact of costs is likely to be taken into account in making the overall order.

Sometimes a husband's solicitors will at an early stage make an offer to include payment of the wife's costs, only up to the date of the financial offer, in order to try to force a settlement.

When costs are paid

The theoretical (and usually the practical) position is that the successful party has to pay his or her own solicitor's bill first and then recover any contribution ordered by the court from the other party. Usually, the solicitor will continue to act by preparing the bill and having it taxed and enforced against the payer.

Sometimes the solicitor may not press his or her client for payment of that part of the costs which are recoverable from the paying party but that is unfortunately entirely a matter of the solicitor's benevolence and his or her assessment of the prospect of the other side paying up.

Costs and the Child Support Agency

If you are seeking or will be paying child support, this will usually be dealt with by the Child Support Agency rather than through solicitors and the courts. Fees may be chargeable by the Agency unless parents are on income support or are otherwise exempt. The fees charged are £34 for assessment of the amount of child support and £44 for collecting and enforcing the payments and these fees are chargeable to each parent (i.e. the total fees could be £68 and £88) and are also payable each year rather than one—off payments. However, in most cases the amount of fees charged will be much less than the equivalent legal costs. (See further Chapter 5.)

CHAPTER 2

FINANCIAL PLANNING FOR DIVORCE

PLANNING for divorce can come at any time. Planning may be something you have been engaged in for some time, waiting just for the right moment to put your plans into action. On the other hand you may be the spouse who has suddenly (and painfully) been left and you cannot see how planning can possibly improve things.

Certainly in times of emotional crisis it is often difficult to make well thought out decisions for the future. In the heat of the moment, when the separation is very recent and often the emotional temperature charged, it can be best to avoid making long-term decisions, concentrating your energies instead on getting through the next week or even day. But as time goes on the importance of planning for divorce, even if you never wanted the separation to happen, cannot be over-emphasised.

By planning you can frequently help minimise the otherwise crippling financial effects of divorce. You can work out in advance how best to divide the income which formerly supported one home but which must now support two homes. Not only can you clarify your existing financial position but also explore how you could improve it: cutting down on outgoings, seeing if there are any ways of increasing your income, minimising the tax consequences of longer term decisions and perhaps seeing whether there would be any financial help from the state (see later in this chapter and Chapters 5 and 10).

Financial planning and child maintenance

Since the Child Support Act 1991 came into force in April 1993, different rules apply about claims for child support. These can affect your control over financial planning following a separation or divorce.

Parents looking after children who need child support from their ex-partner may be required to use the Child Support Agency to claim child support from their partner. If the parent who looks after the children is already receiving income support, family credit or disability working allowance, or intends to claim one of these three benefits after separation, then she (or he) will be referred to the Child Support Agency by the DSS and asked to make a claim for child maintenance. If none of these benefits is claimed, the parent looking after the children can still use the Child Support Agency (but will not be forced to do so – voluntary agreements can be made as an alternative).

The amount of child support will be worked out according to a special quite complicated formula which, together with the procedure for claiming an assessment, is explained more fully in Chapter 5. If you are likely to be making or paying child maintenance, you should read Chapter 5 now before continuing to make financial plans.

Debts

For an increasing number of families, the financial issues involved in divorce are less about dividing up assets than dealing with the heavy burden of debts and who will or should take them on. Although it may be of little comfort, getting into debt has become a common problem. Over 2.5 million families in Britain are estimated to be heavily in debt, two thirds of whom are behind with their mortgage repayments. The stresses caused by financial debts can indeed often be the cause of the family break-up.

Broadly speaking, one spouse will not be responsible for the other's debt incurred by him or her alone. But there are exceptions: one spouse will usually be responsible for the other's unpaid council tax bills and sometimes other outgoings on the home. Spouses also share responsibility for joint debts, say from a joint account or for joint mortgage repayments or rent.

If your spouse has left leaving behind high unpaid household bills, the date of separation is important. If your spouse has failed to pay his or her council tax, you must inform the local authority of the date of separation and thus at least cut off your responsibility for paying your spouse's share of the council tax debt accruing after that. By advising the gas and electricity boards and the telephone company, you can also get the meters read on as near to the separation date as possible and ask for a transfer of the accounts into your own name. This will, obviously, leave you with the responsibility to pay the bills in the future and so may not be appropriate, but it can be one way of avoiding some previously built-up debts.

If on the other hand one spouse is paying maintenance, but the other does not pay the bills, what responsibility does the payer have for the unpaid bills? The answer lies in what the maintenance is due to cover. If the paying spouse makes it clear that the maintenance should cover, for example, the payments of electricity and gas bills (and if the amount of maintenance is adequate for this purpose), then the paying spouse should be relieved of the obligation to pay those bills. Asking the utility companies (for example) to change the accounts into the name of the spouse now living alone in the property clarifies who will be responsible in future.

Working out debt repayments

The first step is to assess the priority of debts with the help of expert counselling – see below. You will probably be advised not simply to pay off the creditor who shouts the loudest. A credit card company, say, may telephone and write a string of letters in an endeavour to get money from you, but that bill may have to be left, if necessary, to enable you to pay for housing. The credit card company may take you to court: at worst the court could send in the bailiffs to take away some possessions, but that would be preferable to losing the roof from over your head.

Once you have worked out the total amount of your debt and (preferably with assistance) worked out a list of priorities for repayment, see also whether you can increase your own income –

perhaps by getting a part-time job or by applying for welfare benefits to which you may be entitled (see below). Look at ways of cutting your own expenditure: say by going to markets instead of superstores, or by walking or cycling instead of going by car. If you belong to a pension scheme you could ask for the payments to be frozen until you can once more afford them.

Although it may be tempting to try to avoid your creditors, you may well find that by contacting them and showing that you are willing to try to repay them you can work out a realistic level of repayment. Creditors will very often accept a reduced payment paid regularly rather than nothing at all and will feel happier knowing that you have not fled the country. Also, it will be less expensive for them to agree a repayment with you rather than incur extra legal costs in having to take you to court.

As an alternative, you may wish to roll up your debts into one loan and then pay a monthly amount. A problem with this is that the loans advertised for such purposes usually charge extortionate rates of interest. Even if your own bank is willing to make you a loan, the interest rates charged may differ little from those charged by credit card companies. Debt advice agencies also advise strongly against taking out a loan to help pay off your mortgage repayments (often termed 'distress borrowing'): this only serves to dig you deeper into debt.

If you find it impossible to pay off your debts (or repay a creditor to whom you own £750 plus) you could ask the court to make a bankruptcy order. If you take this action yourself it will cost you a deposit of £200 plus court fees. You will thus largely be relieved of the burden of your creditors.

However, once you are made bankrupt, there are limitations: you cannot hold a bank account or obtain credit of £50 plus, nor be a company director (or a solicitor, for example). Depending on the circumstances, most bankrupts are discharged after two or three years, when they have a clean sheet. But even if you think this is the only way out of your debts, obtain legal advice before going ahead.

Special help and advice about debts
Whilst there are plans for a new Money Advice Trust backed by the National Consumer Council as a central advice centre, your

best bet is likely to be your local Citizens Advice Bureau, money advice centre or law centre; many of these have special sessions for debt problems. For other agencies and advice try contacting the following bodies.

The National Debtline
The Birmingham Settlement,
318 Summer Lane,
Birmingham B19 3RL
Tel: 021-359 8501 (Mon, Thur 10–4; Tue, Wed 2–7)
Offers free advice plus information pack for those with difficulty in paying their mortgage or rent.

The Office of Fair Trading
P.O. Box 2,
Central Way,
Feltham TW14 0TG
Tel: 081-398 3405
Produces a number of free publications about personal finance, e.g. *Debt – A Survival Guide, Moneyfax – The Crucial Guide to Credit and Debt* and *Creditwise Guide to Trouble-free Credit*.

The Council of Mortgage Lenders
3 Savile Row,
London W1X 1AF
Tel: 071-437 0655
Produces a useful free leaflet called *Assistance with Mortgage Payments*.

Many local authorities and some banks have free information leaflets. You can also get help from your solicitor and green form advice is available if you are eligible (see Chapter 1).

Even if you are not in debt
Even if you are not in debt, you may need to take steps to protect your position.

The home
If your home is registered in your spouse's name alone, you need to register a charge on the property to make sure that outsiders

are aware of your interest in the home. This will also ensure that your spouse will not be able to sell the home or remortgage it without your consent (see also page 155).

Joint accounts and credit cards
With a joint bank or building society on which either of you can draw, there is the risk that the account could be cleared out without the other knowing about it. To prevent this, the bank or building society manager should be told to change the arrangement so that cheques can be drawn only with both signatures. Alternatively, you could ask for the account to be frozen (although neither of you would then be able to draw out funds).

Similarly, where each of you has a credit card or cash withdrawal card for drawing against one account, it is usually wiser, from the main cardholder's point of view, to put a stop on the cards. The card company must be notified and the cards (including if possible the other spouse's card) sent back. A new card will then be issued to the cardholder.

Preventing disposal of assets
If you strongly suspect your spouse of intending to dispose of assets to try to escape his or her financial obligations, you can ask the court to make an application under Section 37 of the Matrimonial Causes Act to prevent him or her from doing so. You will need to instruct a solicitor (see also page 176).

Working out your financial position

The following pages set out guidelines for working out a fairly detailed picture of your and your family's current financial position. It is only once you have filled in the detail of what actually happens now that you may be able to start making future plans. If you can, try to project ahead for the future what your likely income and outgoings might be.

You may not be able to work out all the figures by yourself: your spouse's position may be a blank to you, for example. But you should still fill in as much of the picture as possible: by undertaking this preparation yourself you may well be able to save on a solicitor's time (if you are going to use one) and thus on legal costs.

If you have not been responsible in the past for paying the bills, try to find out how much recent bills have been. Your spouse may be willing to co-operate; otherwise you could contact the companies direct and ask them to send you copies of your old bills, for example the utility companies (about the gas and electricity bills), British Telecom (about the telephone bill) and the local authority (about your council tax).

If you still feel at a loss, use these guidelines to prepare a summary of information for your solicitor who could then help you to sort through them and assist you in planning for the future.

The home
If you own your own home:

- what is it worth now?
  (an approximate estimate can be obtained by telephoning two or three local estate agents to ask them for a rough guide of what your property would be worth if you put it on the market now)
- when was it bought and for how much?
- how did you arrange your finances to pay for the house?
- who put down the deposit, and where did the money come from?
- what substantial improvements have been made to the property since you bought it (e.g. central heating)? when? what was the cost and how was it paid for?
- is the house or flat in joint names?
  (this is important – if you find that the property is in your spouse's name only, it could be sold without your agreement or knowledge but you can take steps to prevent this happening provided that a charge is registered – see page 155)
- is the title registered?

If you own a leasehold property:

- what is the ground rent?
- what is the service/maintenance charge?
- how long is the lease?

If there is a mortgage:

- name, address and account/reference number of the building society, bank or other lender
- how much is outstanding?
- what are the monthly payments?
- when will it be paid off? (ask the building society or other lender for any of these facts if you do not know them)
- if it is an endowment mortgage, when is the policy due to mature and for how much? what is the current surrender/paid-up value of the policy? (ask the insurance company)

If either you or your spouse owns other properties (e.g. a country cottage, villa abroad, time-share, all or part of a parent's home), include its approximate value.

If you rent your home:

- is it rented from a private landlord, the council, a housing association?
- how much rent do you pay (weekly, monthly, quarterly)?
- is there a service/maintenance or management charge? If so, how much?
- what type of tenancy is it?
- in whose name is the tenancy? (check the contract, tenancy agreement or rent book, if you have one).

Car or other vehicle
- do you own a car?
  (if so, what is the make, model, year, value?)
- does your spouse own a car?
  (if so, what is the make, model, year, value?)
- will you and/or your spouse need a car in the future?
- do you or your spouse have the use of a company car? If so, what model is it and how often is it replaced? What is paid for: tax? insurance? servicing? repairs? petrol?
- do you and/or your spouse own a motor-bike? caravan? boat?

Employment
If you are self-employed:

- what income have you had for the past three years?

(Any regular earnings from occasional freelance or part-time work at home should be included.)

If you are an employee:

- name of employer, nature of job, whether full or part-time (if currently not employed, details and dates of last employment and qualifications)
- normal weekly or monthly earnings (form P60 shows gross earnings, tax, National Insurance payments and pension contributions for the previous tax year)
- any other relevant information, such as imminent promotion or redundancy, dates of pay reviews
- any fringe benefits, commission or bonuses regularly received e.g. private medical insurance, subsidised loan, expense account, company car (a company car will be treated as 'deeming' an extra couple of thousand pounds gross income by the Inland Revenue)
- expenses of any clothing and equipment essential for your job
- cost of child-minding or nursery school for your child(ren) while you are at work
- details of additional casual or freelance work.

You will also need to look at details of your spouse's income if known.

Pension

- details of any occupational pension or superannuation scheme or personal plan to which you belong
- does the pension scheme provide benefits for widow or widower? (she/he will probably lose any benefits as a result of divorce).

Try to obtain a copy of the rules relating to the occupational pension scheme and an up-to-date statement showing the present value of your pension and the estimated value on retirement. You can apply for details direct to the pension company or perhaps to your personnel office who should have the necessary information.

Other assets and income

- any joint current accounts or savings accounts you have
- your own savings in building society, bank, National Savings accounts, with details of the account(s) and current balance(s)
- stocks and shares and unit trusts, with a current valuation of your portfolio
- life insurance policies: how much? when do they mature? (ask the insurance company or broker for current surrender values and check whether any policy has been written in your spouse's favour)
- the income from your investments over the past two or three years e.g. dividends, building society account interest
- future income or redemption value of investment that will mature in some years' time
- valuables, such as jewellery, antiques, with estimates of their value and brief details of how and by which of you they were acquired (bought, inherited, gift, etc.).

General contents of the house are rarely realisable, and proposals how to divide these between you should be considered separately. This is better done after you have reached a general agreement on the broader issues – otherwise, you may get bogged down in minutiae.

Outgoings
Summarise as precisely as possible your necessary outgoings. These would probably include:

- tax and National Insurance contributions
- travel to work
- car expenses, including hire purchase payments, insurance, road tax, petrol and repairs
- any other HP commitments
- mortgage payments or rent and service charges
- council tax and water charges
- gas, electricity, telephone
- house insurance and all other insurances
- payments into pension schemes
- housekeeping – food costs, toiletries etc.

- home repair(s) and maintenance
- television rental/licence
- holidays and entertainment
- payments for the children (including child-minding fees).

Try also to project what your outgoings might be in your new home (and, if you can, those of your spouse).

Expectancies and trusts

Are you and/or your spouse likely to come into an inheritance in the foreseeable future? Does either of you have interests under a trust (perhaps as a result of tax planning by you or your parents)?

Child maintenance

Special rules now apply about payment of child support since the Child Support Act 1991 changed the law in April 1993. Instead of working out how much you think you and the children need in terms of maintenance, or how much you think you can afford to pay, maintenance for the children is now usually worked out according to a special formula, which is not only complex but fixed. Although the formula is based on both parents' income, only certain limited outgoings (like tax, National Insurance and housing costs) are taken into account and other outgoings (like debts, travel costs and childcare) are ignored.

The rules are explained in more detail in Chapter 5.

Other maintenance

- any maintenance payments made to former spouse (or an ex-partner of a previous marriage) and/or to your child/ren
- children's maintenance payments received from a former husband or wife of yourself or your spouse
- any regular provision to or from someone else e.g. deeds of covenant from grandparents
- maintenance payments you would expect to receive or pay in the future.

New partner's finances

If you and/or your spouse are cohabiting on a long-term basis with someone else, and/or have plans to marry, you should include what you know of that person's financial circumstances.

Payments from DSS
What money do you receive from the DSS? For example:

- income support
- family credit
- child benefit (including one-parent benefit)
- state pension
- invalidity benefit.

Debts
Make a list of all the money you owe: for example, tax arrears, what is outstanding under any hire purchase agreement(s), bank overdraft, credit card, other loans. For a loan or credit agreement or other liability which requires payment regularly, note the arrears and the total amount outstanding.

Note who is responsible for each debt – you or your partner or both of you. You are not responsible for each other's debts.

Preparing a budget
When preparing the financial summary, the most difficult item to assess can be your outgoings. You do not need to calculate everything precisely to the last penny. But gaining a clearer picture of your current outgoings will help you prepare a budget for your future outgoings.

If you have no idea of how much you do spend on what, get a notebook and write down the cost of your shopping as you pay for it. If your children are old enough to understand, encourage them to note what they spend (it may also make them feel less left out of the future plans which the parent is making).

For major recurring bills, for example, gas and telephone bills, make sure that you try to add these together over a period of say 12 months, before dividing to create a monthly sub-total, to allow for seasonal fluctuations.

You should also make a note of necessary expenditure that may be looming, such as major car repairs, kitting out a child in a new school uniform, and of longer term needs, such as replacing a car, re-roofing the house, and so on.

Not all items will be doubled when you split up: some will be halved, some reduced, and some will still stay the same and may be paid for by either of you. For instance, electricity will be paid twice, toiletries divided, school meals and private lessons unchanged. A probable future spending pattern for each of you should emerge from this.

Making plans for the future

By now you could be thoroughly depressed. You will have spent many hours producing meticulous sets of figures and, almost inevitably, they will paint a grim picture. You may wonder how you ever managed to afford living under one roof – let alone how you will juggle two households.

Try to consider all the possible scenarios for the future. You strengthen your position by having worked out in detail the likely consequences of plans that you and your spouse may each be putting forward, even if (or particularly if) you are convinced that your spouse's suggestions are ridiculously unrealistic.

In practice, you may have little choice, and what options there are will be fairly stark. Inevitably, you will have to make compromises. It is only by having thought through your priorities that you will be able to mould the eventual compromise into a shape that best suits you and your family.

Making plans for the future revolves primarily around accommodation and income.

Where to live

Your first priority will of course be to ensure that the children have a roof over their heads. Work out what it would cost you to stay on in your home, and where you could move to if you were to move, and how either option would leave you and your spouse financially.

The location of children's schools, being near to helpful friends or willing parents – such things can be important considerations, particularly now that you are going to be on your own.

If you own your home but are likely to have to move, ask one or two local estate agents to tell you what they suggest it might fetch. There should be no charge for such a valuation if you explain that you may be selling but have not yet decided. These figures may not be exact (some estate agents undervalue in a depressed house market) but the figures will be a guide. Deduct the likely agent's and conveyancing costs, plus what you still owe on the mortgage, and you are left with the 'net equity'. From that, you would have to pay removal costs as well as purchase costs (survey fee, conveyancing, stamp duty, Land Registry fees, new carpets, redecorations etc.) of possibly two properties – one for each of you. Work out what sort of mortgage you and your spouse could each shoulder and then investigate the property market.

If you are in rented accommodation, and indeed even if you are not, investigate the rented sector – private, council and housing association.

This can be a disheartening business at the best of times, but it is only by exploring what might be possible that you can work out what the options are, and their respective advantages and disadvantages.

What to live on

In respect of capital, look at your schedule of assets, having worked out the net equity in the house (if you own it) and the net value of all other realisable assets after meeting outstanding liabilities (including legal fees for the divorce, if you are consulting a solicitor). What is realisable will depend upon your circumstances – cashing in a life insurance policy or selling the car might be foolish in some circumstances but unavoidable in others. Everyday household belongings are rarely realisable and should preferably be linked to need – the parent with the children, for example, is likely to need the washing machine, and the majority of the furnishings. The other parent, however, may need to buy, either immediately or in due course, his or her own household equipment and furniture.

Starting off calculating maintenance

If you have dependent children, first work out how much child support will be payable under the formula laid down by the Child Support Act 1991. This usually has to be the first step because the amount will be fixed and precise, whereas other payments tend to be up in the air at this stage. Turn to Chapter 5 to work out how much child support is likely to be payable.

A mother who will be looking after children may be able to claim maintenance for herself to top up her child support. As the Child Support Act has increased the amounts of child support payable, conversely the amount she might expect to receive in her own right has (broadly) tended to decrease.

A wife who does not work outside the home or who is on a low income may also be entitled to spousal maintenance from her husband if he earns enough. Exactly how much he should pay is not easy to quantify as the court will take a number of factors into account. If sufficient income is available, a wife could expect to receive enough to meet her reasonable needs (based on the court's pragmatic 'needs and resources' approach—see further Chapters 6 and 10) but the court may also expect a wife who is not currently earning to make endeavours to support herself financially in the future.

Figures and forecast

Once you have worked out what money will be available, compare the figures with a forecast for both new household needs. This may show that one of you has, or both of you have, got nowhere near enough to meet your projected expenses. Remember that a priority will be placed on ensuring that the children have their needs taken care of first.

Looking at your incomes, needs and available capital (if any), a decision must be reached on how things can be arranged but with realistic figures. In many cases, it will just have to be accepted that both of you are going to be very hard up, at least for a while.

Negotiating a financial settlement

You do not need to leave it to the courts to decide how much each of you can have. By negotiating directly with your spouse (or through solicitors) you can save legal costs. It is a good idea, however, to get about an hour's advice from a solicitor to find out properly what your own rights and responsibilities may be before launching into negotiation uninformed.

For reasons of professional etiquette, it is not possible to have the same solicitor acting for both of you. Some solicitors may be willing to see you and your spouse together, strictly on the basis that he or she will act only for one client.

Remember that the amount of child support will usually be fixed and you will then only effectively be able to negotiate about financial matter excluding maintenance for the children.

In your negotiations, your objective must be to achieve a workable financial settlement with your spouse. If you have carefully prepared an overall summary of your financial circumstances and worked out how a division of your income and assets might be in practice, you will have a good idea as to whether the proposals that you intend to make are realistic or not.

Proposals

Once you are satisfied that you have a clear view of the overall financial picture, you can put forward proposals for settlement on a 'without prejudice' basis. This means that if the proposals do not result in settlement and litigation does follow, they cannot be referred to in argument before a court. Your or your solicitor's 'open' negotiations (as against 'without prejudice') would place you in a vulnerable position in that your spouse could later use any admissions you have made in evidence at court. Accordingly, if your solicitor is conducting negotiations for you, he or she will automatically head proposals with the words 'without prejudice'; if you are conducting negotiations yourself, you should do likewise.

Usually it is the spouse who will be paying maintenance and/or a lump sum who puts forward the first proposals; frequently (but not always) these result in counter-proposals from the other spouse. Generally, the eventual agreement will fall somewhere between these two sets of proposals.

You may, therefore, be tempted to pitch your first proposals very low (or very high as the case may be). This is, on the whole, not a good idea. Although whatever proposals you make may be interpreted as just an opening bid, unrealistic proposals will sour the atmosphere and prolong the agony, with inevitable consequences in terms of both acrimony and legal costs. They are also likely to prompt your spouse into being equally unrealistic when it comes to counter-proposals and you will be faced with what appears to be an unbridgeable gulf.

Compromising

Carefully timed, carefully considered and realistic proposals should mean that there is not too wide a gap between you. The question then is one of how to close that gap altogether. Look at the calculations you have made and put yourself in your partner's shoes. You have the advantage of knowing your spouse well and you are likely to know what will be attractive and what will be abhorrent.

Ultimately, you may have to split the difference between you and/or reach a bargain over household goods or the car, for example, to offset an imbalance in terms of hard cash. Reaching a compromise, however, should not mean bullying your spouse into submission or allowing yourself to be bullied. If you feel this is happening, talk it over with your solicitor to get an objective view whether you – or the other one – is being unreasonable. Similarly, if you feel that your spouse is not giving full disclosure or is deliberately disposing of assets, make your worries clear to your solicitor without delay – the court has powers to deal with tactics such as these.

Financial help from the state

When the marriage breaks up and you have separated, you may find that you need – and now are financially eligible for – financial help from the state.

State benefits (that is, payment of one kind or another) have recently been radically reorganised. The old familiar names such as supplementary benefit and family income support have been replaced by new types of benefits.

The five main types of new benefit which you could be eligible to apply for are:

- income support
- family credit
- housing benefit
- council tax benefit
- loans from the social fund.

Both income support and family credit can lead to the recipient being entitled to other benefits, for example legal advice and assistance under the green form scheme (see Chapter 1).

For either income support or family credit, you have to apply to the Department of Social Security (DSS) on the appropriate forms which are available from post offices, social security offices and Citizens Advice Bureaux. There is a free telephone enquiry service (0800 666 555) for general enquiries about benefits and requests for leaflets and forms. Explanatory leaflet IS1 (with claim form) deals with income support and form IS20 is a guide to income support. FC1 (with claim pack) deals with family credit, and RR1 and RR2 give information about housing benefit. FB2 (*Which Benefit?*) tells you about all social security benefits, including the social fund. FC10 (*Family Credit – Extra Money for Working People with Children*), FB8 (*Babies and Benefits*) and FB27 (*Bringing up Children*) might also be useful.

Welfare benefits, child support and court orders

Sometimes a child support assessment or even a court order for maintenance just takes a wife out of her existing benefit entitlement. As a knock-on effect real hardship can thereby be created for her: she may lose her 'passported benefits' like her right to have free school meals for her children, her right to apply for loans from the social fund and her right to legal aid. When it comes to child support assessed by the Agency, there is no flexibility in cases where wives are 'floated off' income support and thereby lose their passported benefits. However, there is no such rigidity when working out spousal maintenance and other financial matters. Here care must be taken when calculating maintenance: consider whether proceeding with a claim through the courts will really be worthwhile.

There are other effects to be aware of when working out entitlement to welfare benefits:

● *Maintenance and welfare benefits*
Payments of maintenance will reduce the amount of income support pound for pound. However, with family credit, housing benefit and council tax benefit, the first £15 of maintenance will be disregarded.

● *Lump sums*

If a lump sum is ordered through the courts, the amount may bring a wife above the capital limit and income support (or family credit) would then cease. The interest which the DSS assumes to be coming from the lump sum may also make her ineligible.

● *Arrears*

If a woman has to claim income support because her husband is not paying the maintenance he was ordered to pay but later he does pay off the arrears, she will be asked to repay any benefits she has received in the meantime.

● *The Child Support Agency*

Since April 1993, claimants of income support, family credit or disability working allowance must approach the Child Support Agency for calculation and collection of maintenance payments. Others can also do so (but they will probably have to pay a fee). For more about this see Chapter 5.

The various benefits and how they will affect you as a one-parent family under the new system are summarised below.

Income support

This benefit has replaced supplementary benefit. It can be claimed by someone who is not working or is not in full-time work (for DSS purposes, full-time work is 16 hours or more a week).

Even an owner-occupier with savings of up to £8,000 who has not paid National Insurance contributions can claim income support. The amount you can get depends on your age and whether there are children in the family, as well as on how much you have coming in from other sources such as social security benefits and part-time work. Savings of between £3,000 and £8,000 will also affect the amount as you will be deemed to have an income of £1 for every £250 (or part of £250) over and above £3,000. After you have returned the tear-off slip on form IS1, you will receive a claim form on which you must give full details of your situation or, if you prefer not to fill in the form, you may be able to ask for an interview with someone from the social security office.

At present (1994/5 rates) the maximum income support for someone over 25 is £45.70 a week plus £15.65 for each child under 11 (more if the child is older), plus 'premiums' for people with extra needs, such as being a lone parent (£5.10 per week for lone parents and £10.05 per week family premium). You may also be able to get help with mortgage interest payments.

Income support and children

After a divorce, absent parents remain legally responsible for maintaining their children. If they do not do so and the mother (or father) has to claim income support for them, the DSS will try to get the absent parent (if he or she can be located) to pay the amount they are giving to the mother (or father) for the children. If he or she refuses, the DSS can take him or her to court.

Although absent parents may be able to afford to pay more, they cannot be forced to do so by the DSS. However, the court can follow guidelines recommended by the DSS. But payments of maintenance will reduce the amount of income support £1 for £1 (unlike family credit, where the first £15 of maintenance will be disregarded when calculating entitlement to benefit).

Family credit

You can claim family credit if you or your partner are working for 16 hours or more a week and have at least one child. The amount you get depends on your income, the income of your partner (if you live with one), and how many children you have.

To calculate how much you might be entitled to, add together your take-home pay, your partner's take-home pay, any social security benefits you are receiving (excluding child benefit and one-parent benefit) and any other money coming in from, say, maintenance payments or rent from a boarder. For these two latter categories, some of the monies received will be disregarded (ignored) when calculating your eligibility:

- maintenance – disregard the first £15
- income from boarders – disregard the first £20 plus 50 per cent of the balance.

If you are self-employed, use the amount of your profit after deducting allowable expenses as the figure for take-home pay.

To get the maximum amount of family credit your net income must be less than £71.70 a week (although if it is more than that you may still be able to qualify). For example, a parent with one child under 11 years old, earning up to the threshold of £71.70 a week, would be able to get £44.30 adult credit and £11.25 child credit (for a child under 11).

You can claim one-parent benefit after you have been living apart from your spouse for 13 weeks, or from the date of your divorce or legal separation if this is sooner. It is not paid if you start living with someone as husband and wife.

Housing benefit and council tax benefit

You can get help to pay your rent and council tax if you are on a low income and have savings of less than £16,000. If you have savings of less than £3,000, your capital will be disregarded; over and above this up to £16,000, again you will be deemed to have an income (called a 'tariff income') of £1 for every £250.

The rates used for calculating payment of housing benefit payment and council tax benefit are generally similar to the premiums that make up income support. The maximum you can get is 100 per cent of your 'eligible rent' (this may not be the same as the amount you pay your landlord) and also 100 per cent of your council tax bill. Other discounts on council tax, for example the 25 per cent sole occupancy discount for occupiers who live alone, may also be available.

If you have more money coming in than the allowances and premiums you qualify for (the money you need to live on, according to official calculations) you get less benefit.

Housing benefit cannot help with mortgage interest payments and other expenses, such as fuel bills. You may be able to get more advice from Shelter or SHAC (see page 79).

Loans from the social fund

There are several types of payment which you may be able to get from the social fund. If you need help to buy things for a new baby and are getting income support or family credit, you may be able to get a maternity payment.

To spread the payment for an exceptional expense you may be able to get a 'budgeting loan'. This is interest-free but repayable, normally from your weekly income support or other benefits.

If you are not receiving any income support, you could still get a 'crisis loan' to help pay for living expenses, or for something you need urgently following an emergency or disaster, if you have no other way of meeting your needs. You have to apply in person to the social fund officer at your local DSS office; however, entitlement to payments depends on available resources and if the fund has reached its limit for the period your application may be refused.

If a single parent is unable to repay a loan, social fund officers are entitled under certain circumstances to try to recoup the money from any person liable to maintain the children.

Making agreements over money

You may be relieved to know that only a small percentage of divorce cases end up in a full-blown battle over money – about 10 per cent. The rest, at some stage along the line, are settled by agreement, which can either be at the very beginning of the separation (or even before) to an agreement made on the very steps outside the court doors just before the final financial hearing is scheduled.

Whenever an agreement is made, the family as a whole is likely to save significantly on legal costs. There are rare cases where a spouse pretends to make an agreement whilst being in reality determined to drag out the process of resolution but as a general rule making agreements will save you money, and the earlier you can do so the more money can be saved on legal fees.

Although you have the option of keeping any verbal agreements verbal and relying on your spouse's sense of honour in not converting them into writing, the problem is that such agreements have a habit of unravelling over time as one or other spouse claims no longer to be able to 'remember' the terms. So, to protect yourself properly, an agreement should be drawn up into the form of a separation agreement or deed, or, far better still, a consent order made by the court.

Financial agreements and child support

Since the Child Support Act came into force in April 1993, agreements about how much child support should be paid cannot always be properly made in practice. Claimants of income support, family credit or disability working allowance will automatically be referred to the Child Support Agency for the Agency to assess child support and collect the amount calculated to be due from the parent who has left the family home. Non-claimants, on the other hand, do have a choice: either to use the Child Support Agency or make a voluntary agreement about how much should be paid. (They will, however, no longer be able to ask the court to make an order for maintenance for the children as the courts have lost their powers in this respect.)

Any agreement about child support will only last for as long as it is a real agreement – if one parent chooses to back out of it, it will be open for him or her to use the Agency for a child support assessment. Even if parents choose to make agreements rather than use the Agency, it is sensible to use the formula for working out how much child support should be paid as a bench-mark – otherwise the payee parent could go to the Agency in the future.

There is one significant practical advantage to making agreements over using the Agency. Currently (1994) the Agency has a huge back log of claims, resulting in waits of many months for those submitting new claims. So where parents are able to make agreements and are not forced to use the Agency, making an agreement that is based on the formula rather than waiting for an Agency assessment could speed up the settlement process for the time being.

Separation agreements

Separation agreements are sometimes simply referred to as agreements, sometimes as deeds. The distinction between the two documents is that the latter is drawn up 'under seal', which is sometimes necessary if the document provides for a transfer of capital assets (like the home). A deed will have small circular red stickers placed by the side of your signatures, which must be witnessed.

Before making a separation agreement, be sure that you are both aware of each other's financial situations, what each earns, owns and owes. It is sensible to consult a solicitor to check the terms you and your spouse have in mind, and perhaps to draft the appropriate documents.

The form of a separation agreement or even a deed is fairly flexible and it can be designed to suit your own particular requirements. The issues that are usually covered include:

- an agreement for spouses to live separate and apart
- agreements about with whom the children will live and how often the other parent will see them and/or have them to stay
- any agreements concerning the house, for example who will live there, whether and when it might be sold, how the sale proceeds will be divided
- agreements to pay sums of spousal maintenance; over what period and how much
- any agreements for the payment of capital sum(s) and/or the dividing up of other assets.

Courts do not like seeing any curbs on their own power, so any provision which supposedly ousts the jurisdiction of the courts (for example, saying that neither party is allowed to go to court over any financial issues) will be void. This effectively means that an agreement or deed could later be challenged in the courts, although the courts are most likely to uphold it unless, for example, it was made with one spouse being unaware of the full extent of the other's wealth or unless one spouse was forced to sign by the bullying behaviour of the other (sometimes known as 'duress').

Care should always be taken about what a separation agreement or deed contains. Even though they may appear quite informal, they pave the way for future long-term financial arrangements and can have serious repercussions in the form of tax consequences (for example, increasing the likelihood of capital gains tax being payable if the home is kept on in joint names in the longer term after one co-owner has left).

Separation agreements or deeds can be enforced if either party later proves reluctant to keep to them by an application to the county court (such applications are rare). Although such agreements and deeds are not absolutely watertight, the court is more likely to uphold the original terms if both spouses had received independent legal advice, there had been full financial disclosure and there had been no duress.

Financial agreements and divorce

Once the divorce has been started, an existing separation agreement or deed should be converted by applying to the court for a consent order to be made. The parties may also reach an agreement over money at some later stage when or after the divorce papers are filed; again, they can then apply for a consent order.

An application for a consent order involves the drawing up of a draft court order which the parties would like the court to make: this is usually called by lawyers 'minutes of agreement and consent order'. This too can be tailor-made to fit your own particular requirements (so can often suit an individual family far better than a court order made by the court after a battle can do).

One of the main reasons why lawyers emphasise that a court order should be drawn up instead of leaving a verbal or written agreement as it stands is the issue of a clean break. The husband and wife may have amicably agreed to a clean break: that they will divide their assets to give the wife a greater share to compensate her for giving up her claims against the husband for maintenance. But so long as no court has formally ordered a dismissal of the wife's maintenance claims, they can still be activated at a later stage. If she were to fall on hard times or were to see her husband's financial standing improve, she would still be able to make a further claim for maintenance from her husband (unless she had remarried). As long as she had included capital claims, say in the petition, these will continue, even after re-marriage, unless dismissed by the court.

To ensure that the form of a proposed consent order is as watertight, tax-efficient and as comprehensive as possible, a solicitor should be instructed to draw up the documents. Note that making a clean break order by consent will not preclude a future application for child support via the Child Support Agency. A recent (1993) case confirmed the long-standing principle that clean breaks can only end a wife's right to maintenance and can never end a parent's responsibility to maintain the children. Parents who previously agreed clean break orders are now often finding that the amount of child maintenence, once taken over by the Agency, dramatically increases beyond their initial expectations.

The consent order

An order made by consent can be much more comprehensive than an order made after a contested hearing. This is because you and your spouse can include undertakings (formal promises) in respect of matters over which the court could make no order: for example, an undertaking by a husband to retain sufficient funds in his own bank account to meet his obligations, to arrange the transfer to his wife of a car owned by a company of which he has control – and so on. Undertakings are enforceable, so make sure that you do not undertake to do anything which might turn out to be impossible.

You can also include 'recitals' setting out the background to the order: for example, that you intend it to be in full and final settlement of any claims, including those under the Married Women's Property Act 1882 (which, in this context, usually refer mainly to claims for household goods). If you have agreed the form of a clean break, it is also wise to include a recital that neither you nor your spouse will be entitled on the death of the other to make a claim against the estate of the deceased spouse under the Inheritance (Provision for Family and Dependants) Act 1975. You can also note 'for the record', for example, that the family home has been sold and the proceeds divided (and, by implication, taken into account in the overall settlement).

And do not forget to include reference to costs, whether for payment by one party of the other's costs or 'no order for costs', and deal, too, with orders for costs 'reserved' on any interim applications where there has been some litigation between the husband and wife before reaching the stage of applying for a consent order.

The words 'liberty to apply' are sometimes written into the wording of consent orders. This confirms that either of the couple can go back to the court for implementation of the order. It does not allow either party to seek in any way to vary the terms of an order for a lump sum or of a property adjustment order.

An application can be made at any time within the divorce proceedings by a couple for an order to be made by consent for maintenance pending suit and interim periodical payments for children. For a final order (lump sum, property adjustment, periodical payments) the application cannot be made before you apply for 'directions for trial' under the special procedure, and the order will not be made until the decree nisi has been pronounced and will not become effective until decree absolute.

To apply for an order, you will need to lodge with the court:

- agreed 'minutes of agreement and consent orders', signed by both parties and their solicitors if instructed in duplicate. Only one copy need be signed
- a short synopsis of the family's financial circumstances (known as a 'Rule 2.61 Statement')
- if financial applications have not already been made, a formal application (form M11 or M13 as appropriate) by both parties.

Rule 2.61 Statement
(This was formerly Rule 76(a) Statement.) A form is obtainable from the divorce court office. The information it seeks includes details of:

- the length of the marriage, the age of each party and of any minor or dependent child of the family
- an estimate in summary form of the approximate amount or value of the capital resources and net income of each party and of any minor child of the family
- what arrangements are intended for the accommodation of each of the parties and any minor children, and what child support payments are being made
- whether either party has remarried or has any present intention to marry or to cohabit with another person
- where the terms of the order provide for the transfer of property, a statement confirming that any mortgagee of that property has been served with notice of the application and that no objection to such transfer has been made by the mortgagee within 14 days from such service
- any other especially significant matters.

There is a very serious obligation on each party to give a full financial disclosure. Just how serious that it was shown by a recent House of Lords decision. In that case, decree absolute was pronounced in April, terms of agreement were reached in August and about one week later the ex-wife became engaged to be married without telling the court or her ex-husband. On 2 September an order was made by consent; on 22 September, in accordance with the order, the husband transferred his half-share in the home to the wife who, two days later, remarried. In these circumstances, the court order was held to be invalid for lack of proper disclosure and the ex-husband was entitled to have it set aside.

These circumstances were somewhat exceptional. You would not be able to have an order set aside on the grounds of failure to disclose some minor matter which would not have made any difference to the order the court would have made.

Financial applications

If the court order is to provide for the dismissal of either party's claims (so as to achieve a 'clean break' situation), it is essential for the court to have the claims before it in order to dismiss them (or to deal with them generally). Both petitioner and respondent should file form M11 or M13 as appropriate, drafted so as to include all the financial applications that each party is entitled to make.

Making of the consent order

Once the consent order minutes, financial statement and applications have been lodged at the court, the district judge will review these. Provided the district judge has sufficient information to be satisfied that the proposed terms are reasonable and both parties are in agreement, he or she is likely to accept the agreement and issue a formal consent order as requested.

If the agreement is put forward by solicitors on each side, the district judge may approve it without either of you having to attend in person, but if you are acting for yourself, the district judge will probably make an appointment to discuss the proposed order with you and your spouse, and may require further evidence, especially if no affidavit has been filed. Approval by a district judge is not a rubber stamping procedure: in certain cases, where the district judge feels that the order is unfair to either party, he or she may refuse to make it (although, again, this is unlikely if you have negotiated terms through a solicitor).

Effect of a consent order
Consent orders, once made, are as effective as orders made by the court after a full hearing. You can apply to have a consent order set aside only on grounds of:

- fresh evidence that could not have been known at the time
- fundamental mistakes, such as wholly erroneous information on which all parties, including the court, relied
- fraud (which may include evidence that the other party had no intention of ever abiding by the terms of the order)
- lack of full and frank disclosure if such disclosure would have resulted in an order substantially different to that which was made
- in certain rare circumstances, where the fundamental basis on which the order was made had been destroyed.

CHAPTER 3

LEGAL ADVICE

AT AN EARLY stage in your divorce/separation process, you should consider obtaining legal advice about your best future course of action. While a do-it-yourself divorce is relatively easy if you agree that there is to be a divorce and on what basis, you will almost certainly need a solicitor's help if there is little or no common ground between you. Wherever financial arrangements and division of property are at issue, or where there is uncertainty about the children, an initial advisory meeting with a solicitor specialising in divorce problems has much to recommend it, if only to avoid giving up rights in ignorance of the law. When faced with the breakdown of your marriage, you are likely to be at your most emotional at the very time when you need to be as dispassionate and rational as possible.

If you can sort out your financial affairs as equal partners, so much the better – although even then it is wise for you both to ask a solicitor whether the arrangements seem fair, and to ensure that they are framed in a watertight manner and do not result in any unnecessary payments of tax.

Using the services of a voluntary conciliation or mediation agency can assist separating couples in reaching agreements over the children; the home and finance can also be covered (see the next chapter). Again, if any agreement is reached via this channel, a solicitor should be asked to review the agreement.

If it is not possible for the two of you to achieve a fair agreement on your own, a solicitor can negotiate on your behalf. It is not usually possible for you and your spouse to instruct the same solicitor as there is a potential conflict of interest between you (although services such as the Cambridge FADC can arrange a joint appointment with one solicitor—see page 73).

A solicitor can be of great help, but try to use his or her services efficiently and economically. Ask yourself whether you want to obtain legal advice or want someone to 'fight' for you. Wanting a solicitor to act for you in a contentious way will involve you in expense which may be out of proportion to anything gained. It is also extremely non-cost-effective to use a solicitor as an emotional support, whatever the temptations.

Time and money are invariably interlinked. The more you use a solicitor's services, the greater the hole that will be cut into your financial budget. What a solicitor can do for you is explained in detail in this chapter. It is of the utmost importance that you consider the question of costs before launching into a major battle. Of course, how much you want to (or are forced to) involve your solicitor may be constrained by how much you can afford to pay. Explanations and warnings about the problem of costs have already been given. If you have not already done so, read Chapter 1 now.

What a solicitor can do for you

A solicitor should discuss your position dispassionately and advise you from the benefit of his or her experience what is likely to happen. Good advice early on may prevent matters becoming complicated, or one party getting less than his or her entitlement, and can generally help to take the heat out of the situation.

Getting your divorce
An undefended divorce is easy enough to do without a solicitor. Do-it-yourself divorce packs are widely available but the packs may contain out-of-date forms, so you should doublecheck these with the court. Be wary of taking important steps without legal advice: investing in a solicitor's time for one hour can be well worth the expense. In any event, if a divorce petition arrives through your letterbox and you are unsure what to do about it, or if your spouse flatly refuses to co-operate in any way, a solicitor's advice would be useful.

Sorting out problems over children
Protracted litigation over the children can be extremely expensive. Also, it is harmful to the children, harmful to you and rarely produces a satisfactory result. If you cannot come to an agreement by yourselves or through mediation, arrange a meeting attended by both spouses and both solicitors. Disputes over children cannot be 'won' or 'lost' and ultimately you are likely to prefer a solution that you reach yourselves, rather than having to accept one imposed upon you by a judge who, however wise and well meaning, does not – and cannot – know you or your children.

Getting court order for maintenance and division of property
A solicitor will know the appropriate court (see page 244) for the particular order you require and the procedure for applying.

Getting information about finances
You may find that you are faced with a long uphill battle to get financial information out of your husband or wife. However much you want to be reasonable over things, and whatever you do, your spouse may refuse to disclose assets.

Withholding information at the early stages does nothing but run up costs and will reduce the amount that there is to go round. If you go to see a solicitor, your spouse may then do so too, and may be persuaded to come clean about details of his or her financial situation.

Getting an agreement about finances
Good solicitors will impress upon both of you the advantages of co-operation and help you negotiate an agreement about finances.

Your resources may leave very limited room for manoeuvre and therefore there may be little point in fighting it out in court. There is no point in getting your solicitor to try to push for more, or for less, if the cost of getting it is going to be more than the amount you are asking for. If money disputes go on for months or even years, the costs will run into thousands of pounds even where small amounts are in dispute. Even if you are in receipt of legal aid and do not initially have to pay your solicitor's charges as they arise, you have to do so ultimately under what is known as the Legal Aid Board's 'statutory charge' (see Chapter 1).

If you have reached an agreement with your spouse and the issues seem fairly clear cut, it may still be worthwhile considering having one interview with a solicitor to check over the terms of that agreement, particularly if you have reached agreement only about the broad outlines of how you are going to split your finances. Sadly, agreements, especially verbal, have a habit of unravelling over time unless all their consequences are thought through and the agreements are recorded officially. Making an agreement formal need not jeopardise amicable relations with your spouse: indeed, doing so can pave the way for a more painless divorce.

A solicitor may also be able to:

- put an agreement into wording that is clear and will be acceptable to the court
- arrange maintenance and the division of property in a more tax-efficient way
- draw up a 'clean break' settlement where appropriate (particularly where there are no young children)
- point out things that you may not have thought of: for example, that a wife may be losing substantial widow's pension rights under her husband's pension scheme
- take into account the effects of any proposed order on welfare benefits entitlements.

Finding a solicitor

When you have decided to consult a solicitor, choose one who is experienced in matrimonial work. This will not necessarily be the solicitor with whom you have previously dealt (perhaps about buying the house or making your will) unless he or she is also experienced in family law. But the solicitor whom you have used before may have a colleague who specialises in divorce matters, to whom you can be referred. If the firm has acted for both of you (husband and wife) in the past, there may be a policy of acting for neither in a matrimonial dispute. A solicitor will not act for you if he or she has previously acted for your spouse.

Ask acquaintances who have been divorced whom they used, although you should be wary of recommendations in cases which are very different from your own. It is also worthwhile making enquiries at your local Citizens Advice Bureau or advice centre or even your local county court (each court keeps a list of solicitors who appear before the court). The Law Society's *Regional Directories* of solicitors practising in the area and showing the categories of the work they undertake are available in Citizens Advice Bureaux, public libraries and court offices throughout the country. The *Directories* and Citizens Advice Bureaux should also be able to point you in the direction of lawyers willing to do legal aid work. If you qualify for legal aid there are significant advantages, not least being exempted from court fees.

When you telephone or write to a firm of solicitors asking for an appointment, say that you wish to be advised in connection with your matrimonial difficulties and ask if they have a solicitor specialising in divorce and related financial matters, preferably one who is a member of the Solicitors Family Law Association.

The Solicitors Family Law Association (SFLA) is in practice a very good source for tracking down a specialist family lawyer. The SFLA is an association of over 2700 matrimonial lawyers who must subscribe to a code of practice designed to encourage and assist parties to reach acceptable arrangements for the future in a positive and conciliatory – rather than in an aggressive and litigious – way. This does not mean that an SFLA solicitor will be 'soft'. His or her advice to you will be positive and so, too, should be his or her manner of dealing with the various issues that arise.

You can ask the administrative secretary of the SFLA – Mrs Mary I'Anson, PO Box 302, Keston, Kent BR2 6EZ; tel: (0689) 850227 – for a list of the solicitor members in your region, but please send a stamped addressed envelope. You can also request a copy of the SFLA Code of Practice. ·

Client care code

All solicitors are now supposed to comply with a 'Client Care Code', which sets out how clients should be kept informed and advised who will be handling their case.

One of the Code's particular objects is 'to ensure that the client who is unfamiliar with the law and lawyers receives the information he or she needs to make what is happening more comprehensible and thus to reduce areas of potential conflict and complaint'.

What this could mean in practice is that at the outset of your case – once you have gone to see a solicitor and informed him or her that you want that solicitor to take on your case – you should receive a fairly detailed letter (sometimes called a client care letter) which complies with the code. This might tell you, for example, the name of the person dealing with your case, the name of the head of the department and information about costs. If your solicitor does *not* send out such a letter, it may be an indication that he or she is not really on the ball – so you may get better service elsewhere.

Low-priced interview

The old-style fixed fee interview, under which you could get up to half an hour's legal advice for £5, was abolished in 1993. However, there is a new scheme in its place called the 'low-priced' interview. Irrespective of your financial means, under this scheme you are allowed half an hour's advice from a solicitor at a reduced cost – the maximum chargeable is £25, and in some parts of the country this half-hour session may even be free. Various local schemes have been set up by Citizens Advice Bureaux, so try your nearest CAB first. Otherwise, you can track down firms of solicitors who offer low-priced interviews (not all do) in the Law Society's Regional Directories.

You must make it clear when making an appointment that you wish to see a solicitor on the low-priced basis. You are more likely to see a junior than an experienced solicitor under the scheme.

When seeking advice from solicitors

Remember that time is money, so try to use your solicitor's time as efficiently as possible. A succinct letter to him or her setting out what you want to do (your 'instructions') may well be more cost-effective than a long rambling telephone conversation. If you can go prepared for your first interview, so much the better. Some solicitors send a questionnaire to their clients before the first interview, to be completed and returned in advance of the interview. Otherwise, try to take along with you, on your first appointment:

- your marriage certificate (if you can find it)
- any correspondence or assessments from the Child Support Agency
- copies of any court orders made in respect of this marriage or any previous marriage – or your children
- typed or neatly written note setting out:
- your names in full, and those of your spouse and children
- dates of birth of yourself, your spouse and children
- details of any children in the household who are not children of the marriage
- your address and (if different) that of your spouse
- your home and work telephone numbers
- your occupation and that of your spouse
- names and addresses of the children's schools
- dates of any previous marriage of yourself and/or your spouse and dates of decrees absolute
- if you have already separated, the date and circumstances of the separation
- a summary of your financial position (include details of your and your spouse's income; details of the home and its approximate value and the name and address and mortgage account number of the mortgagee; any other capital assets and any debts and liabilities)
- any correspondence that you might have received from your spouse's solicitor.

To use your solicitor to the best advantage do not hesitate at any time to ask him or her to explain and discuss any points about which you are not clear. It may help to go prepared with notes of what you want to ask and then to take notes of the advice given. Indeed, this is a sensible precaution as otherwise it is all too easy to forget everything your solicitor has told you.

Remember that you can accept or reject advice as you wish. But before you reject advice, make sure that you understand the point.

Use your solicitor's time wisely and cost-effectively. Do not leave it to your solicitor to do everything: because of the time basis of costing the bill, the more time he or she spends on the case, the higher the bill will be. Quite a lot can be done by you yourself that will save solicitor's costs but tell your solicitor first what you plan to do.

Open your own file at home and be organised about keeping correspondence and any relevant documents safe, and keep copies of letters that you send to your solicitor.

You are entitled to be told at any stage how the case is progressing and how much it is costing. You can ask your solicitor for interim statements of how costs are building up.

Although it can be tempting to forget about the question of costs, this is an area which you ignore at your peril. Running up hefty bills of costs, whether by paying privately, or even by legal aid, will severely damage the ability of both partners to begin their lives afresh. Costs are dealt with at length in Chapter 1: read this now if you have not already done so.

Complaints about solicitors

Occasionally the relationship between a client and a solicitor can break down. If you have a real, not an imagined, grievance against your solicitor (for example, if he or she persistently fails to return your telephone calls or to respond to your letters), it may be worthwhile having a word with the partner who heads the matrimonial or litigation department or the senior partner of the firm. Switching to another solicitor can be an expensive process, as the new solicitor will have to read through all the paperwork that has already been produced: this can itself cause extra delay. So, if a sincere personal intervention can restore a good working relationship with your solicitor, this can often be the best action to take.

If, however, the situation fails to improve, you may wish to complain formally about your solicitor. Address your complaint in writing to the Solicitors Complaints Bureau (SCB) at Victoria Court, 8 Dormer Place, Leamington Spa, Warwickshire CV32 5AE; tel: (0926) 822007/8/9. The SCB also produces a booklet dealing with making a complaint about your solicitor called *What to do, where to go and when to complain*, and you can telephone their helpline for advice on 071-834 8663.

The next stage, if you are still unhappy with the way your complaint was followed up by the SCB, is to write to the Legal Services Ombudsman at 22 Oxford Court, Oxford Street, Manchester M2 3WQ. Appointed by the Courts and Legal Services Act 1990, he oversees the handling of complaints against solicitors, barristers and licensed conveyancers.

Telephone queries of a general nature from the general public are dealt with by the Legal Practice Information Department of the Law Society; tel: 071-242 1222.

CHAPTER 4

Mediation, conciliation and other help

> *No arrangement will work unless those who make it see the sense of it*
>
> Divorce Conciliation and Advisory Service Guidance Notes

In-court conciliation

The following section deals with voluntary or out-of-court mediation or conciliation. There is also a stage in the court process in contested disputes about the children called *conciliation*, or a *conciliation appointment*, which is explained more fully in Chapter 8. Most in-court conciliation is undertaken by a welfare officer from the court's own staff. In a few parts of the country, courts without their own conciliation service may suggest a referral to a local conciliation or mediation agency. If this happens, remember that the decision about whether or not to go is entirely up to you and that what happens in the sessions will be confidential.

Out-of-court mediation or conciliation

If you want to try to resolve problems with your spouse amicably and are worried that seeing separate legal advisers will widen the gulf between your respective positions, consider going to an independent conciliation or mediation service or agency.

Reconciliation and conciliation

First, any potential confusion about the terms that are used here needs dispelling.

'Reconciliation' means a couple trying to get back together as husband and wife. The purpose of conciliation, on the other hand, is to empower parents to create their own tailor-made solutions to the inevitable problems that arise in the wake of a separation or divorce.

Mediation and conciliation

More confusingly, the terms 'mediation' and 'conciliation' have often been bandied about – sometimes to mean the same thing, sometimes to label different processes. Most often the terms are used interchangeably to describe the process by which couples reach their own agreements. However, services specifically described as 'conciliation' services may just cover problems over children, whereas 'mediation', which is becoming the more popularly used term, may deal with children and money. You will need to check what ranges of issues a particular service is able to deal with. If you opt for mediation which deals with financial issues as well as children, ask whether 'comprehensive mediation' is on offer.

The mediation process

Mediation and conciliation take a family-based approach, an alternative to the adversarial approach adopted in the family courts where a husband and wife have to be on opposite sides, which is a distinct drawback when it comes to dealing with the children. Parents need to try to work together to sort out how the children will be looked after when the family separates, and the family-based approach of mediation can often help parents co-operate in planning for their children's and their own futures. For mediation to work, both partners need to attend. With the agreement of the parents, the children themselves may be invited.

The emphasis in mediation is on allowing parents to create their own solutions which enable both of them to remain parents in as full a sense as possible. By meeting in a neutral environment in the presence of a non-partisan, experienced professional (or sometimes two professionals) trained in assisting couples to come to realistic agreements, both partners may find that they can at least (and perhaps at last) communicate directly rather than talking at each other or entirely missing each other's points.

The mediators ought not to superimpose their own views but will try to help the parents to find common ground. Sometimes this process can necessitate the mediators encouraging the more passive partner to put his or her own views and keeping the more dominant partner less verbally active and more able to listen. But each partner will have the chance to make his or her views clear.

Critics of mediation have argued that this form of resolving disputes is biased against women, in that a wife may be too eager to agree in mediation to a settlement which gives her less financially than a court would, for the sake of a quiet life. Both parties should ensure that they receive separate independent legal advice before agreeing any proposals and should be wary of accepting prejudicial terms now, in order to keep the peace, which may in the long term become a source of regret.

Going to an independent mediation or conciliation agency is entirely a matter of choice: the services on offer are both voluntary (no one is forced to go and the sessions can terminate at any time) and confidential. Conciliation can take place at any time: divorce proceedings do not need to have been started. It can even sometimes be of help where the divorce ended years ago but where there are still intractable problems over the children. Nothing said in the context of the sessions can be used in evidence at court, if, eventually, legal action has to be taken. Also, any wish not to disclose an address to the partner will be respected.

Mediation is not appropriate in all cases: there are situations where urgent legal action needs to be taken, for example applying to court for an order returning the children to the caring parent where the other has snatched them, or for an order preventing one spouse from disposing of assets. In these situations, opting for mediation may well involve delays which could undermine the applicant spouse's position. Mediation is not a replacement for the role of family lawyers: it is more of a complementary service and conciliators will always advise their clients to take legal advice about their rights (and will recommend that each spouse's own lawyers separately check the fairness of any agreements reached). But in many cases the service it offers is not only constructive but will be considerably cheaper than a full-blown legal battle.

One-stop divorce centres

For most divorcing couples, getting help in their divorce may well involve visits to different services. However, the progressive Family and Divorce Centre (FADC) may have the key to the shape of things to come.

The FADC (which was set up in 1982) offers at a one-stop venue a range of services to couples facing the breakdown of their relationship. The service begins with a form of diagnostic interview, at which a husband or wife separating from his or her partner is assisted in finding out exactly what help is needed. Referrals can then be made to solicitors (with special Law Society permission the FADC even offers joint information—giving appointments to couples together instead of both of them having to find their own separate solicitor) or to one of the Centre's eight mediators or to counselling services. Part-time child counsellors are also employed. Where the services identified as needed are not available in-house, referrals can be made to outside agencies.

There are currently plans to offer similar forms of service to the pioneering FADC centre in other parts of the country. This style of offering one-stop services has also been given a boost by the recent (December 1993) proposals for divorce reform (see further page 131) which recommend a similar system nationwide.

Family and Divorce Centre (FADC)
162 Tenison Road, Cambridge CB1 2DP
Tel: (0223) 460136

Where to find a mediation or conciliation service

National Family Mediation (NFM)

Charitybase, The Chandlery, 50 Westminster Bridge Road, London SE1 7QY

Tel: 071-721 7658

Most family conciliation services are affiliated to the NFM (previously the National Family Conciliation Council). Your local Citizens Advice Bureau will be able to give you the address of your nearest service or your solicitor can refer you to one. Alternatively, you can write enclosing a stamped addressed envelope and stating what area you need a mediator in.

It is usual to have between two and six sessions, although problems can be resolved in one session alone. The costs vary, the underlying principle being that conciliation services should be available to all regardless of income. Some schemes charge fees (of around £15 per session), some ask for a contribution dependent on income and others are free. If you are receiving advice from your solicitor under the green form scheme (see Chapter 1), the cost of a conciliation report may be met by the Legal Aid Board up to a maximum of £32.50 (made up of £23 for the report and £9.50 for solicitor's costs: April 1994 rates). Some services are also providing comprehensive mediation as part of a pilot project.

Family Mediators Association (FMA)

The Old House, Rectory Gardens, Henbury, Bristol BS10 7AQ

Tel: (0272) 500140; (London office) 081-954 6383

Because of the specialist skills of the trained mediators of the FMA (the FMA pairs experienced family lawyers with qualified professionals experienced as counsellors or in family work), all the questions associated with family break-ups – like arrangements for children, housing, financial and property matters – can be dealt with fully. There are considerable advantages in having a skilled lawyer assisting in the mediation process: although lawyer-mediators do not advise either party individually, they draw on their own experience of family law cases in first of all piecing together an accurate picture of the family's finances and in helping the couple work out realistic (and legally acceptable) solutions.

FMA mediation is available in most parts of the country. The number of sessions is likely to be between two and six. Fees are usually charged but vary regionally (usually £40 to £60 per person per hour, and more in London). However, the mediators have the discretion to reduce fees and a mediation report may be payable by the Legal Aid Board (see above under National Family Mediation).

Divorce Conciliation and Advisory Service (DCAS)
38 Ebury Street, London SW1W OLU
Tel: 071-730 2422

The DCAS offers a neutral setting in which parents who are thinking of separating or divorcing, or splitting up if they are not married, can bring out in the open their confused, conflicting and bewildering thoughts about the situation in which they find themselves. The DCAS stresses that any arrangements made voluntarily between the parents stands a much better chance of working than if it is imposed by an outside authority like the courts. The DCAS also offers a counselling service for people who are considering parting. This allows them to clarify their thoughts and to see what sort of future there is. The DCAS does make a charge but people on income support are seen free and for those who are very short of money fees are negotiable.

Sources of advice and help

Anyone in difficulties over finance, tax, housing, the children, or rights generally, can go for advice to a Citizens Advice Bureau. CAB offices have numerous leaflets and information about local sources of help and services. CABs differ across the country but many can provide you with everything from an impartial listener to representation at social security appeal tribunals or advice about money and county court representation. You can find the address of your local branch in the telephone directory.

The Child Poverty Action Group
1–5 Bath Street, London EC1V 9PY
Tel: 071-253 3406

Produces *The National Welfare Benefits Handbook* (1994/5 edition, £7.95), which covers income support and other means-tested benefits and *The Rights Guide to Non-Means-Tested Benefits* (1994/95 edition, £6.95), which covers other social security benefits (cheques payable to CPAG Ltd – prices are inclusive of postage). Those on welfare benefits can obtain the publications for £2.65 and £2.45 respectively.

The National Council for One Parent Families
255 Kentish Town Road, London NW5 2LX
Tel: 071-267 1361

Works to help parents who are looking after children on their own, and issues a range of books, reports, pamphlets and leaflets on problems that a lone parent may encounter, including taxation, housing, social security benefits, divorce, children and employment. Booklets are free to lone parents.

Gingerbread
35 Wellington Street, London WC2E 7BN
Tel: 071-240 0953

Is a support organisation for lone parents and their families, with over 275 groups in England and Wales. Also publishes advice and information leaflets and operates a national advice line.

Families Need Fathers
Postal address: BM Families, London WC1N 3XX
Office: 134 Curtain Road, London EC2A 3ARTel: 071-613 5060; 081-886 0970 (information line)

Represents non-residential parents and their children, and is primarily concerned with the problems of keeping children and parents in contact after family breakdown. A national network of volunteers provide advice and support on children's issues to separated, divorced or unmarried parents. Publishes booklets and factpacks and a quarterly journal.

Both Parents Forever
39 Cloonmore Avenue, Orpington, Kent BR6 9LE
Tel: (0689) 854343

Provides help and advice to all parents and grandparents involved in divorce, separation or care proceedings. Membership is £6 a year; members receive a quarterly newsletter. An information pack (£6) explains the rights to information about children from schools, social services, medical authorities and so on; parents', grandparents' and children's rights under the Children Act; rights to take a case to the European Commission of Human Rights. Can also help in child abduction cases. Produces a 'Grandparents Only' pack (£1.50).

Family Care Line
Tel: 061-226 7015/7524

Provides a listening and networking service for families in crisis in the Manchester area. Will give out local contact numbers.

RELATE
Herbert Gray College, Little Church Street, Rugby, Warwickshire CV21 3AP
Tel: (0788) 573241

Jewish Marriage Council
23 Ravenshurst Avenue, London NW4 4EE
Tel: 081-203 6311

Provides a counselling service for single, married, divorced, separated or widowed Jews. There is also a get (religious divorce) advisory service: 081-203 6314; and two telephone crisis helplines: (0345) 581999 and 081-203 6211.

Catholic Marriage Advisory Council
Clitheroe House, 1 Blythe Mews, Blythe Road, London W14 0NW
Tel: 071-371 1341

Asian Family Counselling Service
74 The Avenue, London W13 8LB
Tel: 081-997 5749

The National Stepfamily Association
72 Willesden Lane, London NW6 7TA
Tel: 071-372 0844 (office); 071-372 0846 (counselling)

Provides advice, support and information to stepfamilies; confidential telephone counselling service, newsletters and local support groups.

The Family Welfare Association
501–505 Kingsland Road, London E8 4AU
Tel: 071-254 6251

Provides social work and social care services to families and individuals. Staff offer a variety of services to people facing social and emotional difficulties, including family and relationship problems, bereavement, loneliness, poverty, unemployment and homelessness.

REUNITE
National Council for Abducted Children, PO Box 4,
London WC1X 3DX
Tel: 071-404 8356

A self-help network for parents whose children have been abducted.

National Council for the Divorced and Separated
13 High Street, Little Shelford, Cambs. CB2 5ES
Tel: (0533) 700595

Over 100 branches throughout the British Isles which provide a venue where people with similar experiences and problems can meet new friends and develop new interests.

Childline
Tel: (0800) 1111 (calls are free)

A confidential listening and advisory service.

Children's Legal Centre
20 Compton Terrace, London N1 2UN
Tel: 071-359 6251

National organisation designed to improve the law and policy affecting children in England and Wales. Advice by telephone or letter for children with legal problems. Advice line operates weekdays 2–5 p.m.

Shelter
88 Old Street, London EC1V 9HU
Tel: 071-253 0202; nightline (0800) 446441

If you live outside London Shelter can give the telephone number of a Shelter Housing Aid centre near you for help with problems to do with mortgages, occupation of the home, rates, rent and other payments. Nightline operates 6 p.m. to 9 a.m. and all day at weekends for anyone, including those living in London.

SHAC
The London Housing Aid Centre, 229/231 High Holborn, London WC1V 7DA
Tel: 071-404 7447; housing advice line 071-404 6929, 10–1 weekdays
Helps with housing problems within the London boroughs, and also produces publications including *The Housing Rights Guide,. The Rights Guide for Home Owners* (co-published with the Child Poverty Action Group), *A Woman's Place* and *Going It Alone.*

CHAPTER 5

USING THE CHILD SUPPORT AGENCY

EVER since the Child Support Agency began its operations in April 1993 its activities have been hitting the headlines. Usually the reports have been highly critical. The Agency has been lobbied in particular by absent parents shocked at unexpectedly large leaps in child support payments and by parents looking after children who have found themselves pushed into applying for maintenance from ex-partners whom they want nothing to do with.

It is still perhaps early days to judge how well the Agency will fare in the long term. Two of its biggest problems – a huge backlog of unprocessed claims and hence delays in dealing with child support applications, and the harsh rigidity of the formula it has to apply – must be tackled before it can ever succeed in its purpose. That purpose is to provide a fair level of child support, fairly assessed, ensuring that both parents meet their financial obligations towards their children.

What is the Child Support Agency?

The Child Support Agency (CSA) is a governmental Agency which comes under the umbrella of the Department of Social Security (DSS). The CSA was set up by the Child Support Act 1991 to take over responsibility for child support applications, which, nowadays, can usually no longer be made to the courts. The Agency's main tasks are to assess child maintenance payments according to a special, incredibly complex formula, and then to collect and enforce those payments from the parent who is no longer living with the children.

The CSA also has special powers to trace parents who have gone missing – it has access to DSS benefit records and Inland Revenue records, for example. Where there is a difficulty in obtaining information the CSA may use inspectors as a last resort. It will be an offence to fail to co-operate with Child Support Agency inspectors (whose task will be to collect information about liable persons). The inspectors can enter business premises, such as the place of work of a liable person, and make any examination and enquiry that they consider appropriate.

Terminology

Under the Child Support Act, the Agency refers to 'the absent parent' and 'the parent (or person) with care'. The 'absent parent' is defined as someone who no longer lives in the same household as the child and the 'parent (or person) with care' as the person who usually provides the day-to-day care of the child.

When can the CSA act?

Applications can be made to the Child Support Agency as soon as parents separate – you do not have to wait for the divorce to start. Either parent can apply; applications can also be made by non-parents (say a grandmother) if they are looking after the children full-time.

The CSA can be used only for child support claims for natural or adopted children; claims for stepchildren against stepparents still need to go through the courts. The Agency can also deal only with maintenance, not claims for lump sum payments or property transfers for children. If paternity is disputed, then that dispute must usually be dealt with first by the courts before the Agency can act further.

There are other conditions which must first be met:

- the child must be a 'qualifying child' i.e. he or she must be under 16, or under 19 and still in full-time, non-advanced, education

- the child and both parents must all be habitually resident within the UK. So if a parent works abroad and habitually lives abroad, then no application to the CSA can be made (although an application can still be made to court)

In addition, there must (in most cases) be no maintenance agreement or court order made before 5 April 1993 – called 'pre-existing cases'. The operation of the Child Support Agency is being phased in over a period of time – its aim was to deal first with all new cases of maintenance applications. By the end of the phasing-in period, which is April 1997, the Agency will be able to act in all cases – even where a court order or agreement was made before April 1993. In the period between April 1993 and April 1997 the Agency is gradually taking on pre-existing cases under a complex timetable determined first by whether or not the parent with care is claiming income support, family credit or disability working allowance and secondly by the first letter of the surname of the parent with care. Broadly, parents with care claiming one of these three welfare benefits are likely to find that their cases are taken over by the Agency earlier than parents not claiming these benefits, who should come within the jurisdiction of the CSA between April 1996 and April 1997.

If you have an existing court order, it may be possible to bring forward the time when the Agency can take over the case, by applying to revoke the original court order and thereafter submitting an application to the Agency. This approach, however, should be taken only after getting proper legal advice. In a 1993 case the judge ruled it 'inappropriate' for a parent with care to try this strategy, saying: 'It seems to me that an assessment from the Agency is not necessarily in the best interests of the children. It might produce a higher figure, but it may be that other matters outweigh the purely financial.' Here the old court order was reinstated, and the parent with care advised that she should reapply for a variation of the old order.

Another practical problem is that because the Agency has in its first year built up such a backlog of cases it may not be able to offer a swift solution to the problem of getting an increase in maintenance, so an application to court for an upwards variation may get a quicker response.

Clean break orders and the Child Support Agency

One particular matter which has received much adverse publicity is the issue of clean break orders. Previously divorced couples who had opted for a clean break order, whereby the absent parent (usually the husband) agreed to settle a lump sum on the wife and children or transfer the home to the wife in return for no maintenance claims being made against him, found that the Child Support Agency had the right to re-open the case and ask for future maintenance payments for the children.

However, even in the past where a clean break order had been agreed the DSS could apply to the court for maintenance from the liable relative (usually the father). The law would not tolerate a clean break order ending a parent's responsibility to pay maintenance for the children. This principle still applies now that the Child Support Agency has come into operation, with a test case (involving a Mr and Mrs Crozier) confirming that there is an ongoing responsibility of the parents towards the children, to whom the clean break principle never applied.

Getting advice about the Child Support Agency

Solicitors and Citizens Advice Bureaux should be able to offer advice and help about getting or paying child support through the Child Support Agency. However, there are restrictions on legal advice and assistance (the green form) and legal aid for problems concerning the Agency. Solicitors will usually not be allowed under the green form scheme to help a client fill in a maintenance application form or a maintenance enquiry form; green form advice is available only where there are particular legal problems – say over paternity or whether the absent parent lives in the UK – and where, according to the Legal Aid Board, it would be *reasonable* for the solicitor to do the work.

Legal aid is not available for applications to challenge a Child Support Agency assessment through most of the initial appeal stages. So legal aid is not usually available for applications to review an assessment, appeals to the Child Support Appeals Tribunal or appeals to the Child Support Commissioner. However, if there is an appeal from a Child Support Commissioner's decision – which can only be on a point of law, not of fact – then legal aid can be applied for. If you need help in challenging an Agency assessment or decision, your solicitor may however be able to advise you under the green form and then act as a 'McKenzie friend' – an advocate/assistant – on your behalf at a Tribunal hearing. Legal aid is available for taking a case about paternity to the courts.

There is a Child Support Enquiry line on (0345) 133133 (calls charged at local rates) which anyone can telephone for advice and help. This helpline has been beset by problems and it is often difficult to get through, so patience may be called for.

Applying to the Child Support Agency

Applications are made on a lengthy maintenance application form (not unlike a tax return) which asks for full details of your income, assets etc. After receiving this, the Agency will send out a maintenance enquiry form to the payer-to-be who will also be asked to reveal his or her financial position in full.

Originally the CSA was going to deal only with child support applications for those on benefit. However, whilst its remit has been extended to everyone, differences remain in the way it deals with welfare claimants and others.

Welfare claimants

The most important distinction is that parents with care who claim one of the three welfare benefits (income support, family credit or disability working allowance) are compelled to use the Agency. When a claim for income support is made, claimants who are looking after children will be referred automatically to the Agency and asked to complete a maintenance application form (MAF). When signing the form, applicants will also be asked to authorise the Secretary of State to take steps to act on their behalf – namely to recover maintenance. Failure to complete the form as fully as possible or failure to authorise the Secretary of State to act can be termed 'failure to co-operate' and unless an applicant has 'good cause' can result in a benefit reduction of 20 per cent of the adult personal allowance for six months (£9.14 per week on 1994/5 rates) and then 10 per cent for a further twelve months after that.

To show 'good cause' an applicant has to prove that she (or he) would suffer harm or undue distress. Where a woman has fled to a refuge because of violence or abuse and is applying for income support from there, she should be taken to have good cause if she chooses not to go ahead with a maintenance claim against the abuser whom she fears. The Agency says that it will act as a buffer between the applicant and the payer and is under a duty to keep personal details (like addresses) confidential. But if you are in any doubt about this, seek advice from a welfare benefits agency as soon as you can.

People not claiming welfare benefits

People who are not making a claim for income support, family credit or disability working allowance have the option of either using the Agency or making a private, voluntary agreement. They can no longer choose to go to court unless the Agency has no jurisdiction to act in a particular case – say if the absent parent is abroad, for example. (The courts nowadays act as a safety net for all cases which fall outside the jurisdiction of the Agency).

Private agreements will last only as long as they remain real agreements. If either parent is unhappy about the level of payments, then he or she can go to the Agency and ask it to take over the child support case. This is a strong argument for making sure that any agreed amount of maintenance matches the amount of child support worked out according to the formula. The Agency will not, however, be able to collect and enforce child support payments made under an agreement. One advantage of coming to such an agreement over using the Agency is that an agreement can, in theory, be worked out quickly, whereas an application to the Agency can take several months. (Although the Agency planned to deal with applications in under 10 weeks, in their first year most took much longer.)

Unless otherwise exempted, parents with care and absent parents may be charged yearly fees by the Agency: £34 for assessment and £44 for collection and enforcement (if this latter service is also opted for). The fees are payable by both parents, i.e. a total of £68 and £88.

Calculating child support

Calculating child support is the task of the CSA, which must use a formula laid down by special regulations. The regulations (some of which have been based on social security regulations) are complex and very detailed and are designed to cover a wide variety of individual cases. The following is only a summary of the way the formula works – you may well need to get more information to find out exactly how it applies to you (see the summary on page 95).

In very broad terms, the main change that the formula has made is to increase child support payments quite significantly. On average, payments have more than doubled – from around £20 weekly to £50 weekly. The precise amount depends largely on the income of the absent parent, although the income of the parent with care is relevant too, as both parents are viewed as being financially responsible for their children. Payments will vary from the minimum (set at 5 per cent of the adult personal allowance of income support) to the maximum. The maximum sets the ceiling for child support which can be assessed by the CSA. In very high income families, if child support is sought over and above this level, a court application will be required; the court will also be able to order additional amounts of maintenance to cover school fees and extra costs incurred because of a child's disability (again, for wealthy families).

Once the child support level has been set, it will be reviewed every year. As the formula is based on income support rates (which are increased annually), the amount of child support will usually be increased to take account of increases in inflation. The review takes the form of a complete reassessment, so if either parent's financial circumstances have changed, those changes will be taken into account. Parents can also request a review during the year if one is needed, for example if one of them loses a job, although a minimum change in the amount payable will be necessary before a review will be put in train.

Using the formula

The formula is applied by using five different sums (*a.* to *e.*) set out below. Examples have been used to show the different stages of its workings. They should be treated as illustrations only.

a. Maintenance requirement
This represents the day-to-day expenses of looking after children, based on income support rates, adding together sums calculated for the parent looking after the children as well as for the children.

- **The adult personal allowance** for over-25s: this is paid in full when all the children are under 11. Added to this are the family premium and the lone parent premium (where the children are living with a lone parent). The maintenance requirement is always based on the adult personal allowance rate for a single person aged 25 and over (£45.70 in 1994/5), whether or not the parent with care is younger than that or lives with a partner. Adjustments have to be made to the personal allowance element of the maintenance requirement where the parent with care is looking after children of whom the youngest is 11 or over. For example, the £45.70 rate would go down to £34.28 where the youngest child cared for was between 11 and 13, and from 14 upwards the £45.70 rate would go down to £22.85.
- **The personal allowances for children** vary according to the age bands the children fall into. For 1994/5, the DSS rates per week are:

under 11	£15.65	16 to 17	£27.50
11 to 15	£23.00	18	£36.15

Although the maintenance is payable for the children, the maintenance requirement includes the adult personal allowance for the parent looking after the children as a carer allowance. It is the core calculation for child support but it is very unlikely that the amount of child support paid will be the same as the maintenance requirement. The actual amount will be adjusted downwards depending on the other factors below. Child benefit is deducted from the amount of the maintenance requirement.

The maintenance requirement does not limit the amount that the absent parent pays. Where the absent parent is well off, he (or she) is expected to make maintenance payments over and above that maximum. The regulations lay down an extra percentage payment of up to 25 per cent of assessable income, once the maintenance requirement has been met, if the absent parent's circumstances allow for this (see *d*. below).

b. Exempt income

Exempt income applies to both parents' separate incomes and represents what is allowed for each parent's own personal essential expenses, including:

- a personal allowance to cover both parents' day-to-day living expenses *plus* the costs of caring for their natural and adopted children who are living with them, assessed on income support rates (assumed responsibilities for a new partner or his or her children are not taken into account)
- reasonable housing costs of themselves and any natural or adopted children they have living with them (housing costs of anyone else living in the same household such as a new partner or other children will proportionately reduce the absent parent's allowable housing costs).

Housing costs are included only where they are 'reasonable'. Costs which are under the higher limit of £80 per week, or half a parent's net weekly income, are automatically assumed to be reasonable. There are some other special cases where housing costs are taken to be reasonable – for example, where the parent who has left the home has had to take on a high mortgage because he has not yet taken out his financial share of the family home.

Housing costs include rent or mortgage repayments (both interest and capital). Payments of an endowment premium are also included as long as the mortgage is £60,000 or under. They can also include repayments on a loan taken out to install central heating or a kitchen, for example, but do not cover loans taken out to redecorate. They do not cover insurance premiums on the home.

Exempt income does not include other outgoings like child-care costs, travel to work or any debts; parents who have high payments on any of these may find themselves being treated very harshly by the Agency as it will ignore these actual outgoings before assessing what an absent parent can afford to pay.

Parents on low incomes do however get some extra help from the 'protected income' calculation (see *e.* below, which is designed to give a cushion over and above income support rates to try to ensure that parents can afford to continue working).

c. Assessable income

Assessable income is the part of a parent's income used for calculating his (or her) maintenance obligation. This is worked out by taking his (or her) net income (i.e. the amount of income after payment of tax, National Insurance contributions and half the pension contributions) and then deducting from that the *exempt income*.

There are special rules for the self-employed, childminders and other special cases. Whilst not all sources of income count (for example, social fund payments and attendance allowances are disregarded), the Agency can assume a notional amount of income if a parent deliberately deprives himself or herself of a source of income or, in some circumstances, performs services without pay.

d. Deduction rate

Assessable income will be shared equally between the children and the absent parent until the *maintenance requirement* is paid. Once that has been paid, if there is any remaining assessable income, further child maintenance at a lower rate of deduction up to 25 per cent on the excess of income is payable. The 25 per cent rate is payable only if there are three or more children eligible for maintenance. There is a cap or ceiling to the maximum amount of maintenance which can be paid, worked out by adding up the maintenance requirement plus tripling the total of the child premium plus the family premium for each child.

e. Protected income

The protected income is designed to prevent the liable parent's income being pushed down to income support levels or below by the amount of child support which they are obliged to pay. It gives a margin of £30 weekly plus 15 per cent of the total income of the family above income support rates. An absent parent's income should never fall below the protected income level as a result of the calculation of his or her liability to pay child support maintenance.

EXAMPLES

CASE 1: Where the parent caring for the children is not working

1. The weekly maintenance requirement calculation
Mark and Sally have separated. They have two children, Fiona and Brad, aged twelve and five. Using April 1994/5 rates, the maintenance requirement for Fiona and Brad is:

Child allowance:	Fiona	23.00
	Brad	15.65
Family premium		10.05
Lone parent premium		5.10
Adult personal allowance ('parent as carer')		45.70
Sub-total		99.50
Less: Child benefit: Fiona		−10.20
Brad		− 8.25
TOTAL MAINTENANCE REQUIREMENT:		**£81.05**

2. Calculating net income
Calculations about how much an absent parent may have to pay begin with calculating his or her net income.

Gross income
less
(Tax, National Insurance contributions and 50% pension contributions)
equals
NET INCOME

For the purpose of this example, Mark's net income will be taken to be £172.

3. Calculating exempt income

Exempt income is supposed to cover a parent's own personal essential living expenses which must be met first. These do not, however, include all actual living expenses, but those specified in the Child Support Act and its regulations. In most cases this simply includes housing costs and the adult personal allowance for income support. It can also include:

- the costs of caring for the parent's own natural or adopted children if they live with him or her (the children's personal income support plus family premium plus lone parent premium if appropriate)
- an amount equal to the income support disability premium if the parent is disabled
- the carer premium if the parent is caring for a disabled person.

Mark is living alone in rented accommodation costing £55 per week; his exempt income is:

Personal allowance	45.70
Housing costs	55.00
TOTAL EXEMPT INCOME:	**£100.70**

4. Calculating assessable income

Assessable income, the amount from which maintenance will be paid, is calculated as net income *less* exempt income *equals* assessable income. So Mark's assessable income is:

Net income	172.00
Less:	
Exempt income	100.70
TOTAL ASSESSABLE INCOME:	**£71.30**

5. Calculating the deduction rate

Fifty per cent of the assessable income is paid towards the child maintenance requirement, so Mark will pay £35.65 child maintenance. (Amounts are rounded up to the nearest penny.)

CASE 2: Where both parents are working

Sally has now got a job as Brad has started going to school. She receives a total net income of £160 per week. Mark has just been given a pay rise and receives a net income of £200 per week. Sally's housing costs are £80 per week and Mark is still in his flat paying £55 per week.

1. Calculating the maintenance requirement
The children are still the same ages as before, so the maintenance requirement calculation is the same, i.e. £81.05.

2. Calculating the exempt incomes
Mark's exempt income is the same as before, namely £100.70. Sally's exempt income will also need to be worked out:

Personal allowance	45.70
Child allowance: Fiona	23.00
Brad	15.65
Family premium	10.05
Lone parent premium	5.10
Housing costs	80.00
TOTAL EXEMPT INCOME	**£179.50**

As Sally's actual income is less than her exempt income, her income will be ignored when working out how much Mark will have to pay. Her net income would have to exceed her exempt income before the amount that Mark paid would reduce.

3. Calculating the assessable income
Mark's assessable income is now £99.30 (£200 less £100.70), of which he is liable to pay half, i.e. £49.65, towards the maintenance requirement.

If there is a shortfall, as in this example, it will not automatically be made up by the CSA or any other body. The formula simply works out a notional amount of maintenance for the children. (An application for welfare benefits could be made if required.)

CASE 3: Where parents have high incomes
Under the Child Support Act framework, both parents are deemed financially responsible for their children. In practice, as

the parent with care is meeting the costs of looking after the children anyway, her income is often ignored when working out how much the absent parent has to pay. However, for families with higher incomes, the income of the parent with care does more often directly have an impact on the amount the absent parent pays. However, the calculation is complex.

Rupert and Georgina have just separated. Their four children (all under eleven) live with Georgina, who does not work outside the home at present.

1. Calculating the maintenance requirement

Personal allowances	(Georgina)	45.70
	(children – all under 11 –	
	4 × £15.65)	62.60
Family premium		10.05
Lone parent premium		5.10
Sub-total		123.45
Less: Child benefit (1 × £10.20 + 3 × £8.25)		34.95
TOTAL MAINTENANCE REQUIREMENT		**£88.50**

2. Calculating maintenance at the higher level

For the purpose of this example, Rupert's assessable income (net income less exempt income) is £570 per week. As 50% of this (£285) exceeds the maintenance requirement (£88.50), Rupert will be paying a further slice of child support calculated using the 'additional element' of 25%.

To work out how much of his income is used up at the basic deduction rate of 50%, the formula doubles up the maintenance requirement.

Basic assessable income (£88.50 × 2)	177.00
Additional assessable income (£570 − £177)	393.00
Additional element maintenance (£393.00 × 25%)	98.25
TOTAL MAINTENANCE PAYABLE (£88.50 + £98.25):	**£186.75**

Say Georgina were to get a job. Her *assessable* income (i.e. net income less exempt income) for the purpose of illustration is £80 per week. Rupert's assessable income is still £570 per week, and the maintenance requirement is still £88.50 per week. Their joint assessable income is £570 + £80 = £650.

Again, Rupert will still be paying an extra slice of child support of 25%.

To work out how much maintenance Rupert will now pay:

£88.50 × $\frac{£570}{£650}$ = £77.61 (rounding up to the nearest penny)

Basic assessable income (£77.61 × 2)	£155.22
Additional assessable income (£570 − £155.22)	£414.78
Additional element maintenance (£414.78 × 25%)	£103.70

TOTAL MAINTENANCE PAYABLE

(£77.61 + £103.70)	£181.31
	(rounding up)

This is a reduction of £5.44 from the amount Rupert was originally assessed to pay.

For families on very high incomes there is a maximum amount of maintenance which can be assessed under the formula, though applications to court can be made for top-up maintenance.

Effect of child support on welfare benefits

The first £15 of income from maintenance is ignored when calculating a lone parent's entitlement to family credit, housing benefit, disability working allowance and council tax benefit. This £15 provision is referred to as a 'maintenance disregard'; it can be an incentive for the payer who can see a direct financial benefit for the family (as opposed to a simple reduction of payments made by the state).

However, the maintenance disregard does not apply to income support, where the amount of maintenance reduces the state benefits pound for pound.

No flexibility

The amount of child support paid can sometimes float the recipient off income support if it is the same as or more than the amount of the maintenance requirement. This can have the knock-on effect of disentitling the recipient to the 'passported' benefits that are available to income support payees – like mortgage repayments and free school meals – which can cause real hardship to a family. Because the CSA has to apply the formula rigidly, there is no flexibility to provide any financial protection for such families – the parent looking after the children may have to try to find work to help support the family. For working parents, child support can provide real help as a cushion to provide or help towards providing for the extra costs of going to work (like childminding fees and travel). Child support payments will be reduced only if the parent looking after the children increases her (or his) income to more than the amount of her (or his) exempt income.

Summary of steps required to work out the formula

1. Maintenance requirement (MR)
Using income support rates, ADD together:
    Child allowances
    + Family premium
    + [Lone parent premium] if applicable
    + Adult personal allowance
then DEDUCT Child benefit for each child to work out the weekly MR.

2. Exempt income
Using income support rates, ADD together:
    Adult personal allowance
    + [Child allowances] (for natural or adopted children living in)
    + [Family premium] (if natural or adopted children living in)
    + [Lone parent premium] if applicable
    + Housing costs

If the children are older – i.e. the youngest is at least 11 – then the adult personal allowance element will be reduced.

3. Assessable income

Work out first the weekly amount of **net income** i.e. gross income less tax, National Insurance contributions and 50% pension contributions. Then DEDUCT **exempt income** from **net income** to get **assessable income**.

4. Deduction rate

For calculating the maintenance requirement the basic deduction rate is 50% of assessable income. If 50% of assessable income equals or exceeds the maintenance requirement, then an extra proportion of assessable income (up to 25% of the excess) may be payable.

5. Protected income

The protected income calculation is designed to prevent the absent parent's income falling below income support rates as a result of child maintenance commitments – in effect providing a cushion above those rates as an incentive to work.

Phasing in

Where absent parents have a second family and were already paying maintenance to their first family before April 1993, the new amount of maintenance which they have been assessed to pay will be phased in over 18 months, to avoid a sudden high leap in maintenance payments. To qualify for the phased-in payments, the new maintenance requirement per week must be more than £60. During the transitional period, the increase will be limited as follows:

- for the first six months, the old amount plus either 25% of the excess or £20, whichever is greater
- for the next six months, ·the old amount plus either 50% of the excess amount or £40, whichever is greater
- for the last six months, the old amount plus either 75% of the excess amount or £60, whichever is greater.

Challenging a Child Support Agency Assessment

If you feel that your assessment is wrong, you can seek to challenge it. The first stage in this process is an internal review, which will be carried out by a Child Support Officer who is not the same as the original one who dealt with your case. If you are still dissatisfied, you can appeal to a Child Support Appeal Tribunal, and thereafter to a Child Support Commissioner; if you feel the decision was still wrong in law, you can appeal further to the Court of Appeal. All this will cost time and probably money – legal aid is not available until an appeal has been made to the Court of Appeal. If you are on a low income you may, however, be able to ask someone from your local Welfare Rights Advice Agency to come with you to the Appeal tribunal and help you prepare your case.

The Child Support Act and the rules governing the Child Support Agency are very complicated; as space is limited here, only a short summary can be included. For further reading, the Child Poverty Action Group have a very useful *Child Support Handbook* (£6.95). You can also get some excellent help and information from the National Council for One Parent Families (addresses and telephone numbers on page 76).

CHAPTER 6

GETTING MONEY FROM THE COURT BEFORE DIVORCE

IN MOST divorce cases nowadays, where there are children, the first step in getting maintenance before a divorce will be via the Child Support Agency, as the courts have in most cases lost their powers to make court orders for child support in a disputed case. However, even before the divorce begins, you can also apply to court for an order for financial provision from your spouse if he or she is not providing proper maintenance for you.

The courts can still act, however, if the Agency cannot take on a case, say if you wish to make a claim for a stepchild or if one parent lives abroad. However, you will need to get legal advice about whether it will be worthwhile going ahead.

As an alternative, if you and your spouse agree on the terms of separation, you can together enter into a separation agreement which will deal with financial issues (although you may still be required to use the Child Support Agency for child support if you are claiming benefits). If you can agree interim financial arrangements, getting a court order based on your agreement may still be useful or even necessary to ensure that the agreement is watertight. You can ask for a 'consent order' to be made in your agreed terms. Generally, an order is easier to enforce than a simple separation agreement.

Court orders: through the county court

An application can be made to any county court for maintenance or a lump sum payment, even when no divorce is required or possible. You only have to satisfy the court that your spouse has failed to provide reasonable maintenance for you while being in a position to do so.

You will have to submit an application in duplicate, together with a statement in support, providing evidence of your financial resources and needs. The court fees, which have to be paid at the time of submitting the application, are £15.

The respondent (that is, your spouse) is required to file with the court a statement in answer within 14 days of receiving your application from the court. The court will set a hearing date usually some weeks off; the county court district judge normally hears the application in chambers (in private – in the same way as an application for maintenance in divorce proceedings).

Unless there are any special reasons why you should apply to a county court, it is unlikely that you will be able to get a legal aid certificate for such an application. Because the solicitors' costs in a magistrates court tend to be less, the Legal Aid Board will generally only sanction applications for that court.

Court orders: through the magistrates' court

The magistrates' court can make orders for periodical payments for any amount and for lump sums of up to £1,000 each for the applicant and any children. You can apply, for example, for a lump sum to repay you for expenses reasonably incurred in maintaining yourself for the period before the order was made. There is an initial limit of £1,000, but there appears to be no limit on the number of applications you can make: thus you can apply, if the need arises, for lump sums on more than one occasion.

The procedure for applying for a maintenance order in a magistrates' court costs relatively little; no affidavits are required. The application can be made to any magistrates' court in the area where either husband or wife lives, or where they last lived together. Legal aid (or approval for 'assistance by way of representation' under the green form scheme) can be applied for to make or defend such an application.

Proceedings are started by making a 'complaint' in writing or orally. You must be able to prove to the magistrates' court that your spouse:

- has deserted you, or has behaved in such a way that you cannot reasonably be expected to live with him or her (this could include adultery by your spouse), *and*
- has failed to provide reasonable maintenance for you or the children, if this is a case which can still be dealt with by the courts).

If it seems that you have a case, the court will issue a summons for your spouse to appear before the court on a given day.

If you and your spouse have agreed about maintenance, you can go to the magistrates' court and ask for an agreed order to be made along those lines, provided the court has no reason to think it would be unjust. (There is no upper limit on lump sums in 'agreed' orders.)

If the order contains provision for a child (where the court has jurisdiction), the court has a specific duty to check that as far as possible adequate payment is ordered to be made towards the child's needs.

Both the applicant and the respondent will be asked to provide evidence to the court about their income and expenditure and assets. Before making any order, the magistrates' court takes into account all the circumstances of the case, giving first consideration to the welfare of any child of the family.

Other factors are income and earning capacities, obligations and responsibilities, age, any physical disabilities, duration of the marriage, previous standard of living, the contribution each has made to the family and the conduct of each of the parties if it would be unfair not to take it into account.

The interval between applying to the magistrates' court and the date fixed for the hearing varies from court to court; it is likely to be between one and two months.

In a case of urgent need, a court can be asked for an expedited hearing, or for an interim order to tide the applicant over until such time as the case can be heard fully. An interim maintenance order lasts for a maximum of three months but may be extended for a further three months.

If subsequently there is a petition for divorce, details of any magistrates' court order for maintenance have to be given on it, where information is asked about 'other proceedings in any court'.

Because the magistrates' courts tend to deal with people on a low income, and because there used in the past to be a very low upper limit to maintenance orders, the habit of low levels has stuck. The amounts of maintenance and lump sums ordered by the magistrates' court may therefore well be lower than those ordered by either the county court or the divorce court.

Court orders: through the divorce court

Once a petition for divorce (or for judicial separation) has been lodged at the divorce county court, you can apply there for an order for 'financial relief'. (If you have obtained an order for maintenance at the magistrates' court or county court, this will remain in force until there is an order in the divorce county court.)

Maintenance pending suit

A long-term order for maintenance or an order for a capital sum cannot be made until decree nisi and will not take effect until the decree has been made absolute. However, the court has power to order temporary maintenance payments for a spouse until the decree absolute. This is known as 'maintenance pending suit' (MPS). The main point of the MPS order is to keep the wife going until the court can make an order after fuller examination of the financial position. For children's maintenance applications, the court's powers are now much restricted. It is possible that applications can be made for stepchildren, although the courts will usually expect the natural father to pay before making an order against a stepparent. Similarly, for any children of the family, interim payments orders may be made, called interim periodical payments.

An application for MPS can be made as soon as the petition is filed. It takes between three and six weeks (often longer) for the application to be heard and the district judge to make an order. You will have to give the fullest possible information about your needs and provide an affidavit of means (a sworn statement of what you earn, own and owe), as should your spouse.

If your spouse fails to file an affidavit of means, the district judge may make the order for quite a high amount in order to force him to bring his financial affairs into the open – he must pay up, but if he wants to prove that the order is too high for him to manage, he will have to disclose his finances.

An MPS order comes into effect straightaway and may be backdated to the date of the petition. It lasts at most until decree absolute. Its purpose is to tide the payee over until there is a full inquiry into all the financial facts; this is generally reflected in the level of payment ordered – namely MPS will simply cover the payee's immediate needs.

Financial applications for children

As well as reforming the legal framework of the relationships between parents and children, the Children Act 1989 codified the law about financial applications for children. It also enables children over 18 to apply for periodical payments or a lump sum. Since the Child Support Act came into force on 5 April 1993, most children's applications for maintenance will be made in the Child Support Agency, although the courts retain their powers for stepchildren and any other children for whom the Agency cannot act.

A parent, guardian or anyone with a residence order for a child can apply to court for an order that either (or both) parents pay:

- periodical payments (maintenance) (these can be secured; applies only if the Agency has no jurisdiction)
- a lump sum
- a settlement of property
- a transfer of property to the applicant for the benefit of the child or directly to the child (a transfer of property could cover a transfer of a tenancy too).

Applications can be made to either a magistrates' court (Family Proceedings Panel), the county court (Family Hearing Centre) or the High Court, although the magistrates court only has power to order periodical payments or a lump sum.

The court must look at all the circumstances, including the income, earning capacity of the parties (and the financial position of the child), their needs and obligations, any physical or mental disability of the child and the way in which the child was (or expects to be) educated or trained (this approach is often summed up as 'needs and resources').

See also Chapter 5 about applying for child support under the Child Support Act 1991.

Applications by sons or daughters over 18

A son or daughter over 18 can apply for periodical payments (like weekly or monthly payments) or a lump sum if he or she is in full-time education or training (although this would also cover situations where the son or daughter was working in the evenings to supplement his or her income whilst in continuing education). The courts will take the approach as outlined above.

There are, however, some restrictions on applications: they can be made only if the parents (whether married or not) are no longer living together in the same household and there was no previous maintenance order in existence before the child's sixteenth birthday. In other words, this provision is primarily intended for sons or daughters who plan to go on to further education and whose parents have comparatively recently split up and where the parental part of the grant (for example) is not being paid. Instead of the parent being forced to go to court to chase up maintenance payments the son or daughter is able to make his or her own application. Students are also able to apply only if they are not covered by the Child Support Agency, i.e. they are 19 or over.

CHAPTER 7

GETTING A DIVORCE

THERE is only one ground for obtaining a divorce in England or Wales, namely that the marriage has irretrievably broken down. In order to prove this irretrievable breakdown, you will have to prove one or more of 'the five facts':

Fact 1: adultery and intolerability
Fact 2: unreasonable behaviour
Fact 3: desertion for a period of two years
Fact 4: separation for a period of two years with consent of the other party
Fact 5: separation for a period of five years.

The full wording of the facts which you will have to prove, and an explanation, are set out later in this chapter.

A petition for divorce cannot be presented until one year has elapsed since the marriage took place, whatever the circumstances. But you do not have to start off divorce proceedings to apply to the court about problems over the children (for more of this see Chapter 5). Applications for a residence or contact order, for example, can be made at any time. Similarly, you can also ask the Child Support Agency for maintenance for the children (or the court for maintenance for yourself) before the divorce proceedings start. So there is no need to begin an application for a divorce until you have finally made up your mind that that is what you want.

Even if you can establish the facts for going for a divorce now, you might also want to consider whether to make a separation agreement with your spouse now and then apply for a divorce on the 'no fault' ground (Fact 4) later. Applying for a divorce when you have lived separately from your spouse for at least two years and where you both consent to the divorce going ahead can help to remove some of the bitterness and difficulties often associated with divorce.

Jurisdiction

Whether you got married in England or Wales or abroad is not relevant in determining whether an English court has jurisdiction to hear your petition. Either you or your spouse must be 'domiciled' in England or Wales or have been resident there for at least one year before the date of presenting the petition. Short absences (for example holidays) can be ignored. It is advisable to consult a solicitor straightaway in connection with any proposed divorce where there is doubt about domicile or where neither of the couple lives in England or Wales.

The law in Scotland and the procedure in Northern Ireland is different and are dealt with in Chapters 15 and 16. Domicile or residence in Scotland, Northern Ireland, the Channel Islands or the Isle of Man is not sufficient to enable you to get divorced in an English court.

Where to apply

Divorce proceedings are usually started in your local divorce county court or a county court which is classed as a 'Family Hearing Centre' (see the chart on page 244: 'Which Court?'). Not all county courts deal with divorce proceedings, so telephone your county court first to check whether it does. It is possible to start divorce proceedings at any court in England and Wales; this can be useful, in sensitive cases, if you want to avoid publicity. Usually, however, you should choose the court that is most convenient for you (and your spouse).

Your case may be transferred to the High Court (also now known, under the new court structure, as a 'care centre') if the divorce proceedings become defended or, in a very small number of cases, where the financial proceedings or the proceedings relating to the children are extremely complex. In London, the Divorce Registry acts both as a county court and High Court.

Judicial separation

Judicial separation proceedings can be used where the parties do not yet accept that the marriage has irretrievably broken down, or do not want to divorce, for example for religious reasons. The facts that have to be proved are precisely the same as for divorce.

The effect of a decree of judicial separation is that the husband and wife are technically relieved of the obligation to reside with each other. But they remain married, in law, so that neither can marry anyone else and on the death of one partner, the other would be his or her widow or widower. This can be particularly important in the case of an elderly couple when a wife would lose substantial widow's pension benefits on divorce. The decree does, however, affect inheritance rights: if either spouse dies without making a will, they are considered as if they were divorced.

A decree of judicial separation does not preclude a divorce later and the facts relied on to obtain the judicial separation decree (except for desertion which formally ends on a decree of judicial separation) may be relied on in the later divorce proceedings. The procedure for obtaining a judicial separation is similar to divorce but there is only one decree with no interim stage. Applications for judicial separation are made much less frequently than applications for divorce: if ultimately what you want is a divorce, applying for judicial separation in the meantime will only double your costs.

The procedure for getting a divorce

Whichever of a couple formally starts off the divorce process is called the petitioner. The other becomes the respondent. Under current law, it is not possible to file a joint petition (but see page 131 for divorce reform proposals). You should try to agree between yourselves who is going to file the petition and on what facts. Some people find offensive the idea of being the respondent and admitting adultery or unreasonable behaviour. It will not, however, affect how a court decides related issues to do with money or the children unless the petitioner specifically alleges in those related proceedings that the other's conduct has been so bad that it should be taken into account. There is a practical advantage in being the petitioner because it is the petitioner who is in the driving seat and who can, to some extent, control the pace of the divorce. In certain cases, it is possible for a respondent to file a cross-petition. However, this merely adds to the expense and is rarely worthwhile (see page 119).

In an undefended case, a solicitor is not needed for the actual procedure of getting divorced. However, you may want advice from a solicitor before embarking on proceedings. You may want to check whether there is a basis for divorce in your case and that you understand what has to be done, by whom and when, and what the implications are of the questions you will be required to answer on the various forms that have to be completed and submitted to the court.

If you have children, it would be wise to discuss with your solicitor the arrangements that you propose to make for them. Under the procedure brought in by the Children Act, the petitioner must try to agree the contents of the form called 'Statement of Arrangements for the Children' with the repondent before the divorce proceedings start. You may want some advice about how to complete the form and what approach to take with your spouse. It is also useful to get some advice on financial matters at an early stage.

Undefended divorce – the special procedure

Undefended divorces are dealt with by what is known inaptly as 'the special procedure'. The divorce process is carried out on the basis of paperwork and you will not have to attend any hearing in respect of the divorce petition. The facts in the petition (and the subsequent affidavits) are considered by the district judge of the divorce court without either spouse being present. If you have children, the district judge will also review the arrangements for them: he or she must then decide whether or not any order should be made about the children. If the district judge considers that no reply should be made, then again the divorce will proceed just on the paperwork and you will not be asked to go to court. If there are doubts or problems, the district judge can ask for further evidence, which may require personal attendance at court. In practice, the majority of divorces will not have any order made about the children, leaving it up to the parents to make their own arrangements. Court orders about the children will be made only if there are disputes or if in some other way a court order will be better for the children.

Documents needed
To start off divorce proceedings, you need to send the following to your local divorce county court or the Divorce Registry in London (Somerset House, Strand, London WC2R 1LP):

- the completed form of petition for divorce, with a copy for the other spouse (the respondent) plus an extra copy in an adultery case where the co-respondent is named
- the marriage certificate or a certified copy of it.

A photocopy of your marriage certificate is not acceptable. A certified copy can be obtained for £5.50 if you go in person to the Public Search Room, St Catherine's House, 10 Kingsway, London WC2B 6JP, or by post (£15) from OPCS, Smedley Hydro, Trafalgar House, Birkdale, Southport PR8 2HH. You could also obtain one from the Register Office in the district where the marriage took place. (The marriage certificate will not be returned to you after the divorce).

If your marriage certificate is in a foreign language, you will also need a formal notarised translation of it.

In addition you need to send:

- a fee of £40 (or a completed 'fee exemption form' if you are exempted because you are in receipt of income support or family credit or legal advice under the green form scheme)
- a statement of the proposed arrangements for any relevant children (see page 115), with a copy for the other spouse. Try to get this completed form agreed in advance with your spouse and countersigned by him or her.

If your solicitor is filing the divorce petition for you, he or she will also need to file a 'certificate of reconciliation' stating whether any advice has been given about reconciliation (except where you are being advised under the green form scheme).

Blank forms for the petition and the statement of arrangements for the children are available from divorce court offices and the

Divorce Registry, without charge, and also a free booklet on the subject. There is a standard printed form of petition for each of the 'five facts', which prove that the marriage has irretrievably broken down. The court supplies notes for guidance which you should read carefully before completing your petition. In some courts, the staff will help you complete the forms but they are not allowed to give you legal advice. If you are dealing with the divorce proceedings yourself, always keep a copy of any documents you supply to the court and/or your spouse.

You will be sent by the court a letter confirming that the divorce proceedings have been lodged, which states the reference number allocated to your petition. This must be quoted on all communications to the court.

The petition
In the petition, you must give the full names of yourself and your spouse and the date and place of the marriage (copied from the marriage certificate); the address at which you and your spouse last lived together and your present address(es); the occupations of yourself and your spouse, the full names of children and dates of birth if they are not adults; details of any previous court proceedings relating to the marriage or property.

The form assumes that the petitioner is domiciled in England or Wales; if you are not, you must make it clear that you are relying on your spouse's domicile or the fact that you or your spouse have been habitually resident in England or Wales, which means at least one year's residence ending with the date on which the petition is presented. Addresses and dates of residence must be given.

You must set out one or more of the five facts on which you rely to show that the marriage has irretrievably broken down. Later in the proceedings you will have to swear on oath that the facts that you have alleged are true. If you have any doubts about or difficulties with completing the petition form which the court office is unable to help you with, you should consult a solicitor.

Fact 1
That the respondent has committed adultery and the petitioner finds it intolerable to live with the respondent

In the petition, no more need be said than that the respondent has committed adultery with someone else (called the 'co-respondent'). The petitioner must, in addition, state that he or she finds it intolerable to live with the other spouse.

If you know the name and address of the co-respondent, you can include it but you do not have to. Also, if you do not know the co-respondent's identity, you can state, for example, that the respondent 'has committed adultery with a woman whose name and identity are unknown to the petitioner'.

You are asked to say when and where adultery has taken place, so far as you know. You can ask the respondent to provide a 'confession statement' admitting adultery at a specific time and place with a person (stating his or her name and address or stating that he or she refuses to disclose the identity). Such a statement can be admitted as evidence and you can copy the details given onto the petition.

If the co-respondent is named, you will need to send to the court an extra set of papers for serving on the co-respondent too.

If your spouse refuses to admit to adultery and you have no proof of it, there is a risk that the divorce will become defended (with all the expenditure of money and time that this necessitates), so another of the 'facts' on which to base the divorce may be more sensible.

Fact 2
That the respondent has behaved in such a way that the petitioner cannot reasonably be expected to live with the respondent
There is no simple definition of unreasonable behaviour. Violence or serious threats of violence to the petitioner or to the children, homosexual or lesbian conduct, persistent nagging, refusal to have sexual intercourse or to have children knowing that the other spouse wishes to have them, financial irresponsibility such as gambling to excess – these are some serious examples of what can amount to unreasonable behaviour. But many less grave matters are sufficient.

The test is whether the court feels that between this particular husband and wife the behaviour complained of is sufficiently serious to make it unreasonable to expect the petitioner to carry on living with the respondent. Usually, there will have been a number of incidents to evidence the breakdown of the marriage but one very serious incident (such as considerable violence) can be enough. Mere incompatibility is not enough unless it has driven one or both partners to behave unreasonably – for example by showing no sexual interest or affection, being abusive and derogatory, and so on.

If the behaviour of one of the spouses has forced the other to leave home, this would be evidence of the unreasonableness of the behaviour.

In the petition, you should give as precise details as you can. You can allege in general terms the types of behaviour but then you should insert specific incidents, giving details with the approximate dates and places, preferably in date order. But try to be concise – a few short paragraphs giving the bare bones of the allegations will usually be sufficient.

If you have continued to live together, it is particularly important that instances of unreasonable behaviour within the last six months are included in the petition. Further evidence can, if necessary, be given in the affidavit that follows the petition.

Fact 3
That the respondent has deserted the petitioner for a continuous period of at least two years immediately preceding the presentation of the petition

Desertion as the basis for divorce means a period of separation of at least two years brought about by a husband or wife leaving the other against the deserted party's wishes. You have to state the circumstances, the date on which he or she left and that it was without your consent.

Fact 4
Separation with consent: that the parties have lived apart for a continuous period of at least two years immediately preceding the presentation of the petition and that the respondent consents to a decree being granted AND

Fact 5
Separation without consent: that the parties have lived apart for a continuous period of at least five years immediately preceding the presentation of the petition

In order to establish separation as proof of the breakdown of a marriage, a couple must have lived apart for at least two years if the respondent consents to a divorce, or for five years if there is no consent. If you are still living under the same roof as your spouse but in separate households, you may be required to give evidence of details of your separation later in the proceedings. In order to be considered to be living apart, you have to be sleeping separately, eating separately and not carrying out any domestic tasks (like cooking or cleaning) for each other.

The date of the separation should be stated accurately in the petition. If the separation has been for more than two but less than five years, the respondent's positive consent to being divorced – not just lack of objection – is necessary. The respondent confirms his or her consent by completing the acknowledgement of service. If there is a real risk that the respondent may withdraw consent after the divorce papers have been served, it might be worthwhile considering filing for a divorce based on another fact, if appropriate.

After five or more years' separation, the respondent's consent is not required (but there is provision for opposing the divorce on the grounds that it would cause grave financial or other hardship).

In all separation cases, the respondent may request that his or her future financial position be considered by the court before the decree is made final. The respondent's financial position as a result of being divorced will then be closely scrutinised and, in order to obtain a decree, the petitioner may have to safeguard the respondent's financial position.

Six months for attempted reconciliation
On the affidavit that has to follow the petition, there are questions about times when husband and wife have lived in the same household. To allow for attempts at reconciliation, you can have gone on living together for a period of up to six months, or several short periods which together add up to less than six months, without affecting the facts on which the petition is based.

Six months for attempted reconciliation after adultery
After a petitioner became aware of the other's adultery, a period of living together which exceeds six months would prevent a decree.

Time begins to run from the date that you knew of the actual adultery which is referred to in the petition. Knowledge does not mean mere suspicion. If you had suspected your spouse for some time but only properly found out about the adultery after you had confronted him or her about it, for example, the six-month period would start to run only from the date of your confrontation. If the adultery is still continuing, you can rely on the latest incident, rather than the date you first knew about it.

Six months for attempted reconciliation after unreasonable behaviour
Where unreasonable behaviour is alleged in the petition, the period of living together is counted from the last act of unreasonable behaviour referred to in the petition and will be taken into account in deciding whether the petitioner can reasonably be expected to live with the respondent. Living together for more than six months would not necessarily prevent a decree being granted, but the court would require a detailed explanation and might well conclude that the respondent's behaviour was not unreasonable.

Six months for attempted reconciliation after separation
Although periods of living together (up to a total of six months since separation or desertion) will not invalidate the divorce petition, any such period does not count as part of the two or five year threshold. For instance, if you lived together for three months in an attempt at reconciliation and then parted again, the petition cannot be filed until two years, three months and one day have elapsed since the original separation.

The prayer
The last page of the petition asks the court for various things:
- a prayer (request) for the marriage to be dissolved (ended)
- an order for costs to be made against the respondent and/or co-respondent; in the case of a petition for adultery, or unreasonable behaviour or desertion, it is usual to ask the court to make an order for costs against the respondent

- under the heading of 'ancillary relief', orders for maintenance (called periodical payments), lump sum payments and property adjustment. Such applications are made in general terms at this stage, so do not specify any actual amounts
- any orders sought for the children (for example, a residence or contact order).

Under the Children Act procedures, in theory you should include the application for an order about the children only if you really want an order to be made. In practice, some divorce petitions still include a claim for a residence or contact order even if the spouses agree that no order is necessary.

It is better not to cross off the claim for financial relief because it may be complicated or even impossible to apply later. A petitioner would have to make a special application to the court for leave (permission) to apply later for any required order if a claim for ancillary relief were deleted. Such an application is not certain to be granted if it is made after a long time lapse or if, for example, the respondent says that he or she decided not to defend the petition only because of the absence of any request for ancillary relief. So, even if you have agreed with your spouse that no financial claims will be made, you should nevertheless include them in the petition so that they can be formally dismissed (only if claims have been made can they be dismissed and a full and final settlement order be made). But to avoid misunderstanding when your spouse receives the petition, explain to him or her that the claims are being included only so that they can be dismissed later.

Similarly, you can include a prayer for costs even though you may agree or decide not to follow this request through. What you are claiming here is costs only in respect of the divorce itself (not ancillary issues such as finance or custody) and these costs will be comparatively low. In the case of a divorce based on periods of separation, the petitioner and respondent often agree that costs will be divided between them, so the petitioner would only seek an order for half the costs to be paid by the respondent. It is possible to seek costs against a co-respondent, but it would be wise to discuss this with a solicitor.

The last page of the petition should be signed by you if acting in person or by your solicitor if he or she is acting for you. You should also include the names and addresses for service of the respondent and co-respondent and your address for service. Usually home addresses are addresses for service but if solicitors are acting for either or both of you, their address(es) will be inserted instead here.

Statement of arrangements for children

All 'children of the family', whatever their ages, have to be named in the petition. Children of the family are, in broad terms, children who are:

- children of both husband and wife
- children adopted by them both
- step-children
- other children who have been treated at any time during the marriage by both as part of the family – but not foster children.

'Relevant' children are those under the age of 16, or under the age of 18 and still in full-time education, or undergoing training for a trade, profession or vocation (even if the child is also earning). If your child is over 16 and under 18 but is in full-time employment or is unemployed (i.e. no longer in the education system), it is important to say so because he or she is no longer a 'relevant' child.

A statement about the present and proposed arrangements for relevant children must be prepared by the petitioner. (A blank printed form of statement is available from the court office: you will need a completed copy for the other spouse.) The petitioner should try and agree its contents with the respondent in advance of starting the divorce, and get his or her countersignature if possible. If the respondent refuses to co-operate, the petitioner can file his or her own statement of arrangements and the respondent will have the opportunity of producing his or her own statement of arrangements later. If the respondent has not signed the statement of arrangements, some courts will want you to confirm that you have tried to obtain his or her signature.

The Statement of Arrangements form is eight pages long and requires detailed information about the children of the family. Although it is long, it is fairly jargon-free. You will need to set out details about the home where the children currently live, their education or training, any childcare arrangements, amounts of maintenance payable for the children (whether this is paid or agreed), details of contact (access), their health and if there are any other court proceedings about them. If you do not agree with current arrangements, there are spaces in the form for you to set out your proposed changes. At the end of the form you will be asked whether you would agree to attend conciliation with your spouse if arrangements are not agreed.

The aim of making the form more comprehensive is to ask parents to look at the realities of their children's changed lifestyles in some depth. As the courts will not be able to ask the parents in person about the children (most divorces now proceeding on the basis of paperwork alone), they want to have as complete a picture as possible of arrangements for the children. If your future is uncertain, it may be difficult to complete the form fully; if so, just include as much information as you can, indicating where necessary what arrangements have yet to be decided upon.

Service of the petition

The court posts to the respondent, at the address given in the petition, one copy of the petition and of the statement of the arrangements for any children.

The court also sends an 'acknowledgement of service' form, which the respondent has to complete and return to the court within eight days (although this time is not always adhered to). If adultery is alleged and a co-respondent is named, a copy of the petition is also sent to him or her, again with an acknowledgement of service form to be returned to the court.

The court has to be satisfied that the respondent (and co-respondent) has received the divorce papers or that all reasonable steps have been taken to serve the documents on him or her. Service is normally proved by the return of the acknowledgement of service form to the court. If, however, the acknowledgement of service form is not returned, the petitioner can apply to the court for a fresh set of documents and arrange for 'personal service'.

The petitioner cannot personally serve the petition, but any other person over the age of 16 can effect service by delivering the set of papers to the respondent personally and then completing an

AGREED ARRANGEMENTS FOR CHILDREN: A QUICK GUIDE

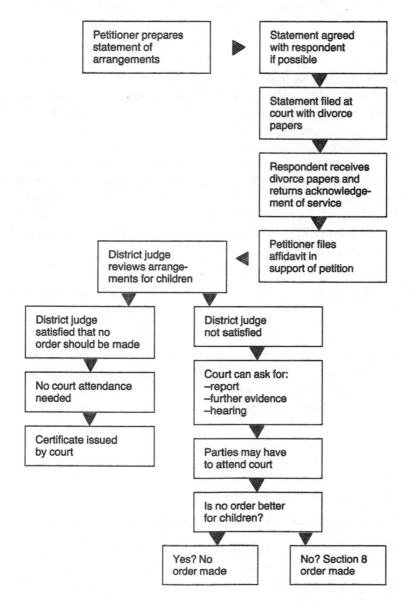

affidavit of service and taking or sending it to the court. If the petitioner has had difficulty in serving the papers, he or she can apply to the court for the petition to be served by the bailiff of the county court for the area in which the respondent lives, or can employ an enquiry agent to act as process server.

If the respondent (or co-respondent) fails to return the acknowledgement of service form but has acted in a way which makes it clear that he or she has received the petition, an application can be made by the petitioner for service of the petition to be deemed to have been effected.

If service turns out, in practice, not to be possible, the petitioner may be able to get an order dispensing with service.

The respondent's response

With the documents sent to the respondent are explanatory notes called 'notice of proceedings' telling the respondent some of the implications of the answers he or she may give on the acknowledgement of service form.

The acknowledgement of service is not only an acknowledgement that the petition has been received but also includes questions about the respondent's intentions, namely:

● **whether he or she consents to the divorce proceedings**

In an adultery case, the respondent is asked to indicate if he or she admits adultery, and he or she must sign the acknowledgement of service even if a solicitor is also signing. In most other cases, if you have instructed a solicitor, the solicitor's signature suffices.

In a separation case, the respondent has to reply to the question on the acknowledgement of service form whether he or she intends to apply to the court to consider the financial position as it will be after the divorce.

Where the divorce petition is based on separation with consent, the respondent has to confirm that consent by writing 'yes' and also putting his or her signature on the form.

● **whether he or she objects to a claim for costs; if so, why**

If a prayer for costs has been made in the petition, you are asked whether you object to paying the petitioner's costs and, if so, why. You may, for example, have agreed with the petitioner that no order for costs will be pursued against you and your comment to this effect on the acknowledgement of service form should remind the petitioner to delete that request in the affidavit following the petition.

- **whether he or she wishes to make his or her own application for an order about the children**

If you do not agree with the proposed arrangements, first make sure that what you are objecting to are actual proposals and not mere intentions. Try to discuss them with your spouse. If there is underlying disagreement, send to the court your counter-proposals by filing your own statement of arrangements.

All financial matters and any disputes about the children are dealt with as separate issues, irrespective of whether the divorce itself is defended or undefended.

The respondent has to sign the acknowledgement personally where there are children and a statement of arrangements has been filed.

Cross-petitioning

As an alternative to a fully defended divorce petition, the respondent can file an 'answer' not necessarily denying the allegations but seeking a divorce on other facts (a cross-petition).

You might want to do this if you felt that the facts in the petition did not represent the true picture, and you wanted to give yourself some breathing space while you negotiated with your spouse. Bear in mind, though, that this tactic could backfire and increase your costs in the long term.

If the petitioner does not dispute this, the divorce will proceed on the respondent's petition and the special procedure will again be adopted. It is also possible (but unusual and expensive) to obtain cross-decrees: the petitioner obtains a decree on the basis of the petition and the respondent on the basis of the answer.

After an answer has been filed by the respondent, the petitioner may file a reply. Once these divorce documents have all been sent to the court, either party can apply to the district judge for directions for trial. Courts go out of their way to discourage defended petitions and the district judge will try to see if there is any way of avoiding a defended divorce. Only if these efforts fail will the district judge allow the case to go forward to a hearing of the divorce.

The full divorce hearing will be in open court before a judge. Each party should instruct his or her own solicitor who may in turn instruct a barrister for representation in court.

Getting back together

Some couples find that there is a chance of saving the marriage when the divorce procedure is well under way but feel that they are bound to continue with the court action until the end. This is not necessary. If you feel at any stage that you and your spouse might like to give the marriage another try, you are quite free to do so; it is best to tell the solicitor and the court what is happening. You can apply to the court to dismiss the petition when you feel the reconciliation is working. It is particularly important to tell the court if you have obtained an order to get or keep your spouse out of the house and/or not to molest you. Such an order will automatically lapse once you start living together again.

Recent studies of divorced couples suggest that not only did some of them regret the decision to get divorced, but also many started to feel uneasy about the process long before getting the decree but felt unable to halt the impetus that had been created.

You may want to consider whether some or all of the differences with your spouse can be resolved with outside, non-legal help. A fresh viewpoint can often be useful. Such help can, for example, be obtained from a marriage guidance counsellor (look in the telephone directory under RELATE); see also Chapter 4.

Continuing proceedings

The next stage to get an undefended divorce under way is to apply to the court for a date for the decree nisi to be pronounced, by completing the court form 'request for directions for trial (special procedure)'.

The petitioner can make this application only if he or she can prove that the respondent and any co-respondent have been served with the petition and have had the opportunity to defend it. Usually, proof of service is provided by the respondent's filing the acknowledgement of service. The court then sends a copy of this to the petitioner, usually together with a blank form of 'request for directions for trial' and a blank form of affidavit.

The petitioner must complete the 'request' and affidavit and lodge them with the court. In the 'request' form, you should fill in only the top part by inserting the name of the court, the number assigned to the petition, the names of the petitioner and respondent; then date and sign it. The rest of the form will be completed by the district judge and court staff.

Affidavits

The 'special procedure' affidavit is a fairly straightforward document, mostly in the form of a questionnaire. The questions refer to the petition, asking for confirmation that its contents are true and for any alterations or additions. (Knowingly giving false information is perjury which is a criminal offence.) You also have to state whether you are going to pursue any requests for costs made in the prayer of the petition.

There is a slightly different form of affidavit for each of the five facts on which a divorce can be based.

In the unusual circumstances of a divorce being based on two facts – for example, unreasonable behaviour and adultery – two affidavits would have to be completed.

Except where the respondent has failed to file an acknowledgement of service, the acknowledgement of service is referred to and sworn with the affidavit as an 'exhibit'. Where there are children the statement of arrangements also has to be exhibited and the truth of its contents sworn to.

Affidavit where the 'fact' is adultery

You must insert the facts on which you base the allegation of adultery. Refer to the relevant numbered paragraphs on the petition and state that the allegations are true to the best of your knowledge and belief. If the respondent has admitted the adultery on the acknowledgement of service form or by making a written confession statement, you should identify the respondent's signature on the document (and similarly if the co-respondent has supplied a confession statement). A co-respondent does not need to have admitted the adultery for the divorce to go through, provided that the respondent has made the admission or that the petitioner can prove the adultery.

If the adultery has not been admitted by the respondent (and provided that you can prove service of the petition on the respondent and co-respondent), you should give all the first-hand information availabl , such as the date of confession of adultery or details of circumstances to show that the respondent has committed adultery.

'Hearsay' evidence, that is, indirect information from some-body else, is not usually acceptable: you may need to supply further affidavits by people who can give first-hand information to back up the allegation. In the past, an enquiry agent's report often provided additional evidence, but this form of investigation is used less often now.

You also have to confirm in the affidavit that you find it intolerable to live with the respondent.

Affidavit where the 'fact' is unreasonable behaviour
Further evidence to substantiate any allegations made in the petition may – but does not necessarily have to – be given. There is no need for a blow by blow account of every incident, provided that the respondent's conduct has been adequately set out in the petition. If the district judge is not satisfied with the information given, he or she will call for further evidence to be supplied, such as a medical report or a witness's affidavit.

In order to clarify whether, and for how long, you have gone on living with the respondent, you are specifically asked whether the behaviour described in the petition is continuing and, if not, when the last incident took place. You then have to say whether you have lived at the same address for more than six months since then; if so, you have to describe what arrangements you had for sharing the accommodation. This involves giving details of sleeping arrangements, cooking and cleaning.

Affidavit where the 'fact' is desertion
The date on which desertion began has to be given, and you must state that you did not agree to the separation and that the respondent did not offer to return.

Affidavit where the 'fact' is separation

Where you and your spouse have been living in separate households for the whole of the period apart, the relevant dates and separate addresses should be given and when and why you decided that the marriage was at an end. Merely living apart is not necessarily sufficient; separation starts from the time you considered the marriage had actually broken down.

You are asked to say when you came to the conclusion that the marriage was at an end – not when you decided to get divorced, which could well have been at a later date.

You may have had to continue living at the same address because it was impossible or impracticable to live completely apart, even though the marriage was at an end. You may not consider that you have been 'living together' if you have merely been under the same roof and, for example, sleeping separately, not having sexual intercourse, and barely communicating; but a court could hold that you have in fact been living together in one, unhappy, household and would need to be convinced that there were, to all intents and purposes, two households. You will therefore have to give the fullest possible information about the separateness of the households. (If the space provided in the standard affidavit form is inadequate, attach an extra sheet dealing with this point.)

If the district judge is still in doubt about the circumstances, he or she may remove the case from the special procedure list, to be heard in open court so that fuller evidence can be given. If this happens, you should consult a solicitor; if your financial position makes you eligible, you can apply for legal aid to be represented at the hearing.

Completing the affidavit

With the affidavit, you must return the copy of the respondent's acknowledgement of service form sent by the court. If the respondent has signed it personally, you must identify the signature on it as being that of the respondent by inserting the respondent's name exactly as he or she has signed the acknowledgement of service.

If the respondent's acknowledgement of service has been signed by his or her solicitors alone, you cannot identify the signature and thus you must delete the relevant sentence in the affidavit.

An affidavit is sworn by taking it to a solicitor other than the one acting for you, a commissioner for oaths or the court office. Most solicitors' firms are very willing to offer this service and you can go to a firm convenient for you. A solicitor or commissioner for oaths makes a small charge (at present £3.50 plus £1 per exhibit, that is, any document attached). There is no fee for swearing an affidavit before a court official.

The completed affidavit, signed and sworn, has to be sent or taken to the court with the application form requesting directions for trial.

District judge giving directions

About the divorce
Provided that the district judge is satisfied as to the service of the petition on everybody concerned and that an opportunity for defending has been given and, in a consent case, that the respondent's consent has been confirmed, and that all the paperwork is correct, he or she gives directions for the case to be entered in the special procedure list.

If the district judge is not satisfied with the information in the affidavit, the petitioner (or a witness) may be asked to lodge a further affidavit or give additional information on the points of concern.

If the district judge still does not accept that there is sufficient evidence for a divorce, he or she may direct that the petition be removed from the special procedure list. A fresh application then has to be made for directions and for a date to be fixed for a hearing in open court before a judge.

When the district judge is satisfied that there is sufficient evidence to support the petition, he or she certifies that the petitioner is entitled to a decree nisi of divorce (or decree of judicial separation). The court then fixes a date for the judge to pronounce the decree nisi.

About the children
At the same time as the district judge looks at the divorce papers, he or she must also consider the arrangements for the children

[continues on page 130]

UNDEFENDED DIVORCE BY SPECIAL PROCEDURE: THE STEPS

	Time stage	Who acts	Action required and documents involved
1	–	spouse wanting divorce	–may go to solicitor for advice on grounds for divorce and for help with completing petition –gets appropriate form of petition and, if relevant, statement of arrangements for children, from divorce county court office or Divorce Registry –completes statement of arrangements and tries to agree its contents in advance with the respondent if possible; if other spouse (respondent) agrees, he or she countersigns the form
2	any time after 1 year from date of marriage	petitioner (spouse wanting divorce)	–lodges at court office: i) completed petition plus copy for spouse (and named co-respondent, if petition based on adultery) ii) certified copy of marriage certificate iii) two copies of completed statement as to arrangements for children, where relevant –pays fee of £40 to court office (or completes form to get exemption of fee)

[continued]

125

	Time stage	Who acts	Action required and documents involved
3	within a few days of (2) depending on the court's workload	court office	sends to respondent copy of petition, statement of arrangements for children, notice of proceedings, and acknowledgement of service for completion (in adultery case, all documents except statement about children also sent to co-respondent, if named)
4	within 8 days of receiving documents in (3) (longer if respondent living outside England or Wales)	respondent (and co-respondent)	must return acknowledgement of service to court (strict time limits apply), plus, if desired, any counter-proposals about arrangements for children
5a	if acknowledgement(s) of service not returned	court office	notifies petitioner and gives information about alternative methods of service
b	once acknowledgement(s) of service returned	court office	sends copy of acknowledgement(s) of service to petitioner, plus form of request for directions for trial and form of appropriate affidavit in support of petition, to be completed

6	after 8 days from service of petition if respondent (or co-respondent) has not indicated intention to defend on acknowledgement of service **or** after 21 days from filing acknowledgement of service if respondent (or co-respondent) indicated intention to defend but no answer has been filed	petitioner	—completes affidavit in support of petition, takes it to a solicitor or court for swearing, plus copy of statement of arrangements (if there are children) and acknowledgement of service, identifying respondent's signature (and, in adultery case, any confession statement from respondent) —completes request for directions for trial (sent at 5b by court office) and takes/sends to court plus i) completed affidavit with any relevant supporting documents ii) copy of any previous court orders relating to the marriage or the children
7	when request for directions for trial received	district judge	reads and considers the documents

[continued]

Time stage	Who acts	Action required and documents involved
8a if all in order	i) district judge	−enters case in special procedure list −certifies entitlement to decree (and to any costs claimed, if appropriate) −certifies there are no children or that the court need not exercise its powers over the children
	ii) court office	fixes date for pronouncement of decree and issues certificate of satisfaction about arrangements for children; sends notification of date to petitioner and respondent and co-respondent
b if district judge not satisfied	i) district judge ii) petitioner iii) district judge	requests further evidence or information has to supply required evidence or information to court considers further evidence or information supplied
c if district judge then satisfied	i) district judge ii) court office	grants certificate as in 8a(i) fixes date for pronouncement of decree by judge sends notification of date to petitioner and respondent
d if district judge still not satisfied	i) district judge ii) court office	removes case from special procedure list informs petitioner and respondent

9	on date given in 8a(ii) or 8c(ii)	i) judge	pronounces decree nisi (petitioner and respondent need not be present)
		ii) court office	sends copy of decree to petitioner and respondent
10	six weeks and one day after (9) (provided certificate of satisfaction about children issued)	petitioner	applies to court (on form available from court office) for decree to be made absolute; pays fee of £15 to court office (or completes form to get exemption of fee); if petitioner fails to do this, respondent must wait a further three months before applying for decree absolute
11	when application (10) received	court office	—checks court records that no reason why decree should not be made absolute —issues certificate making decree nisi absolute —sends copy of decree absolute to ex-husband and ex-wife

and whether *no* order is better for the children. If so, a certificate of satisfaction will be issued to this effect and the decree nisi pronouncement will go ahead.

If, however, the district judge has doubts or concerns about proposals for the children, or if there is a clear dispute between the parents, then further evidence will usually be called for. The district judge can ask for the parents to attend a special appointment at court, or for affidavits or a welfare report to be filed. In that case the decree nisi will usually be postponed until the district judge is again satisfied that no court order needs to be made, or a residence and/or contact order will be made where appropriate.

Decree nisi and decree absolute (final decree)

The decree nisi is a provisional decree and does not end the marriage. It entitles the petitioner to apply to the court for the decree to be made absolute after a period of six weeks and one day have elapsed. Until this is done, you are still married.

A decree can be made absolute earlier than the six weeks if the petitioner applies for this when the decree nisi is pronounced and attends to explain to the judge in person the reason for the application. The respondent must be given notice of the application by the petitioner. An application will be granted only in urgent circumstances, for example to enable one of the couple to marry again before a child is born.

The procedure for applying for a decree absolute is simple. The form 'application for decree absolute' (obtainable from the court office) is completed by the petitioner by inserting the date of the decree nisi, the date of the application and his or her signature and lodging this form together with a fee (currently £15) at the court office. A certificate of decree absolute will then be issued by the court and sent to the petitioner and respondent (and co-respondent).

If the petitioner does not apply for the decree nisi to be made absolute when the time comes, after a further three months have elapsed (i.e. six weeks and one day plus three calendar months after decree nisi), the respondent may apply to the district judge for the decree to be made absolute, with an affidavit setting out the reasons why it is he or she who is applying rather than the petitioner.

If decree absolute has not been applied for within twelve months of the decree nisi, the delay must be explained when the application for decree absolute is lodged, giving the reason for the delay and stating whether the couple have cohabited since decree nisi and whether the wife has borne any more children. A district judge may require further explanation or even affidavit evidence before the decree is made absolute.

It is important to keep your certificate of decree absolute in a safe place as you will have to produce it if you want to marry again.

Defended divorce

If the divorce petition becomes defended, the respondent will state that he or she intends to defend the petition on the Notice of Proceedings form and must also file at court an 'answer' to the petition within 29 days of service of the petition. The answer can consist of a simple denial of the facts contained in the petition or can go into more detail by including the facts which the respondent states to refute the allegations in the petition. The petitioner then has the opportunity of filing a 'reply' 14 days after receiving the respondent's answer if he or she wants to dispute allegations made in the reply.

The court will usually then fix an appointment for a pre-trial review which will state whether any further evidence needs to be filed and the case will usually be transferred up to the High Court. The court may try to find out if a settlement can be reached.

Defended divorces are costly not least because they culminate in a full hearing before the court, which both parties (and any witnesses) must attend, plus their legal representatives (usually solicitors *and* barristers). Some sort of compromise (perhaps by the petitioner agreeing to amend some of the more hurtful allegations in the petition) can usually be made (and should be made wherever possible). Defended divorces are indeed very rare – only 50 or so a year.

Divorce reform: new law

In December 1993 the Lord Chancellor's Department (the governmental body which deals with new laws) published recommendations for changing the legal process of divorce. The key proposed change is a switch away from the **fault-based** divorce to a **time-based** divorce. The sole ground for divorce would still be that the marriage had irretrievably broken down – but the means of proving the breakdown would be different. Under the new suggested system, after filing for divorce (which could be done jointly instead of one spouse having to initiate proceedings) spouses would have to wait for 12 months before the divorce was granted. During that year, couples would be expected to think about whether they really wanted a divorce and, if so, plan ahead for their future lives without each other. Separating couples would also go to a meeting with an adviser, who could then refer them on to a solicitor or mediator, or even a counsellor, whichever was felt to be appropriate.

The divorce reform proposals may not become law until 1995 at the very earliest and as they are likely to prove controversial may well be delayed further. But check with your solicitor or CAB as to whether the law has yet changed.

CHAPTER 8

CHILDREN AND DIVORCE

DIVORCE is a decision reached by adults and often comes as a great shock to children, even when to their parents the strains in the marriage have become only too clear. The instinctive reaction of a child may be similar to your own or your spouse's reaction – disbelief, denial and a frantic attempt to make it not happen. It is important that you find time to allay a child's fears by explaining what is happening and by providing reassurance. This can be far from easy when you yourself are in a state of emotional turmoil and stress.

When you are trying to put the past behind you and start a new life, it may be difficult to accept that your children's needs are different from yours and may even conflict with yours to some extent. For example, children often say very little about wanting to see the parent who has left home because they are aware that this may upset the person they are living with. Their silence does not mean that they are not missing the other parent. Both parents need to reassure the children that they do not have to choose one and reject the other, and that their separation is in no way the children's fault.

Your status as a husband or wife will finally be over when the decree is made absolute, but not your status as a parent. Your children will always have two parents and your link with your former spouse will continue as long as you have children. This enduring bond is indeed now legally acknowledged by the Children Act 1989 which states that both parents (if they were married when the children were born) will continue to have 'parental responsibility' for their children even after the marriage break-up (see later).

As parents, you are related to each other by blood through your children and you need to shift the focus of your relationship from that of husband and wife to that of being parents.

A fundamental issue is how the children are going to keep in touch with the parent with whom they are not living. Working out arrangements for access (or, to use the new term, contact) that both parents can cope with takes a lot of effort. Be aware of the fact that your former spouse is likely to behave in the same kind of irritating way that he or she did while you were married (and that the same is probably true of you), so you will both need to behave with greater consideration than before. Be careful not to play out, in the guise of disputes over contact, what are really matrimonial disputes.

Sorting out arrangements concerning the children will be a continuing process, but it is one that gets increasingly easier – as emotions die down, as the children get older and as routines become established. Initially, you may find great difficulty even in discussing proposed arrangements with your former spouse. This is a time to consider the possibility of mediation with professional help (see Chapter 4).

It is worthwhile persevering. Whilst the most important factor affecting how well the children cope with divorce is the emotional and psychological health of the parent who looks after them, another key factor is the maintenance of strong links with *both* parents. Studies have shown that children of separating parents who see the 'absent parent' regularly are able to cope better with the emotional stresses of divorce. This is particularly true in the period just after the separation, which is most traumatic for the children. Although it may be tempting to wait for a 'cooling off' period before the parent who has left home sees the children again, this would be laying trouble in store. The children are most needy just after the separation and seeing regularly the parent who has left can help them adjust gradually to the fact of the family break-up.

There is a financial incentive in this, too. Other studies have shown that fathers who have contact with their children are more likely to pay maintenance on a regular basis.

There are other ways in which you can help your children. Psychologists have identified the effects of 'secondary' divorces suffered by all who go through divorce, but particularly by children (through moving house, school, leaving grandparents behind, for example). If you can keep the family home, so as to provide the children with the security of a known base, this will help them considerably. Maintaining their links with their school friends and grandparents also can help them to cope better.

Both you and your spouse need to affirm frequently your continuing love for the children and assure them that they are in no way to blame for the break-up. If you are able to, you should work together with, rather than against, your spouse in your approaches towards the children. Tell them jointly, if you can, about the separation and do not give the children any opportunity to play you off one against the other. Your children, as well as you, will need time to come to terms with what has happened.

The focus of the advice contained within this book is practical and legal. There are many good books now on the market which give valuable advice for parents who want to help their children overcome the adverse effects of divorce, such as *Divorced Parenting: How to Make it Work* by Dr Sol Goldstein (published by Mandarin).

Parental responsibility

Since the Children Act 1989 came into force in 1991, parents who were married to each other when children were born (or who married each other later) both automatically have 'parental responsibility', the new legal concept which defines the framework between parents and children. As a major change from the old law, *both* parents will retain parental responsibility until their children are eighteen, even after marriage breakdown. So the continuing blood tie with the parent who will no longer be looking after the children on a day-to-day basis is formally acknowledged. He (or she) will keep the duty and right to have a continued involvement in a child's upbringing. The courts cannot take away parental responsibility from married parents unless an adoption order is made.

The fact that each spouse will always have parental responsibility is intended to encourage absent parents (usually fathers) to take an active interest in their children's welfare. It means that fathers will lose out less on divorce since they keep parental responsibility (unlike under the old law, when they often lost custody).

In another major change, the new law also now gives parents who want to co-operate with one another much greater flexibility to make their own arrangements for the children; courts will in future make no court order unless 'it would be better for the children to do so'. Advocates for the change argued that as the courts never usually intervened to divide the children up between the parents during a marriage, why should a marriage breakdown automatically give them that right? Parents, they argued, are the best people to create their own tailor-made solutions to the problems arising on family breakdown. So if the parents can work out answers to the problems by themselves, the courts should not interfere.

So, in reality, in most divorce cases nowadays, the courts will not make any orders about with whom the children will be living, thus encouraging the parents to work out arrangements for the children. But if there is conflict between the parents which they cannot resolve by themselves or through negotiation (through solicitors or conciliators), then either parent can apply for a court order under section 8 of the Act, like a residence order or contact order.

What it means in practice
Parental responsibility is defined as 'all the rights, duties, powers, responsibilities and authority which by law a parent of a child has in relation to the child and his property'.

In practice this means the responsibility (and right) to make choices over all the issues that are necessarily involved in bringing up a child, like:

- where a child will live
- where a child will go to school
- what religion a child will be brought up in
- what medical treatment a child will have.

If you have parental responsibility you are also able to apply for a passport for a child.

Having parental responsibility is not exactly the equivalent of being a parent, as unmarried fathers do not automatically have parental responsibility but must acquire it (either by making a formal agreement with the mother or by successfully applying to court).

In some more unusual circumstances, other people may acquire parental responsibility: anyone who has a residence order in their favour automatically acquires parental responsibility too if they do not already have it. So a grandmother who permanently looks after a grandchild can apply for a residence order and if she gets it will also have parental responsibility – in other words, the right and duty to make decisions about how the child is brought up. But the fact that the grandmother acquires parental responsibility does not mean that the parents lose it. Now three people have parental responsibility: the mother and father (if they were married) and the grandmother.

Orders the courts can make

All of the following orders are made under section 8 of the Children Act 1989 and are thus referred to as 'section 8 orders'. All of them restrict in some way the exercising of parental responsibility. They are intended to be more focused than the old court orders and easier to grasp. So, instead of the old confusion about (for example) whether 'custody' meant legal custody or care and control (physical custody), there is now a residence order.

Residence order

This settles the arrangements about with whom (and thus where) a child will live. In most cases it will be with one parent (usually the mother), but a residence order can allow for shared parenting where children divide their time equally between their parents' homes. In theory it could also be applied for by two people together, for example a parent and step-parent.

Contact order

This requires the person with whom the child lives to allow contact (thus shifting the burden more to the parent looking after the child). It can be visits or stop-overs, or can be by way of telephone calls or letters, or all or any of these.

Specific issue order

This gives directions for the purpose of determining a specific question connected with parental responsibility, for example which school the child should go to.

Prohibited steps order

This has the effect of restraining in some way the actions of a person in relation to the child. No step stated in the order can be taken without the consent of the court. This could be used for example to stop another parent from changing a child's surname or stop them from taking the child out of the country without the other parent's or the court's consent.

Both specific issue and prohibited steps orders have their origins in wardship proceedings, which are now thus much less likely to be used. Both types of order can be applied for in an emergency 'ex parte', in other words, without the other party having the opportunity of putting his or her side to the court.

The courts may attach conditions in certain circumstances to the new orders. For example, they could state that contact should only take place in the home of the parent who looks after the children or that another adult is present during the visit.

Who can apply for section 8 orders?

Either parent can apply for an order, if necessary even before the divorce itself has started. The new court orders can be used much more flexibly than before, and indeed other people, such as relatives, or even the child him or herself may also be able to apply where appropriate (see further page 152 and Chapter 14 on Stepfamilies).

The courts themselves can make a section 8 order in any family proceedings, thus widening their own powers. But the courts are supposed *not* to use section 8 orders without proper consideration: court orders can be made only if it is better for the children to do so. If the parents can decide between themselves about who should be looking after the children and when the other parent should see them, then it is likely that no formal court order will be made, and the situation will continue fluidly with both parents having parental responsibility and thus both deciding together about how the children will be brought up.

Neither partner will be in a stronger position than the other, although in practice the parent having the day-to-day care of the children will be in more of a position of influence over choices made in their upbringing. Parental responsibility can be exercised independently, so that each parent is able to make up his or her mind about issues relating to the children (though effective co-parenting needs a measure of co-operation between the parents). The fact of independent rights and responsibilities can be useful in an emergency: if the child were in an accident, then one parent could sign the necessary consent form without having to consult the other parent. But, again, if in future the parents reached stalemate about any particular issue involving the children, a section 8 order (say a specific issue order) could be applied for.

The role of the court

No divorce decree can be made absolute without the court considering the arrangements for the children of the family. The court has to look at the arrangements and decide whether it is satisfied that a court order need not be made. In the vast majority of cases no formal court order will now be made and the courts will leave it up to the parents to sort out arrangements between themselves. This will also mean that no court attendance will be necessary, so that unless there are financial applications which have to be heard by the courts the whole divorce will be able to proceed on paperwork only.

'Children of the family' means the couple's own children (including adopted children and those made legitimate) and any child treated by them as one of the family, so arrangements made for a stepchild will also have to be put before the court.

Normally, only arrangements for children under 16 have to be set out for the court. Whilst parental responsibility lasts during the children's minority (until they are 18), court orders (i.e. section 8 orders) will be made for children over 16 only in exceptional circumstances. What this means has not been defined by the Act, but the courts may feel it is appropriate to make a section 8 order if, for instance, a child is disabled and dependent on an adult and a full court order is needed.

Applications for maintenance for the children will now usually be dealt with by the Child Support Agency (see Chapter 5). Other applications (such as for capital lump sums for the children) can still be made to the court under the Children Act 1989 (see Chapter 10).

Agreed arrangements

1. Where the parents are in agreement about arrangements for the children, the petitioner (the spouse starting divorce proceedings) should prepare a statement of arrangements for the children in advance and try to get its contents agreed with the respondent and countersigned by him or her if possible.
   (If they cannot agree the respondent can file his or her own statement of arrangements later, but this is more likely to mean that the court will ask for further evidence and that personal attendance at court will be required.)
2. After the divorce papers have been served, the respondent has filed an acknowledgement of service and the petitioner has filed an affidavit in support of the petition, the papers go before a district judge for consideration.
3. If there are 'children of the family', the district judge has to consider whether the court needs to exercise its powers to make an order under section 8. If the district judge decides that the court does not need to make a section 8 order, he or she issues a certificate to this effect (called a section 41 certificate). A date for decree nisi is fixed and neither party need attend a court hearing about the children.
4. If, however, there are problems (for instance, if there is an application for a section 8 order, if there is some dispute or if the district judge otherwise considers that the arrangements might not comply with the principle that the welfare of the child is paramount), the district judge can:

   • ask for further evidence
   • ask for a welfare report to be prepared
   • ask for the parties to attend a court hearing.

5. Once that direction has been complied with, the district judge either issues a certificate saying that no court order needs to be made or makes one.
6. Decree absolute can be applied for six weeks and one day after the date of decree nisi.

Sometimes, one spouse may want a section 8 order to be made even if the arrangements are otherwise agreed – say, for example, the local authority is insisting on the production of a residence order before re-housing (although strictly it is not entitled to do so). In this situation it will be up to the applicant to persuade the court that a court order should be made and that it is better from the children's viewpoint to do so. It would be sensible to obtain legal advice about what approach should be taken.

Contested arrangements

In any case involving disputes over children, it is wise to consult a solicitor and obtain further legal advice. Court disputes are costly, both financially and in emotional terms. There is rarely any winner in battles over who will have primary care of the children on a day-to-day basis.

Wherever possible, you should try to negotiate with your spouse either directly, or through a mediation agency, or through solicitors, to avoid a full-blown battle over the children. In such battles, you are forced to wash your dirty linen in public and will be making damaging accusations against each other to the effect that the other parent is not fit to have the day-to-day upbringing of the child. In all cases, consider carefully whether, from the child's viewpoint, it is best for you to go ahead with an application to the court.

The procedure

An application for a residence or contact order (or other section 8 order) is triggered off by an application to the court, stating clearly what order you are seeking. Since the Children Act was implemented, however, the need to make the 'right application' is not absolute, as the court has the power to make an appropriate section 8 order even where the wrong order was sought. No evidence should be filed at this stage. If your court has set up a type of 'in-court conciliation', as most have, the court will fix a conciliation appointment before the district judge for you, your spouse and any legal representatives; and a court welfare officer will also be in attendance. The children may also be asked by the court to come, depending on their ages – not if they are less than about ten years old.

The aim of the conciliation appointment is to help the parents to reach a solution acceptable to both in a supportive, relatively informal, private setting. The court welfare officer or other appointed conciliator talks with both parents and will be concerned to try to defuse the parents' competition to 'win' the children. If a settlement is potentially achievable but cannot be reached in one session, the courts can fix other appointments to allow the conciliation process to continue.

If the conciliation process is not successful, or in courts where conciliation processes have not yet been set up, the district judge will then make an order for directions concerning the evidence to be filed. This usually consists of the original application, the answer and witness statements. All of these are similar to affidavits but they are not sworn.

The district judge will also order that a court welfare officer (not the same one who assisted in the conciliation process) should prepare a report. Time limits will be set which must be strictly complied with (the Children Act specifically recognises that delay may be harmfully prejudicial in a children application). You should also be told the 'return date' – in other words, when the case will next come to court.

In your evidence, try to confine yourself to setting out the facts, rather than inserting emotional arguments. 'The facts' can extend in children cases to hearsay evidence (information you learned secondhand) but the courts are far more influenced by clear, concise, factual and accurate information than by gossip.

The welfare officer will usually interview both parents and the children. The older the children are, the more their views will carry weight. The court welfare officer may also make enquiries of the children's schools, and from other relevant parties – for example, a child's grandmother, if it is proposed that she will be looking after the child while her child (the child's parent) is at work. The welfare officer prepares a report which sets out the facts and circumstances and his or her impressions, and occasionally includes a recommendation to which the court will pay great attention (although will not necessarily follow).

A copy of the welfare officer's report will be sent to the parties directly or through their solicitors, if appointed. It must not be shown to any third parties without prior permission of the court. Before a final hearing the court may have set a date for an interim hearing to try to resolve which issues are in dispute. Again at this stage the date for a final hearing will be fixed.

The court's considerations

The overriding principle is that 'the child's welfare shall be the court's paramount consideration'. In applying this welfare principle, the court now has a checklist of matters it must look at in particular:

- the ascertainable wishes and feelings of the child (in the light of the child's age and understanding)
- the child's physical, emotional and educational needs
- the likely effect on the child of any change in circumstances
- the child's age, sex and background and any characteristics the court considers relevant
- any harm the child has suffered or is at risk of suffering
- how capable each of the child's parents, and any other person in relation to whom the court considers the question to be relevant, is of meeting the child's needs
- the range of powers available to the court.

The checklist is not an exhaustive and exclusive list, but one which lays out simply what the court *must* consider. The court *may* of course consider that other factors are important in an individual case. For example, the parents' wishes and feelings, although not listed, may often have an important bearing on the eventual outcome of a case.

The wishes and feelings of the child

The fact that the child's wishes and feelings have been placed at the top of the checklist highlights the child-centred approach of the Children Act: children should, wherever possible, be put first. At a hearing, the judge may ask to see the children in private in chambers, without parents or legal advisers present, to talk to them and ask them what they want. If so, the court will ask the parents to bring the children along to court (usually this applies only to children of about ten or over). Far more often children's wishes and feelings will be explored by the court welfare officer when preparing the report.

The older the child, the more persuasive his or her views. Teenage children in any event often 'vote with their feet' over where they want to live whereas younger children may find it very difficult to put what they want into words. In practice, this factor is extremely influential. The views of mature children from around 10 upwards, who have sound reasons for choosing a particular outcome, will often be the decisive factor. But if the court suspects that children have been coached by one or other parent, 'their' opinions will carry little weight. Although children's views will be respected, they should not be forced to choose unwillingly between two people both of whom they love. Ultimately, especially for younger children, it is up to adults to make decisions.

The child's physical, emotional and educational needs

If the child is very young or sickly or otherwise especially needs a mother's care, a residence order is more likely to be made in favour of the mother. In the past the courts have usually decided that a child's welfare is best protected by being with the mother rather than the father. One case decided since the implementation of the Children Act 1989 confirmed the presumption that a baby would stay with his or her mother. There is thus an in-built bias in favour of mothers, although that bias becomes less strong as the child gets older. It is not unusual, for example, for a court order to provide for older boys to live with their fathers. The courts will always look at each individual family: whichever parent has primarily looked after the children and with whom the children have the closer bond is likely to have a residence order made in her or his favour.

The effect of change

The courts have long recognised that changing an established status quo can compound the difficulties of a child adjusting to the parent's separation. So a parent who is already looking after the children usually has a much stronger claim. This however does not apply if the children have been snatched from their usual home environment: the courts can act quickly to return children to the parent best able to care for them.

Likewise, splitting the family is almost always regarded as undesirable, so that wherever possible siblings (sometimes even half-brothers and -sisters) should be kept together.

The child's age, sex and background

The inclusion of this factor in the Children Act is an attempt to get away from trying to impose a stereotypical view of the family which does not 'fit' an individual family unit. So if, for example, it is the cultural norm that the parents go off to work whilst the grandmother cares for their children, the court might well feel it is best for the children to continue to be cared for by the grandmother. Each case will be decided on its own merits.

Harm or risk of harm

Alcholism or violence (whether towards the mother or the children) will prejudice a parent's case. Also, if there is a real risk of sexual abuse by a parent, that parent would definitely not get a residence order. A contact order might be given, but only if it would be in the child's best interests (for example, if there were a strong bond between parent and child, if the parent were seeking treatment and if the contact were supervised properly). In the past the courts have been prejudiced against homosexual parents to the extent that they have overlooked that parent's capacity to bring up his or her own child. A case decided in 1991 stated that while a parent's homosexuality will now be a factor taken into account it will not necessarily be decisive (unless the court thinks the children will be adversely affected).

It is still sensible for a homosexual parent to obtain professional advice from a solicitor experienced in this area. There are several organisations concerned with lesbian and gay parenting; for most of them the first point of contact would be to ring the **London Lesbian and Gay Switchboard** (24 hours on 071-837 7324), who can make a referral if necessary.

Capability of the parents
This can range from practicalities, such as whether a parent works outside the home, to an ability to respond to the child's needs. Overall in deciding on an application for a residence order between the parents, it is a matter of trying to assess which parent will be better able to look after the children during the week (contact orders may be made for weekend visits); sometimes the claims of both will be equal. Note that this factor does not refer to the parents' conduct as individuals and a distinction must be drawn between a person's behaviour as a parent (which will be looked at) and as a partner (which will often be ignored).

A parent who can offer a stable home life (perhaps particularly if remarrying) will usually have a stronger claim than an unreliable parent. A parent who abandons the children and puts the interests of a lover first is likely to be at a disadvantage in applying for a residence order.

Where relatives or other people (like childminders or full-time nannies) are involved in bringing up the children, their capabilities too may be explored.

The courts' powers
As the courts' powers under the Children Act are wider and more flexible than before they might be expected to come up with more creative solutions than in the past. For example, residence orders could be split between both parents: if both parents were equally capable and the children wanted to share their time with each parent, the court could make a residence order specifying that the children would spend two weeks with the father and then two with the mother so that the parents had the opportunity of sharing the care of the children. But the parents would have to tailor their own lifestyles around the children's needs (for example, both living near to the children's schools) and the children must usually also really want to spend equal time with each parent to convince the court that such unusual arrangements were really in the children's best interests.

Appeals
Successful appeals against decisions made by the trial judge are extremely rare. The trial judge (the one who originally hears the

case) has a wide discretion and appeals will only be allowed if the first decision can be shown to be 'plainly wrong'. This is so even if the appeal court feels it would have come to another decision itself. But if further important evidence comes to light, then an appeal might work.

An appeal against a decision of either the county court (now called a Family Hearing Centre) or the magistrates' court (the Family Proceedings Panel) will go straight to the High Court. From the High Court an appeal will lie to the Court of Appeal.

Challenging an old order

If a parent wishes to vary or change an old court order made before the Children Act 1989 came into force (14 October 1991), then usually the application will be made under the Children Act 1989. Whilst an application to re-open an old decision has a better chance of success than an appeal, the situation would have to have changed fundamentally before it would really be worthwhile going to court again.

Before the Children Act
Prior to the Children Act's implementation there were three different legal concepts applicable to children: custody, care and control, and access. The legal usage of some of the words was (and is) different to ordinary English usage. Because these terms are still popularly used even though they no longer apply, it is useful to be aware of what they mean. (You may also have an old court order which uses these concepts).

Custody
This meant the bundle of responsibilities that parents have towards their children, for example, the right and duty to take major decisions concerning their upbringing, their religion or education.

There were two different court orders for custody: sole custody (for one parent) or joint custody (for both). Joint custody was the court order that resembled most closely the pre-divorce role towards the children. In a sense, the effect of a joint custody order was primarily psychological because it confirmed for the parent who did not look after the children the fact that he or she had a recognised role to play towards his or her children. ('Parental responsibility' now fulfils this function.)

Care and control

This meant the actual physical possession of the child. Orders were made only for sole care and control: an order for care and control could not be split (unlike the new residence orders). Care and control is what most people meant when they talked about custody.

An order for care and control was granted to the parent with whom the children were living on a regular basis. Even in the unusual cases where children divided their time equally between their parents, one parent used to have to have an order for care and control.

Access

This meant the visiting periods for the parent who did not have care and control. This could have been 'staying access' (when the child stayed with the non-custodial parent) or 'visiting access' (where the non-custodial parent simply visited or took the child out for the day for an outing).

Where parents were able to agree, the courts usually made an order for 'reasonable access' which left the terms of the access visits, or periods of staying access, up to the parents to agree between themselves. Where the parents could not agree, the court may have made an order for defined access, determining when the child would visit the non-custodial parent, sometimes specifying the time when the child should be collected and brought home again.

Other issues

Changing a child's surname

If a child is to be brought up in a new family, a parent (usually the mother) may want to change the child's surname to that of her new partner when or after they remarry. Whether there is anything in the law preventing her from doing so depends on whether there is a residence order (or an old custody/care and control order) in force.

If there is such an order, there will automatically be a provision stating that the child's surname cannot be changed without the consent of the other parent or the court. But if no such order exists, the mother can in theory change the child's surname: she has parental responsibility which she can exercise independently. If the father objects, he should apply to the court for a specific issue order. The court application will be decided by the principles that the child's welfare is of paramount consideration and that no court order will be made unless one is better for the child.

It is likely that the courts will be influenced by the old caselaw which broadly disapproved of changes of surname. The courts usually took the line that the link between a child and his or her natural parent, as symbolised by the surname, should not be broken, so changes of surname were usually refused.

However, the child him or herself may apply for a change of surname by way of a specific issue order too. If the child has strong feelings about wanting to be included in the new family and sound reasons for making the application, this may well persuade the court to make an order for a change, given that the child's wishes and feelings rank number one on the welfare checklist.

Taking a child abroad for a holiday

The usual rule is that a parent who wants to take a child abroad (this includes going to Scotland) should obtain the other parent's written consent first. This is because it is a criminal offence to remove a child from the country without the written consent of both parents or the consent of the court.

Where a parent simply wants to take the child on holiday, if he or she has a residence order in his or her favour, he or she can take the child abroad for a period of up to a month. If the other parent objects, an application can be made to court for its permission by way of a section 8 order. (See also Chapter 13 on child abduction.)

If there is no residence order, the civil law says nothing either to permit or prevent a parent from taking a child abroad. Again, if parents are in dispute, one or other should apply for a section 8 order. But whether a residence order exists or not, the criminal law still applies.

Applications by grandparents and others

When a marriage ends, sometimes the contact between children and one or other set of the grandparents ends too, as families divide into opposing camps. This is rarely good for the children: often children can be helped to cope with their distress by grandparents (or other close relatives or friends – say perhaps a godparent) who can give a helping hand to guide the children through their trauma.

Grandparents (or for that matter any other interested relative or family friend) can now apply to the court for a contact order or other section 8 order. They do not have to wait until divorce or other proceedings have been started (as under the old law). Children Act applications are not just limited to new cases either: if an old order is already in existence, an application can still be made for a section 8 order under the new law.

Before such an application can proceed, the court's permission may first have to be sought. The Children Act gives some categories of people the automatic right to make an application. So, if the potential applicant has had the child living with him or her for three years or more *or* has the consent of the person with a residence order in his or her favour, *or* has the consent of everyone with parental responsibility (or has the consent of the local authority if the child is in care), he or she can apply as of right to the court for a contact order or other section 8 order. Otherwise, the court's permission must be obtained before the application will be given the go-ahead. The court will then take into consideration:

- the nature of the proposed application
- the applicant's connection with the child
- the risk of harmful disruption to the child's life.

If applicants, for example grandparents, have lost contact with the children over many years and formerly had a bad influence on the children, it is possible that their application for permission to apply to court will fail. But usually the court will grant permission to apply and leave a full investigation of the facts to a proper court hearing involving all sides.

Applications for contact by grandparents are likely to be granted unless there is deep bitterness between the families which would be exacerbated by making a contact order. Contact orders can be in the form of letters, cards and telephone calls, so the court may make an order for contact in stages, building up contact from letters and telephone calls before a face to face meeting if the last time that the grandparents met their grandchildren was some years ago.

Applications for residence orders may well be unlikely to succeed unless the natural parents (or the local authority if the child is in care) are fully in support and the child has established a pattern of living with a grandparent.

Legal representation for children

In some cases where the parents are presenting opinions of the children which are totally at odds with one another, it may be helpful to ask the court for the child to have separate representation – in other words, to have his or her own advocate at court.

In public law cases (where the local authority is concerned), children are usually represented by a 'guardian ad litem', a person skilled and experienced in dealing with children, who will put the arguments for what is in the child's best interests. Occasionally the courts have taken the step of appointing a guardian ad litem in private law proceedings (i.e. those involving disputes between private individuals). In other cases the court has asked the Official Solicitor (a public official – a lawyer – who acts for children and others who do not have full legal capacity) to intervene and present the case from the child's viewpoint.

Appointing a legal representative such as a guardian ad litem or the Official Solicitor is still an unusual step and only usually taken where allegations about the children are particularly serious – say where there is an allegation of abuse. The issue of costs also can prohibit such an appointment. The costs of the guardian ad litem or the Official Solicitor will have to be met and where neither party can afford them privately, the law is not yet clear about where the costs should fall. As an alternative, it may be possible for the child to make his or her own application.

Applications by a child

The Children Act also allows children themselves to make an application for an order under section 8: the extra hurdle that the child has to overcome is to show that he or she is of 'sufficient understanding' before an application will be allowed to proceed.

Legal aid will be available on the grounds of financial eligibility (assessed on the basis of the child's own resources, if any) and merits.

Whilst as yet applications by children in their own right are relatively rare, a lot of publicity has been given to the handful of cases where, according to the media, children have applied to 'divorce' their parents. In law using the term 'divorce' in this context is incorrect. Children cannot actually divorce their parents: parents will still continue to have parental responsibility and thus be legally connected to their children. The courts have endeavoured (not always with success) to protect the privacy of children who have made their own court applications, on the basis that conducting family battles in the full glare of the media is not conducive to resolving family problems calmly and reasonably. More often than not the cases brought by children have been sorted out without a full court battle: the much publicised case of a teenage girl who wanted to live with her boyfriend and his parents eventually ended amicably with the teenager agreeing to go back home to her mother.

It is still early days since the Children Act was implemented, but so far the new right of children to make their own court applications has not yet been fully tested. Cases have been brought by children to ask the court for a residence order that they live somewhere else or for a contact order that the parent who has left the home be made to see them (sometimes against that parent's will) – but no case has yet been reported about the outcome of the latter applications.

In general, remember that court applications by children must cross two hurdles. The court must first be asked permission for a child's application to go ahead; only if that stage is passed will the court then look at the merits of the case. In general, the court will want to be convinced that the child making the application is mature and has sound reasons for asking the court for help, and is not just making the application on impulse because of a row with a parent.

Once the first hurdle is crossed, the court may sometimes appoint the Official Solicitor to act for the child in place of an ordinary solicitor. If a child wants to ask the court for help, care should be taken to get the advice of a solicitor experienced in dealing with children cases. Contact the Solicitors Family Law Association (address on page 65) or the Children's Legal Centre, 20 Compton Terrace, London N1 2UN (tel: 071-359 6251). The law may not be the best remedy for sorting out children's problems – also consider mediation or a form of therapeutic help.

CHAPTER 9

THE FAMILY HOME

LAWYERS often refer to the family home as the 'matrimonial home'. This term is used in the context of divorce to refer to the home – house or flat – acquired by husband, or wife, or both, to be lived in by the family during their joint lives.

Before the divorce

The spouse who does not legally own the family home – that is, whose name is not on the title deeds – has certain rights of occupation:

- the right not to be evicted without a court order if he or she is in occupation
- the right (if the court thinks fit) to return to the home if he or she has left it
- the right (if the court thinks fit) to exclude the owner spouse from occupying the home for a period.

The same occupation rights apply if the home is rented.

These are short-term rights of occupation while the marriage is still in existence (until decree absolute is granted). The long-term decisions about the rights to live in the home or to get a share of the proceeds if it is sold will have to be made as part of the divorce financial settlement. If violence has been threatened or used against you, making it unsafe for you to live in the family home, you can apply to the local magistrates' court or Family Hearing Centre to protect yourself (as described in Chapter 12).

Registering occupation rights: owner-occupied homes

If you are a sole occupier or joint owner of the family home, you do not need to register your rights of occupation separately. Third parties (for example a potential buyer or mortgagee) will become aware of your interest by carrying out a search of the property title, so your spouse cannot try to sell or mortgage the property without your consent.

If, however, your spouse, not you, is the sole owner of the family home, you must register your rights of occupation to ensure that they are protected against third parties.

How you register your rights of occupation depends on whether the title to the family home is 'registered' or 'unregistered'. 'Registered' here means registered at the Land Registry. Most homes will have titles registered at the Land Registry as the whole country is now subject to compulsory registration of title, but if your home was, until recently, in an area of voluntary registration, the title to your home may not yet have been registered if, for example, you bought it some time ago.

If you do not know whether the title to your home is registered or not, you may be able to find out from your bank or building society (if the home is mortgaged). If they have a 'Charge Certificate' (a Land Registry document), then the home is registered. If there is no mortgage and your spouse has a Land Certificate, then again the title is registered.

As an alternative, if you do not wish to ask a solicitor to register your rights of occupation, you can carry out an 'Index Map Search' at HM Land Registry (fee £5) to find out whether the title to the home is registered. HM Land Registry's address in London is Lincoln's Inn Fields, London WC2A 3PH (tel: 071-917 8888).

If the title is registered

The district land registry for your area will advise you how to register your rights of occupation and should provide the various forms and tell you about the procedure. HM Land Registry in London can advise you which is your local Land Registry.

If the title is unregistered

A 'class F' land charge should be registered at the Land Charges Department, Burrington Way, Plymouth PL5 3LP (tel: 0752

779831). The form to be used, K2, is available from law stationers' shops and the fee for registration is £1 per name.

The information required includes the full name in which the property-owning spouse bought or acquired the property. If you are unsure of the precise name shown on the conveyance, register the charge against all possible permutations: for example – John Smith, J Smith, John Peter Smith, J P Smith. The charge is ineffective unless it is in exactly the right name. If you are in any doubt, or time is short, apply to register at both the Land Registry and the Land Charges Department until you have sorted out the position. If you find that the title is registered you should cancel the charge at the Land Charges Department.

The green form scheme allows for a solicitor to deal with registration of a land charge or a notice if you are financially eligible.

All Citizens Advice Bureaux can help with filling in the forms to register a right of occupation and some have a supply of the necessary forms.

The effect of registering a charge or notice
Anyone buying the property or granting a mortgage on it would, as a matter of routine, check the appropriate registry and discover your notice or charge protecting your rights. (Even if a buyer or mortgagee does not actually search the register or has no knowledge of the registration, the effect of registering a land charge or notice amounts in law to notice of a non-owning spouse's right of occupation.) If he or she then buys the house or gives the mortgage, he or she does so subject to your right of occupation and cannot turn you out unless you have agreed to release your rights.

The effect of registration normally ceases once a decree of divorce is made absolute. If the question of the family home has not been settled by then, the non-owning spouse should ask the court, before the decree is made absolute, for the registration of the class F land charge or the notice to be renewed after the decree absolute. Alternatively, if you are making a claim for a share of a property, you should register a 'pending action' claim, which similarly puts third parties on notice of your interest.

Finding out if your spouse owns a second home

Sometimes there may be good reason to suspect that your spouse has bought another home – say if she or he has moved in with a new partner in a newly bought home which she or he says belongs to the new partner. There is now an easy way of checking who legally owns the home, again via the Land Registry. As long as you have the postal address of the new home, you can ask the Land Registry (address on page 155) to supply the name and address of the registered proprietor of land identified by its postal address. The fee is £5.

If your suspicions are confirmed and your spouse is shown as a legal owner, once you have made financial claims in the divorce proceedings, you may also be able to register a 'pending action' claim on the title of the second property if you think that your spouse may try to sell it to avoid paying money.

Moving out

If you hope eventually to have the home to live in permanently, it is tactically best to try to stay there, if possible. Even if you are not planning to remain in the long term but want to persuade your spouse to make other financial provision for you, staying put may help you in your negotiations. However, the strategy of staying put can sometimes be counter-productive: remaining at close quarters with your spouse once the decision to separate has been made can give rise to tensions which may undermine the prospect of successful negotiations. It may be helpful to discuss with your solicitor the pros and cons of moving out, whether on a temporary or permanent basis.

It may be tempting, if the situation between you and your spouse has become very volatile, to lock your spouse out of the home while he or she is away. Remember, however, that your spouse has a right of occupation to the property, at least while the marriage is in being, and can apply to the court for an order restoring to him or her the right to occupy the home.

Severing a joint tenancy

If you and your spouse own your home (or any other land or buildings) jointly, you need to check whether the ownership is held under a 'joint tenancy' or a 'tenancy in common'. Check the title deeds to ascertain this information (if you have a mortgage, the building society or bank can be asked).

Under a joint tenancy (the most popular method for spouses to hold the matrimonial home), each spouse's respective interest in the property is not determined: both of you own the whole of the house (or flat) jointly. And when either of you dies, the whole property automatically passes to the survivor, irrespective of any provision you may have made in a will. Under a tenancy in common, on the other hand, the interests of each spouse are fixed (usually on a 50/50 basis but it can be in any proportion) and separate, so that each of you can separately dispose of your share by will.

Many solicitors advise that you should end the joint tenancy and, pending a financial settlement or a court order, divide your respective interests in the property by becoming tenants in common. Either of you can do this by sending a 'notice of severance' to the other spouse at any time. The notice can simply take the form of a letter to your spouse, stating 'please accept this letter as notice of my severing the joint tenancy in our property known as [insert address of property]'.

A notice of severance will convert your ownership into that of a tenancy in common. It does not affect your status as co-owners but, if one of you died, the deceased's share of the property would fall into his or her estate and would be distributed under the terms of his or her will or according to the rules of intestacy.

Whether it would be in your interest to sever the joint tenancy is something you may like to discuss with a solicitor.

The matrimonial home in divorce proceedings

The kinds of order that the divorce court makes are:

- for a sale, with division of the proceeds
- for outright transfer of one spouse's interest to the other
- for a transfer of one spouse's interest to the other with a lump sum adjustment
- for a postponed sale – usually until the children complete their education but sometimes beyond that, the house then to be sold and the proceeds divided in specified proportions.

No special rules specifically lay down when and what order the court should make: the courts have a fairly wide discretion. A sale and 50/50 division of the proceeds is appropriate in many cases (especially where the marriage has been short and there are no children); in many others, this would operate unfairly against one or other of the parties. The court's decision in each case depends on whether or not there are children, the ages of husband, wife (and any children), the length of the marriage and whether the spouse who will move out has potentially secure accommodation.

Rented property

The court has power to make a transfer order on divorce with regard to 'property', which includes some but not all rented property, under section 24 of the Matrimonial Causes Act 1973.

The Matrimonial Homes Act 1983 gives the court power to transfer certain tenancies from one spouse to another on granting a decree of divorce or at any time after that. The power is contained in section 7 and schedule 1 to the 1983 Act and covers:

- protected and statutory tenancies under the Rent Act 1977
- statutory tenancies under the Rent (Agriculture) Act 1976
- secure tenancies under the Housing Act 1985
- assured tenancies under the Housing Act 1988.

If a non-tenant spouse has been deserted by the tenant spouse it is important that he or she should ask the court for a transfer of tenancy order *before* the divorce decree is made absolute.

This is because the occupation of the accommodation by the non-tenant spouse is keeping alive the protected, statutory, secure, or assured tenancy because of the 'deemed occupation' rules contained in section 1 of the 1983 Act.

Once the marriage is ended on divorce (decree absolute), these rules no longer apply, and the tenancy will lose its protected, secure or assured status, or in the case of a statutory tenancy will simply cease to exist. If there is no longer a protected, statutory, secure, or assured tenancy in existence, there is nothing for the court to transfer under the 1983 Act.

Tenancies can, however, be transferred only if they do not contain an express or implied clause against the tenant assigning the tenancy. Most 'short-term' residential tenancies do contain suah a clause. Furthermore, it is doubtful whether a statutory tenancy created for example under the Rent Act 1977 counts as property for this purpose and so it cannot be transferred.

Council tenancy
Any council tenancy is 'property' and can similarly be transferred as part of the financial arrangements on divorce.

Owner-occupied property

If the property is in joint names and expressed on the title deeds to be for the benefit of both parties equally, each technically has a half-share in the 'net equity' (or value) of the home. Occasionally, the deeds may express a different division of the property, say 60/40, but this is more common where two cohabitees buy a property. Where spouses buy a property together this is usually done on an equal basis.

Whatever the title deeds may say, the court can act on its own discretion about how to divide up the equity of a home.

The court needs to assess what the financial interest of husband and wife is in the home, but in most cases this is only the first stage of the process by which the court decides what is to happen. The court has a fairly wide discretion and each individual case is decided on its own merits.

Whose name the house is actually in – husband's, wife's or jointly – and who put up the deposit and who paid the mortgage are obviously important, but by no means the decisive, factors when making decisions on divorce.

Where the home has dropped in value
In times of recession, it is not uncommon for the equity of the home to be less than the amount of the mortgage, especially if the original mortgage was for 100 per cent of the purchase price. Even for properties where the value is slightly higher than the unpaid mortgage, the added costs of selling the home involving legal and estate agents' fees may mean that the home is worth nothing or even less than the mortgage itself.

In this situation, you will need to weigh up carefully what your best course of action might be. In favour of retaining the home and carrying on meeting the mortgage repayments would be the facts that a spouse and any children would keep a roof over their heads and that property prices may later rise to make the investment worthwhile. Sometimes estate agents may suggest a very low price for the home just to ensure a sale, whereas keeping the property for a year or so until the market improves can raise the price that the home would eventually fetch.

On the other hand, continuing the mortgage repayments if the home is unlikely to increase sufficiently in value to cover your indebtedness may only be throwing good money after bad, so it may be better to hand the keys in to the mortgagee (the bank or building society) and leave it to them to sell. The drawback of following this course is that the mortgagee may sell the property at a considerable loss and try to look to you for the balance at a later stage.

None of the options that you face may look attractive, and you may be forced into choosing the least unattractive, namely the one that costs you least. Ask several estate agents for a free valuation of the home and for their views on the property market. Although some of what you are told may be speculative rather than factual, you should get a clearer picture on which to base your decision. Talk to your bank or building society to see whether they offer any schemes to help out home-owners in your situation. Make sure that you also talk to your solicitor or Citizens Advice Bureau to discuss your options before finally making up your mind.

Where there are no children

Where there is a divorce after a short marriage, the court may look mainly at what financial contributions relating to the house or flat had been made and decide that the person who put in the most should have the most out. The longer the marriage has gone on, the less the court is interested in who put in what, in money terms, and the more it is prepared to recognise the other party's non-money contribution. For instance, the wife's contribution in keeping the home going may count as much as the husband's financial contributions.

The main consideration is likely to be whether the net proceeds of sale of the house are likely to be sufficient to enable each spouse (with the aid of such mortgage loan as each might be able to obtain) to buy an adequate new home. If so, the court may well order a sale of the house without delay. Even if one of them wants to stay on, it may not be practicable or fair to the other for him or her to do so because the other one would need his or her share of the value of the house in order to buy a new home. The house may have to be sold where the combined resources of husband and wife are insufficient to keep up the mortgage repayments on the existing home and to provide accommodation for the other spouse.

Where the home has been bought from the local authority under the 'right to buy' with a discount and it is sold within three years of buying, you have to pay back to the local authority part of the discount you were allowed. This may well be an argument for asking the court to defer a sale until the three-year period is up.

Division of proceeds

When determining how best to share out the money from the sale of the house (or flat), the court will take into account direct financial contributions by the non-owning spouse towards the purchase (payment of part of the deposit or part of the mortgage repayments) or for the improvement of the house. It will also consider indirect financial contributions – for example, where the wife has worked for all or part of the marriage and has used her earnings to pay some of the household bills, food, clothing or has paid her earnings into the couple's joint bank account.

If the wife's share would be insufficient to enable her to buy a new home, particularly if her earning capacity puts her into a less favourable position for getting a mortgage, the court could order that the wife should get a greater share of the proceeds of sale. The court may compensate the husband by ordering him to pay relatively low maintenance to the wife – or none at all.

Not selling

A sale of the family home may, however, not be the right solution. The expenses of selling, and of buying two other houses, will have to be met, and the net proceeds of sale may not be sufficient to enable either spouse to buy another home. (Moreover, if either was legally aided, the Legal Aid Board may claim part of the proceeds for the legal aid fund's statutory charge.) The court could order that the wife remain in the house:

- until she wants to move out, or marries again, or cohabits permanently (this is normally taken to be the case after, say, six months of living together, but preferably should be defined in the order) or she dies; *or*
- for a period of time specified by the court.

After that, the house would be sold, and the net proceeds divided in the proportions decided by the court at the time of making the order (these cannot be varied later).

The wife might have to compensate the husband in the meantime by a (notional) payment of rent. In practice, this might be achieved by an appropriate reduction of his maintenance obligations to her.

An arrangement which leaves the wife with uncertainty as to her future home, and the husband having to wait a number of years before he receives his capital while he has to continue paying maintenance, can cause bitterness. The courts try to avoid some of these difficulties by arranging a 'clean break': for example, it might be fair for the house to be transferred outright to the wife and the husband compensated by dismissal of the wife's claims for maintenance for now and the future.

If an order is made for the transfer of the whole of the home into one of the spouse's sole name or from one into the joint names, a transfer or conveyance will have to be drawn up. On the transfer of property by court order following the break-up of a marriage, no stamp duty is payable irrespective of the value of the property. Where a solicitor is required for the conveyancing, the work can be done under the green form scheme or a legal aid certificate.

One spouse 'buying out' the other
An alternative 'clean break' arrangement is for the spouse who is going to remain in the house to buy out the departing spouse, by

paying him or her a lump sum for his or her share in the house. If the spouse who remains has to borrow the money or to raise an extra mortgage, there will be tax relief on the interest on the amount of mortgage up to £30,000.

If the person who has been bought out uses the money towards buying another house and borrows the rest on mortgage, he or she will get tax relief on the interest on a loan of up to £30,000. In other words, both ex-spouses can take advantage of the full amount of tax relief on mortgages for a house each.

Beware, however, the danger of a delay in the lump sum payment if the house market is volatile. In a recent case (*Hope-Smith v. Hope-Smith*) the husband had been ordered to pay his wife a lump sum of £32,000 within 28 days and if he failed to do so, the matrimonial home should be sold forthwith and £32,000 of the proceeds given to the wife. The husband unsuccessfully appealed against this order, but three years later the house was still unsold. His former wife then successfully appealed against the original order and the court substituted a larger payment to the wife because of the increase in house prices over the three years.

Wherever there is likely to be a delay in payment, it may be better to express the payment in percentage terms of the equity of the house, rather than as a fixed lump sum.

Where there are children

The court's priority is that an adequate home should be provided for the children. Recent cases continue to stress that, while the court has a number of matters to take into consideration, the first consideration is for the interests of the children.

The Child Support Act has made a significant impact on the way the courts and lawyers deal with the home following divorce where there are children. In most cases it has taken away the courts' power to decide on the amount of child support and switched to calculating child support amounts according to the new formula.

The full extent of the changes has not yet been fully tested in the courts so there is as yet no clear guidance about what differences the Child Support Act will make with regard to the home. One thing, however, is clear – the fact that in general child support payments have more than doubled – on average from around £20 weekly to around £50 weekly.

Because the spouse who has left the home (called the absent parent) is likely to end up having greater outgoings in the form of child support payments, one knock-on effect is that he may no longer be able to afford to transfer his share in the home to the parent remaining to look after the children. So the advice which follows here must be tempered by the consideration that there may not be enough money both to achieve proper child support payments and changes in ownership of the family home. As payments of child support are usually fixed, the absent parent may have to retain a share in the family home unless there are sufficient funds both to meet child support payments and the costs of his re-housing (see also Chapter 5 for more information).

Selling

It is unlikely that the court would order a sale unless selling the home would bring in enough money to buy other adequate accommodation for the parent (usually the wife) who is going to have the children to live there with her.

The house would, however, have to be sold if the wife could not keep up the mortgage repayments with whatever assistance by way of maintenance the husband could finance. More economical accommodation would then have to be provided for her and the children out of the proceeds of selling the house.

Not selling yet

In order to secure the house as a home for the children, the court may order the husband to transfer it into joint names if it has been in his sole name. When a house is in joint names, it cannot normally be sold without the agreement of the joint owners, but either party can apply to the High Court for an order to enforce a sale. To prevent this, the divorce court normally directs that the house shall not be sold for a specific period while the wife and the children live there – usually until the youngest child reaches school-leaving age.

A more usual alternative is to transfer the house into the wife's sole name, subject to a charge securing to the husband whatever sum or proportion of the net proceeds of (eventual) sale the court thinks proper. A 'charge' over the property means that when it is sold, the charge (which is like a mortgage) comes into effect and the other spouse will get his or her money out of the proceeds. The husband does not have the right to intervene in respect of the property by virtue of such a charge – his position becomes just like that of a bank or building society to whom money is secured on the property. The husband may have to pay Capital Gains Tax on the money he eventually receives. Normally, the provisions for inflation and his personal exemptions cover this but it may be worth bearing in mind if there is an anticipated gain, or if the husband is likely to use up his exemptions in some other ways.

In either case, the court specifies at what point the husband can realise his interest in the house. This is likely to be when the youngest child of the family comes of age or when any child undergoing full-time education ceases to remain normally resident in the home. The husband can then enforce the sale.

Selling much later

The difficult problem is whether the house should be kept as a home for the ex-wife even after the children have left home. The court will take into account whether the wife's share of the proceeds, if the house were sold then, would enable her to buy another house, and also the husband's need for the capital. The court can only gauge what the situation is likely to be – possibly 12 or 15 years ahead – what money the ex-wife would receive from the sale of the house, her likelihood of employment and earnings and mortgage capacity. Her share would need to be sufficient for her to buy a flat or a smaller house at an age when she may be unable to raise much by way of mortgage. Meanwhile, the husband will have been able to start afresh with another mortgage because of his lower age and possibly higher earnings at the time of the divorce.

The cons of selling later

A disadvantage of delaying a final resolution of a division of the parties' capital assets is that, when the time eventually does come for a sale, the ex-wife may well be reluctant to move out, particularly if she sees her former husband doing comfortably in another property. In a sense, this type of order can prolong the agony of a divorce. But sometimes there is no alternative.

If it seems likely that the ex-wife will have insufficient to enable her to buy another house, when the children are no longer dependent, the court may either award her a larger share of the value or defer the sale (or enforcement of the ex-husband's charge) for the remainder of her life (or until she remarries or cohabits). The court may not make such an order if by not selling, the ex-husband's problems are likely to outweigh the ex-wife's.

Where either party was legally aided and the Legal Aid Board's statutory charge applies, this will not be levied until the house is sold. By then, the rise in house prices may have reduced the practical effect of the charge (but there will be accrued simple interest at 8 per cent (1994 figures) per year on the charge to be paid in addition).

When the house is eventually sold, liability for capital gains tax may arise for an ex-spouse who is still a joint-owner but who had moved out of the house.

If there is no mortgage to be paid off, the ex-wife will effectively be living in the house at the ex-husband's expense. The court therefore may make an order requiring her to pay the ex-husband an occupation rent from the time that the children cease to need the house as a home. If she is paying off the mortgage on the house, the ex-wife will be contributing to the value of the ex-husband's eventual share of the proceeds of sale.

If the house or flat is mortgaged

Mortgages cannot simply be transferred and the court has no power to order the transfer of a mortgage – only transfer of the property subject to the mortgage. The consent of the building society or other mortgagees is necessary, otherwise the mortgagor (usually the husband) remains liable for the mortgage even if the property is transferred. The mortgagees must be served with notice of an application to the court for a transfer of ownership and have the right to object.

It may well be the ex-wife who is going to be responsible for meeting the mortgage repayments in future, possibly out of an income from maintenance payments on which the building society or bank would not have agreed to make a mortgage loan. It is advisable for her to contact the mortgagees as soon as possible to discuss ways of making repayments if and when the house is transferred.

The building society or other mortgagee must agree before the transfer can take effect. If they do not agree to the transfer, it may be necessary to try to pay off the mortgage and find a new mortgagee – if necessary through a mortgage broker (although remember that mortgage brokers usually charge fees at around one per cent of the amount borrowed).

It is not uncommon for building societies to ask a former husband to guarantee a mortgage that is being taken out by a woman whose income comes from his maintenance payments either in whole or in part. The ex-husband would have to meet the mortgage repayments only if his former wife defaulted. (He can ask her for an indemnity so that she is liable to compensate him if this did happen.) In practice, her default is likely to happen only if he defaults on the maintenance.

Where there is an endowment mortgage

A mortgage on an endowment basis is linked to an insurance policy that should pay out enough to repay the loan (with a surplus if it is a with-profits policy) at the end of the mortgage term or on the policyholder's death. In the meantime, only the interest has to be paid on the loan, plus the premiums on the insurance policy. Doubts have recently been raised about whether in reality endowment policies will realise sufficient to cover the mortgage, especially if the policies were affected by the stock market crash in 1987. It may be worthwhile checking with your mortgagee or insurance company how financially healthy your particular endowment is.

The application for a property adjustment order where there is an endowment mortgage should include an application to transfer the husband's beneficial interest in the insurance policy to the wife (or vice versa). If this is not transferred, the ex-wife would be in a position of getting nothing under the policy and would have to pay off the whole mortgage loan out of the proceeds of sale of the house. When the mortgage term comes to an end, a decision has to be made regarding any bonuses on the policy over and above the amount required to repay the loan. This surplus could be ordered to go to the ex-husband to compensate for the loss of use of capital, or to the ex-wife, particularly if she has been paying the premiums for many years, or to be shared between them.

Capital Gains Tax

Capital Gains Tax (CGT) is payable on gains arising on the 'disposal of assets'. Before the Finance Act 1988, capital gains were treated differently from income for tax purposes. For disposals made after 6 April 1988, the amount of your chargeable capital gains is added to your income. You are charged the appropriate income tax rate (20, 25 or 40 per cent) calculated by treating the capital gain as the top slice.

A specified amount of gains in any one tax year is exempt. Both the husband and the wife each have their own £5,800 annual exemption (1994/5 figures).

So long as a husband and wife are living together, and for the rest of the tax year after the separation, no chargeable gain results where there is disposal between them. But when the asset is eventually transferred or is sold to someone else, the gain (or loss) is calculated over the whole period of ownership, not just since the date of transfer to the ex-spouse.

For the calculation of gain on disposals of property that was owned before 1982, the base cost is the market value of the asset on 31 March 1982 (subject to certain special rules mostly dealing with business). To calculate the inflation since that date, reference is made to the increases in the retail prices index (RPI) based on the figure at March 1982.

On divorce or separation, the major areas where disposals are likely to arise are:

- household contents
- other assets such as a car, a second home, stocks and shares, savings ('assets' means practically everything capable of being owned and sold or transferred)
- the home.

Most consumer goods decrease in value, so the question of 'gain' does not arise. Most chattels with a lifespan of less than fifty years are exempt from CGT, anyway.

Cash and cars are specifically exempt from CGT, and so are any sums received on the surrender of life insurance policies. So if, for one reason or another, you cash in an endowment policy which is linked to a mortgage, there is no question of liability to CGT. A sale of other assets, such as stocks and shares, can give rise to CGT.

The home and CGT

Any gain made on the sale of a person's principal private residence (PPR) is normally exempt from CGT. But CGT liability arises when the home is sold if you had stopped living there more than two years ago.

On divorce, it is likely that you will do one or other of three things with the home:

- sell it and split the proceeds
- transfer it to your spouse outright
- put it into joint names (or leave it in joint names) and postpone sale and division of the proceeds until a future date.

Sale and division of proceeds

If you sell the house and split the proceeds within two years of one or other of you ceasing to reside there, you will be entitled to claim 'principal private residence' (PPR) exemption provided the home was your only, or main, residence throughout the period that you owned it.

If at any time you have two or more homes, either of them is potentially eligible for the PPR exemption. If, therefore, you have bought another home and the old home has not been sold, you may make a choice, within two years, as to which one you wish to have treated as your PPR. (If you do not, your tax inspector will.) It may make sense to claim the exemption in respect of the house that is being sold, if this is at a gain.

Where the sale takes place more than two years after one of you has left, the person who ceased to reside there will not be fully exempt. Only a portion of the gain will be exempt: namely, the period of his or her actual occupation plus the last two years of ownership. (The last two years of ownership are always exempt.) Thus, the longer you wait beyond two years after separation before selling your old home, the greater the possibility of CGT having to be paid by the person who left. The person who remains will not be liable for CGT provided he or she has remained permanently in residence.

Transfer of the home to your spouse outright
Although no money changes hands, the transfer would in theory be a 'disposal', based on the market value at the date of disposal. Quite apart from the fact that there may well not be a capital gain anyway (after taking inflation into account and the current year's exemption), the transaction would qualify for PPR exemption if made within two years of the transfer or leaving the home.

Even if the transfer were made outside the two-year period, provided that it was made as part of a divorce settlement and provided that you had not elected to declare any other home as your PPR, the Inland Revenue should treat the disposal as exempt by 'concession'.

House in joint names sold much later
Transferring the house into joint names will not attract CGT liability.

When the house is sold many years later and the proceeds divided, the spouse who has remained in the home will not have to pay tax on his or her share because that will be fully covered by the PPR exemption. But the one who moved out will be liable to some CGT. The same applies if the house is not in joint names but the one who moves out has a charge on the property. On realisation of the charge, the husband will be liable for capital gains tax on the increase in the value of the charge after taking into account the increase in the RPI and his annual exemption.

Second home
Selling a second home to raise money may render you liable to capital gains tax if there is a sufficient gain. (By 'second home' in this context is meant a property for which PPR did not apply while you were living together.)

It could make more sense to transfer it to the spouse who is moving out of the matrimonial home for him or her to live in it as his or her PPR. When it is eventually sold, it will be possible for him or her to claim PPR exemption on the whole of any gains from the date when the property had first been acquired – provided that the transfer between the spouses took place before the end of the tax year in which they separated.

Advice

You may well feel that you need specialist advice about capital gains tax, perhaps from an accountant. For someone in receipt of legal aid, it might be better for the solicitor to instruct the accountant since he or she will then pay the accountant's fee and may be able to recover the fee from the legal aid fund as an expense reasonably incurred, but would need to obtain the authority of the Legal Aid Board to incur the accountant's fees before instructing him or her. If the accountant were instructed directly, the client would have to find the money more or less straightaway (whereas a legal aid statutory charge may not be payable until considerably later).

CHAPTER 10

Money in divorce

Money and the Child Support Agency

Since the Child Support Agency has in the main taken over responsibility for child support, there have been radical changes in the way money in divorce is dealt with – unless of course there are no children, in which case the courts' powers remain the same.

Where there are children, the most important change is the approach to the way that money will be divided up. Because the child support formula provides, in theory at least, a clear and precise answer to the question of how much child support should be paid, child support is usually the place to start (see Chapter 5).

You can then see how the remainder of the income and assets (if there are any) should be divided. Because of the likely increase in overall support payments paid by the absent parent, there may be less money to go around to be able to afford capital divisions. Many lawyers predict a decrease in the numbers of clean break orders being made, for example, because an absent parent may not be able to afford to buy a new property and thus will need to keep his share in the old one.

The Child Support Act is still in its early days. The formula for working out child support may not be particularly easy to apply where the parent who has left the home (or even just plans to leave sometime) has not yet bought or rented a new home, as the housing costs will be a question mark. No cases have yet been reported and therefore no guidelines have emerged about the best way of going about dividing up capital and income on divorce. So in the meantime, during the teething period of the Child Support Agency, the advice given here must be tempered by the fact that no-one yet knows with certainty how much the old approach to money in divorce has been changed.

Money and the courts

It is perfectly possible to obtain a divorce without dealing with the question of finances but it would be unwise to leave this unresolved and uncertain. If you have reached an agreement with your spouse on other financial matters, your agreement should be drawn up in the form of a consent order (see page 56) to ensure that it is as watertight as possible. If you are unable to reach a satisfactory agreement, you will need to start off financial proceedings (often known as 'ancillary proceedings') at the court.

A further warning about costs is appropriate here. Many spouses have found themselves engaged in time-consuming and costly legal battles over money. Money swallowed up in legal fees will not be available for distribution from the family's 'pot' of resources at the end of the day. Even if you are legally aided, the likelihood is that through the statutory charge you will have to meet the legal fees incurred by your solicitor during the course of the financial proceedings.

If, however, you are faced with a recalcitrant spouse who demonstrates a refusal to cooperate and who is likely to delay deliberately a financial settlement, your best bet may be to follow the practice of some solicitors who from a very early stage prepare the evidence for as much of their client's case as possible. Some solicitors make it their practice to submit to the court right at the start, in difficult cases, an application for financial relief supported by an affidavit, with valuations of any relevant property and a list of the documents to be relied on. This has the immediate effect of placing the ball firmly in the court of the uncooperative spouse. It also means that future endeavours by the solicitors can be concentrated on extracting information from the unwilling party.

A legal aid certificate covers work in connection with financial applications, including representation at the hearing, although the work covered will generally exclude child maintenance, which is now usually dealt with by the Child Support Agency.

The procedure

The formal claim for financial relief is usually included within the prayer in the petition and/or, where the case is defended, in the prayer of the answer. To trigger off these claims, the petitioner or the respondent will have to file another application (form M13 or form M11), supported by an affidavit, giving notice to the court that he or she wishes the financial issues to be dealt with.

If for any reason the prayer of the petition did not include a claim for financial relief, the court must be asked for permission to make such a claim before an application can be made by the petitioner, or by a respondent who is defending. Maintenance applications for an ex-spouse can be made, in any event, only if the applicant has not remarried.

After divorce in another country
A court in England or Wales can make orders for financial provision in cases where a marriage has been dissolved or annulled or the couple have been legally separated by judicial or other recognised proceedings outside the British Isles. However, permission to pursue such an application has first to be obtained from the High Court which has to decide whether, bearing in mind the domicile and other circumstances of the applicant, England or Wales would be an appropriate jurisdiction to hear the application.

An affidavit explaining all the circumstances must be filed with the request for leave to apply. It would be foolish not to consult a solicitor before embarking on this.

After separation
Where a divorce is founded on the basis that the parties have lived separately for a period of two years and each agreed to the divorce, or have lived apart for five years, the respondent can indicate on the acknowledgment of service form that he or she intends to apply to the court to consider what his (or, more usually) her financial position will be after the divorce. This is

known as a section 10 application (because the matter is dealt with in section 10 of the Matrimonial Causes Act 1973).

A special form for a section 10 application (form M12) can be obtained from the court office and must be filed at court. The decree absolute cannot then be granted until the district judge is satisfied that the petitioner is going to make fair and reasonable financial provision for the respondent, or the best that can be made in the circumstances.

A section 10 application is advisable where the respondent wife is around 40 upwards and is particularly concerned about the loss of her pension rights. Solicitors acting for such clients will usually advise submitting a section 10 application unless the wife specially asks them not to take this step.

The orders
An application can be made for all or any of the following:

- an order for maintenance pending suit (i.e. before decree absolute is granted)
- a periodical payments order
- a lump sum order
- an order for secured provision
- a property adjustment order.

If you make a claim for a lump sum order, the court can order only one lump sum; there is no provision for the court to order an interim payment of capital.

Preventing a spouse from disposing of assets
If your partner has assets in his or her sole name and is threatening or scheming to try to dispose of these assets in order to thwart your claims, you can apply to the court, ex parte if necessary, for an injunction preventing or restraining him or her from so doing. If another person is involved, that person (for example, if a second home is being sold subject to a mortgage, the mortgagee of that property) must also be served with notice of your application.

You must file an affidavit setting out full details of your need for such an order. But it is wise to obtain legal advice before applying for such an injunction.

Starting off your claim

You should consider filing your application for financial provision at an early stage. Maintenance payments can only be backdated to the date of the application. For the petitioner the date of application is the date of the petition; for the respondent this is the date of the application itself. An application (other than for maintenance pending suit) will not be considered by the court until the decree nisi. If you are still negotiating about financial matters with your spouse, make it plain to him or her, however, either directly or through solicitors, that filing a formal application should not be interpreted as an unwillingness on your part to try to negotiate an agreement. On the contrary, by setting out your own financial position in the affidavit supporting the application, you are paving the way to productive negotiations.

If you are the petitioner, you apply by *Notice of intention to proceed with application for ancillary relief made in petition* (form M13); if you are the respondent, you apply by *Notice of application for ancillary relief* (form M11). Both forms are available free from divorce court offices.

Two copies of the notice of application have to be completed (and keep an extra one for yourself) and both have to be lodged at the court office. They must be accompanied by an affidavit of means in support of your application. The fee for lodging an application for ancillary relief is at present £20.

Do not fill in the space on the application form for the date of the hearing. This will be dealt with by the court office.

List the orders you are seeking, but do not state the amounts you wish to claim for the maintenance payments or lump sum. These will be decided during negotiations or at the hearing. It is usual to make a claim for all the available orders to enable the court to consider the financial position comprehensively.

Where the application includes a property adjustment claim, the address of the house or flat or description of any other property which you wish to be transferred should be given with particulars, so far as you know, of any mortgage, whether the title to the property is registered or unregistered and the title number if it is registered and the name and address of the mortgagee. If there is a mortgage, the mortgagees (building society or bank) will have to be sent a copy of the application and, if they request it, a copy of the affidavit in support of the application.

Once an application for property adjustment has been made, you can register a 'pending action' against the title to the property, which may be useful if the registration of your right to occupy the matrimonial (family) home is about to be overtaken by decree absolute or if the property in question is not jointly owned by you and is not the matrimonial home.

The affidavits

Standard blank forms of affidavit may be obtained from the divorce court office or from law stationers' shops. You do not have to use the standard form but it is a useful guide to the relevant information to be given in your own affidavit. Once the affidavit has been sworn, the original needs to be lodged at court, one copy to be sent to the other spouse with the application and one for you to keep. If a magistrates' court order for maintenance is already in existence, a copy should be sent to the divorce court with the affidavit. The application will be sealed (that is, officially stamped) at the court office and handed back to you. You must then send this copy of the application to your spouse (together with a copy of the affidavit you lodged with the application), within four days. If your spouse does not turn up at any subsequent hearing, you will have to satisfy the court that the application was sent.

The application form requires the other spouse to file an affidavit of his or her means within 28 days of receiving the notice of application. This requirement was rarely honoured before the Children Act came into force. However, under new Family Proceedings Rules, time limits under Children Act applications have become much stricter, which has had a slight knock-on effect on other applications. So do your utmost to comply with time limits.

Information in the affidavits

The foundation of the evidence set before the district judge is contained in the statements sworn by each spouse. It is therefore important to make sure the information given in your own affidavit is complete and accurate and contains all the information that the district judge is likely to require. It is equally important to ensure that your spouse discloses all relevant information. Affidavits are written in the first person and in concise numbered paragraphs.

It is not necessary to go into very detailed explanation and summaries of your income and expenditure (for example) will often suffice. At the end of your affidavit put the paragraph: 'Save as set out above, I have no other source of capital or income' – and this should be the truth. Remember that an affidavit is made on oath; false statements amount to perjury and can lead to your being penalised, probably by having to bear a greater share of the costs of the case if you have misled the court.

If you are the applicant, you will have the opportunity later, once the recipient has filed an affidavit in reply, to lodge with the court a further affidavit which can cover and clarify matters which you feel may have been misrepresented by your spouse or on which it is necessary to give further evidence to the court.

Give clear and accurate details of your own capital and income and liabilities as well as what you know of the financial position of anyone you may be planning to marry or live with on a permanent basis. It will be helpful for the court if at this stage you set out a summary of your needs in the form of a budget, putting outgoings either on a weekly or monthly basis and giving a total – but you may consider that, tactically, from the point of view of current negotiations with your spouse, this would be best left until later.

As much information as possible should be given about any property that you want to have transferred to you: its value, when it was bought and the price paid for it and by whom.

For a house or flat, whether or not you want to have it transferred to you, details should be given of any mortgages on it (including any insurance policy which is collateral security for a mortgage) and the amount still owing to the mortgagees.

Where several properties have been owned during the marriage, try to give details of each and the dates of purchase and sale (approximately), the prices paid and obtained for each property and the contributions made by each spouse to the purchase (including loans or gifts by in-laws) or to the improvement (particularly structural) of each home.

Also include any relevant information you have about your spouse's other property.

Details of any other substantial assets should be included, for example, a car, insurance policies, and, if the marriage has been long-lasting, pension schemes.

If yours is the first affidavit, you can set out what you know of your spouse's finances, especially areas which you think might be 'forgotten', such as valuable personal belongings or fringe benefits. If your partner has already filed an affidavit, you can comment on any omissions or inaccuracies in it.

What accompanies the affidavit

It is usual to attach to the affidavit copies of several recent pay slips (for example, for the last three to six months) and your P60 (a form issued to all employees at the end of each tax year, and giving details of gross pay and tax deducted). If you are self-employed, at least your most recent sets of accounts should be attached.

Attachments to the affidavit are described as 'exhibits' and should be numbered chronologically: for example, in the affidavit of John Smith, a self-employed bookseller, 'I produce and exhibit marked "JS1" copies of business accounts for the last three financial years'.

'Directions' and preliminary hearing

There will generally first be an appointment for 'directions' at which the district judge gives directions about the steps that need to be taken so that all the required information will be available to the court at the eventual hearing. This 'directions hearing' is a preliminary hearing; the district judge will not make a decision about the application (but, in some courts, it may be coupled with a hearing of a claim for maintenance pending suit or for an agreed order).

Certain courts will automatically fix a date for the hearing of directions. In other courts, you will have to apply for a specific date. Check with your local court for details.

Other courts issue standard directions automatically after the filing of a financial application (for example, as to when further affidavits must be filed, how an owner-occupied home should be valued).

You yourself can apply for a hearing for directions if one has not been fixed or if you want an interim order for maintenance. Notification of the date of the hearing is sent by the court to both parties.

At a directions hearing, the district judge can make orders for further affidavits (or order that there shall be no further affidavits without the court's permission), for information or documents to be supplied, for discovery of documents relevant to the applications, for either or both parties to give oral evidence, for valuation. The courts are becoming increasingly concerned that such an exchange of information does not get out of hand (and thus run up huge legal bills). So two valuations would usually be regarded as unnecessary for a family busines, for example, especially if that business could not be sold on the open market. The parties would be expected to try to agree an appointment of a valuer.

If you want to be sure that your spouse will be physically present at the full hearing to give evidence, ask at the preliminary hearing for the district judge to make an order that he or she should attend for cross-examination.

Interim order

If your affidavit contains some reasonably up-to-date information about your spouse's financial position, this may enable the district judge to make at least an interim order at a preliminary hearing even if your spouse has failed to file an affidavit in time. You can apply for a hearing for your application for maintenance pending suit or an interim order, although if the district judge feels that such a hearing was unnecessary, he or she may order you to pay your spouse's costs or expenses in attending.

Some district judges are willing to listen to an application for an interim order for spousal maintenance based on a wife's estimate of her husband's income and a general assessment of his likely liabilities. Others prefer the husband to file an affidavit even if he has shown himself unwilling to do so. The courts have a discretion in this respect.

If the husband is clearly not cooperating at all, a district judge might well make a high interim order for periodical payments, with the deliberate aim of forcing the husband to disclose his means in order to obtain a reduction of the order. Otherwise, it is often the case that a maintenance pending suit order is pitched at a lower level than a later periodical payments order, as it is rare for district judges to have the opportunity of a full examination of the facts at a preliminary hearing. The courts will also take account of any child support application made to the Child Support Agency and if assessment is already in place may reduce the spousal maintenance in the light of what the husband can afford to pay.

An interim order can be replaced later by a lower (or higher) order back-dated to take effect from the date of the interim order.

Getting an affidavit from an unwilling spouse

If your spouse has failed to file an affidavit and you think that he or she is going to continue to be difficult about this, do not allow matters to drift on too long; delaying may be a deliberate tactic. You can apply to the district judge for an order requiring that an affidavit be filed within a set period and to have what is known as a 'penal notice' endorsed on the order. If this is done and a copy of the order is served personally (by you or someone acting on your behalf) on your spouse, he or she will be in contempt of court in still failing to comply, and an application can be made to the judge to commit him or her to prison.

Finding out more about your spouse's financial position

When you receive a copy of your spouse's affidavit, go through it carefully to see whether he or she has omitted any major assets or sources of income.

You can respond to specific inaccuracies or points made by filing a third affidavit. If allegations were made which you believe to be false, these could also be commented on in a further affidavit – but do not let the number of affidavits spiral uncontrollably. (The court may have given directions limiting the number that can be filed.)

If your spouse in an affidavit 'puts you to proof' of information, you must provide this and may do so in an affidavit.

At the directions hearing, the district judge can either have provided for an exchange of information by each party supplying a list of documents to the other side or, more likely, by means of 'rule 2.63' questionnaires (the old name for these is 'rule 77' questionnaires).

Information given in an affidavit can be checked, investigated or clarified by means of a written questionnaire sent to a spouse or his/her solicitor. Rule 2.63 of the Family Proceedings Rules 1991 states:

'Any party to an application for ancillary relief may by letter require any other party to give further information concerning any matter contained in any affidavit filed by or on behalf of that other party or any other relevant matter, or to furnish a list of relevant documents or to allow inspection of any such document . . .'

It is quite usual to ask for this kind of supplementary information and documentation. What it is appropriate to ask for depends on how comprehensive the other person's affidavit is and how complicated his/her other finances are. Requests may be made, for example, for:

- copy of pay slips for, say, the past three to six months
- copy of form P60
- copy of forms P11d, tax returns and notices of assessment for the past three years
- copy of contract of employment or statement of terms of employment
- copy of bank statements for, say, the past 12 months and building society passbooks
- statements of current surrender values of insurance policies
- statement of value of pension scheme and copy of pension rules
- valuations of antiques, jewellery etc. (market value, not insurance value).

If the information or documentation is not supplied in response to your questionnaire, you can then apply to the district judge asking for an order that your spouse provide such information or documents. Whether or not you will be successful in obtaining such an order depends on the reasonableness of your request.

Just as it is usual to make an application to the court for financial relief even though you hope to negotiate an out-of-court settlement, it is also quite usual to make requests in the form of a 'questionnaire' in order to clarify the financial picture before proposals are made or agreed. If in the end you can reach no agreement and there has to be a court hearing, a spare copy of the questionnaire and answers should be made available for the court.

Property valuations

If you can include in your affidavit an estimate of the value of the property you or your spouse own, do so.

You may have asked a local estate agent to tell you what a reasonable asking price would be for your home, but your spouse may think the value is over (or under) optimistic. It is then generally best, if possible, to agree to instruct one valuer to carry out a formal valuation – for which you will then have to pay a fee – agreeing that you will each accept what that valuer says. Otherwise, if you each instruct a separate valuer, their reports may disagree; if there is then a contested hearing, each valuer may have to be called as a witness (adding to the cost) and the court will have to decide what value to attribute.

If there is delay before the final court hearing, it may be necessary to get the valuation updated, particularly in times of fluctuating property markets.

If your spouse has other assets, such as a business, it may be necessary to get his or her interest in the company valued. A direction on this point will usually be made by the district judge at the directions hearing.

Before you decide to ask for a direction for a valuation of a business in which your spouse is involved, consider carefully the question of costs. An investigation of a company's business, which will usually be carried out by an accountant, can be expensive and is worthwhile only if:

- you have serious concerns that your partner is attempting to disguise its true worth, *and*

- the asset is important from the point of view of capital as well as providing income for using, *and*
- the business itself is valuable.

Warnings about excessive amounts of costs are constantly being made in the courts. One judge, Mrs Justice Booth, issued these guidelines to lawyers in 1990:

- affidavit evidence should be confined to relevant facts
- professional witnesses should avoid taking a partisan approach
- extra care should be taken to decide what evidence should be produced; non-material emotive evidence should be avoided
- care should be taken to avoid duplicating documents
- both parties' solicitors should agree a chronology of material facts
- if a case looks to be substantial, a pre-trial review should be arranged to see if settlement can be reached.

Coming to an agreement

Once affidavits have been filed, it is wise to send to the other side an offer setting out the terms on which you would be willing to settle the case. The letter, which should be marked 'Without Prejudice' so that it cannot be used in evidence against you (except on the point of costs), is known as a Calderbank letter (from the name of the case which decided this principle). Briefly, it is a 'without prejudice' offer of financial settlement which, if not accepted and the case goes ahead, will be made known to the court at the end of the financial hearing. If the court has awarded less than the offer that was refused, the offeree will usually have to bear the offeror's legal costs. The very fact of your sending a Calderbank letter can bring issues to a head because if your offer is fair your partner is running the risk (if he or she decides to continue the case) that the costs incurred after the making of your offer will be awarded against him or her. The courts have indicated that each spouse is under a *duty* to try to settle financial disputes by making a Calderbank offer. Either side can make an offer, or counter-offer, although the initiative usually lies with the wealthier spouse (in most cases the husband).

Making a Calderbank offer can be viewed as a gamble, but an experienced solicitor can help reduce the odds. In some cases the gamble pays off even if the offer is slightly on the low side, especially if the other party refuses to negotiate or make a counter-offer.

CASE

The husband made a Calderbank offer of £400,000 which the wife rejected. After a contested hearing the wife beat the offer and was awarded £435,000. But the judge refused to award the wife her costs because of her refusal to negotiate over the original offer, so she had to pay her own legal bill instead of this being awarded against the husband. [S v. S (1990)]

Fewer than one in ten financial applications ever reaches a full hearing. Many are settled well before you get to court, although a number are settled on the steps leading up to the court on the date of the hearing. The earlier that you can settle your case, on reasonable terms for you, the greater savings you will achieve in terms of legal costs, time and harassment.

Getting a hearing date

When you are satisfied that you have obtained as much information as is necessary to enable the court to make a realistic judgement, you, jointly with your spouse, can apply for a hearing date. If you have instructed a solicitor, the solicitor (or a barrister if one will be representing you at the hearing) will prepare a 'certificate of readiness for trial and time estimate' and lodge this with the clerk to the district judge, with a request for a hearing date. How quickly your case will be heard depends on the relative pressure of work on the court which will hear your application, and on how long your case is likely to take. The date you will be given is likely to be more than three months away.

Preparing for the hearing

Before a contested hearing, it is useful to prepare a summary of the financial position of each of you in both income and capital terms, together with details of any debts and liabilities. If the marriage has been long or the financial dealings are otherwise complex, a chronological listing of events can help. Such information will help to present the case clearly to the district judge and many solicitors now prepare and agree with the other side a financial schedule to summarise the facts.

Both parties should attend the hearing, together with any witnesses, whether or not they are legally represented. Your solicitor may have instructed a barrister (counsel) to represent your case to the district judge. You may well have had a meeting to discuss your case (known as a conference) with the barrister before the hearing. Make sure you take to court all the relevant documents, including copies of all affidavits and any questionnaires, and check with your solicitor whether any up-dating financial information is required.

Because of the potentially profound effect of costs on a case, both parties should prepare for the district judge a summary of their legal costs up to hearing, and an estimate of costs including the hearing. If you are legally represented, these will include the solicitor's fees, VAT, and disbursements (which can include estate agents fees for valuing your house) and counsel's fees plus VAT.

The hearing

The hearing is 'in chambers' – that is, not open to the public. Each spouse has an opportunity to state his or her case, either in person and/or through a solicitor. You may have to give oral evidence on oath, if only to bring your affidavit up-to-date. Where there is oral evidence, the applicant gives evidence first and can be cross-examined by the other party – who can similarly be cross-examined on his or her evidence, if appropriate.

If you have to give oral evidence, here are some tips:

- always listen carefully to any questions put to you
- answer the questions clearly and simply and do not ramble or mumble
- take a deep breath before answering any questions and try to speak slowly: often the other party's solicitor and the district judge (as well as your solicitor, if instructed) will be taking notes of what you are saying

- avoid becoming heated or emotional in response to the other party's questions; the district judge will want to confine his or her enquiry to the facts.

If any witnesses are called, they will not be able to come into the district judge's room until they give evidence – sometimes this may entail a long wait. Witnesses should give evidence only about matters that have been raised before the court hearing – you should not try to spring something on the other side (although where a new piece of evidence has only just come to light and is relevant in the proceedings, the district judge will usually use his or her discretion to hear it).

When oral evidence is not asked for, neither side is subject to cross-examination, but both sides can make submissions or comments after the affidavits are read.

How the court decides

The court no longer has free rein in deciding how the family income can be divided, as the Child Support Agency usually has jurisdiction over child support. After that, the lawyers (and ultimately the court if the case proceeds to a full hearing) will usually work out how much is left for division and will apply the court-based rules given below.

The other important question to be decided is with whom the children should live (in cases involving children) and whether the matrimonial home needs to be retained. From these decisions, all other matters will flow.

Before deciding on the amount of **maintenance** to order, the district judge will look first at the shortfall between the child support and the needs of the parent looking after the children. Factors particularly relevent to maintenance are:

- the gross income of the husband and any necessary expenses of his work that can properly be set against his gross income
- the gross income of the wife and any necessary expenses of her work that can properly be set against her gross income

- the needs of the children, now and in the foreseeable future
- the needs and outgoings of husband and of wife
- the possibility of each being financially self-sufficient ('a clean break')
- the effect of tax on any proposed order
- the effect of any order on welfare benefits entitlements.

When dealing with a request for a **property adjustment** or a **lump sum** order the district judge will consider:

- the full extent of each party's capital and details of any other assets
- the value of the family home and of any other properties owned by either the husband or the wife or by both
- the amount owing on any mortgages
- the needs of each for accommodation
- whom the children live with
- the financial contributions or other contributions made by each towards the purchase or improvement of the family home and any previous homes
- if husband or wife is legally aided, the effect of the Legal Aid Board's statutory charge on a property adjustment or lump sum order (and in all cases, the overall question of costs).

In deciding whether to make financial orders on a divorce and if so what orders, statutory guidelines require a court to take account of:

- the income, earning capacity, property and other financial resources of both spouses, both now and in the foreseeable future, including any increased earning capacity which the court could reasonably expect either person to try to acquire
- the financial needs, obligations and responsibilities of both spouses, both now and in the foreseeable future
- your standard of living before the breakdown of the marriage
- your ages
- the length of the marriage
- any physical or mental disabilities

- the contributions of each spouse to the welfare of the family including any contribution in caring for the family or looking after the home, both in the past and in the foreseeable future
- in some circumstances, your or your spouse's conduct
- the value of any benefit, such as a pension, which either spouse would lose the chance of acquiring as a result of the divorce.

These guidelines are set out in section 25 of the Matrimonial Causes Act 1973, as amended by the Matrimonial and Family Proceedings Act 1984. The 1984 Act altered the previous guidelines in various ways and specifically directed that the court must give first consideration to the welfare of any child of the family under 18 when considering all the circumstances of a case. In practice, the needs of dependent children have long determined what course the court could reasonably follow in making appropriate orders, but the specific endorsement of this principle gives recognition to the role of the parent with whom the children make their main base, while also discouraging any assumption that that parent is automatically entitled to life-long support without further question, purely as a result of having looked after the children.

The 1984 Act abolished an old and quite unrealistic objective, namely that the court should try to place both spouses in the financial position they would have been in if the marriage had not broken down, insofar as was practical and just. The thrust of the guidelines is now more clearly forward-looking – but only after taking careful note of the circumstances relating to the marriage and the family. The court must still consider the standard of living enjoyed before the breakdown when considering appropriate provision for the future.

Part of the emphasis of the 1984 Act was that the guidelines now specifically mention contributions that will be made to the family's welfare in the foreseeable future (as well as those made in the past).

Earning capacity
The court is specifically directed to consider whether either spouse could reasonably increase his or her earning capacity. The

1984 Act reflected the desirability of a husband and wife aiming at financial independence from each other after divorce, to the extent that this may be realistic. Courts recognise, however, that women who have long been out of the job market may not be able to return straightaway and, even if a job is found, it may well turn out to be with low earnings, little job security and few career prospects.

Generally speaking, a young woman with no children would be expected to go out to work. If there are very young children at home, a court would not expect a mother to go out to work unless she had been working before the breakdown of the marriage, in which case she would be expected to go on earning if practicable. This is also true of a father if the children live with him, except that it may be more realistic for him to go out to work, particularly if his level of earnings would mean that he could afford a housekeeper or childminder.

As the children grow older, the courts expect mothers to be able to return to work, at first perhaps part-time, or after a period of retraining.

A woman who has not worked at all throughout the marriage, who has grown-up children and is herself only a few years from retirement age is recognised as having a very limited earning capacity, perhaps none. The extent to which it might be reasonable to expect her to find paid employment would depend very much on how realistic an option this is, set against the background of the marriage, the husband's earnings, her health and all the other circumstances.

The court cannot order anyone to get a job but it can 'deem' a level of income which it considers either spouse could reasonably get. This can work both ways. If a wife is felt to be unreasonably refusing to work when there are job opportunities available, her maintenance order might be reduced. If a husband gives up his job simply to avoid paying maintenance, a bullish court might still make a maintenance order against him based on the amount that he should realistically be earning, in the hope that this will spur him back to work. The court will, however, take account of economic realities.

Conduct

The old provision was that the court had to take the conduct of each party into account 'so far as it was just to do so'. This was interpreted by the courts as meaning conduct which was 'gross and obvious' or such that it would 'offend one's sense of justice not to take it into account'. The courts are now directed to have regard to conduct if it is such that in the opinion of the court it would be inequitable to disregard it. Many lawyers and judges thought that the new wording would have no significant effect on the way courts considered the question of conduct, and this has been borne out by more recent cases decided since the passing of the 1984 Act. Bad conduct as a partner, for example having an affair, will usually be ignored.

In practice, only in exceptional cases will conduct be brought into account and then only where one party's conduct was 'gross and obvious' whilst the other party's conduct was comparatively blameless. Where both parties behaved extremely badly, the court is likely to disregard conduct. Even where conduct is relevant, it is only one of the factors to be put into the balance together with all the other factors the court must look at.

Pension rights

One factor that the court has to consider is the possible loss by a divorced woman (or, less frequently, a man) of a right to a widow's pension under an occupational pension scheme of which the husband is a contributing member.

Although in other countries court orders can be made dividing a pension, this is not the case here. The courts are much influenced by the discretion given to trustees of a pension scheme. The trustees have to abide by the rules of the scheme. These usually allow discretion on the part of the trustees to decide who should get what. The rules may stipulate paying the widow's (or widower's) pension to the legal widow (or widower) rather than the first ex-wife and, if there is no legal wife, a pension may be paid for the benefit of any children or any adult dependant (such as the common law widow). A pension cannot normally be divided between a wife and an ex-wife. Although an ex-wife cannot claim any share of a widow's pension, she could try to claim a dependant's benefit or (perhaps part of) the scheme's lump sum benefit. Employers' schemes normally include a lump sum death benefit of up to four times an employee's pay on his death before retirement. The trustees would normally take into account the member's wishes in the 'expression of wish' which he will have completed when the scheme was joined. It should, however, be remembered that a scheme member can at any time alter the nominated 'beneficiary'. On the death of a divorced husband, the trustees may be able to use their discretion where appropriate to divide the lump sum between the ex-wife and any current wife or cohabitant.

Many pension schemes provide that on the death of a member after retirement, the widow will be entitled to a proportion, perhaps one half, of the pension which would have been received by her late husband. Under the majority of pension schemes, a divorced former spouse is not likely to be eligible. Some pension schemes may allow a member to give up part of his own pension at retirement to provide, in return, a pension for his ex-spouse after his death.

What the court can do

The court can try to have the wife compensated for loss of what her pension entitlement would have been.

In one 1993 case a court was able to treat a pension as a type of post-nuptial settlement, which it could then divide and give a former wife an annuity now plus a pension later. But such cases are few and far between. This case involved a wife who had been employed by her ex-husband's company and the pension provision had been made by the ex-husband. Occupational pension schemes will not be affected by the decision.

This case, however, added to the clamour for divorce reform. An influential 1993 Pensions Management Institute report (which was endorsed by the Goode Committee's review of pension law the same year) recommended some fundamental changes to allow courts to divide up pensions. Two main recommendations were that pension rights should be valued and part of the value should be paid over to another pension for the ex-wife where divorce takes place before retirement. For divorces after retirement part of the pension could be earmarked and paid over directly to the ex-wife.

But such reform is as yet far off. In the meantime there are a few other options. Whilst the court cannot order the husband to take out life insurance (for a widow's pension) or an annuity (for the ex-wife's own pension), it can order the husband to provide capital by way of a lump sum to enable her to buy a deferred annuity for that amount. An alternative solution is to increase the wife's share in the family home or provide for a greater lump sum by way of compensation for her loss of pension rights.

Where the divorce is based on separation and the court is asked to consider what the respondent's financial position will be after divorce, the court may refuse to allow the decree to be made absolute unless and until a satisfactory insurance policy has been taken out for the benefit of the wife respondent.

In practice, the loss of pension rights will be brought into account only where the marriage has been fairly long-lasting and both parties are coming up to retirement age. If the wife is, say, under 40, it is most likely that the court will ignore the question of pension rights, particularly where there are no children.

New relationship

If either or both of you have formed a new relationship, this may make the break-up of your marriage less financially damaging. The fact that the other is moving out to live with somebody else, although emotionally hurtful, may be the best thing that could happen as far as accommodation costs are concerned. It reduces the biggest financial strain of all – the cost of two homes from one income. Where an ex-spouse's living expenses and accommodation costs are substantially reduced because of a new partner's contribution, there is more of the ex-spouse's money to go around and be shared out. (See also Chapter 14 on Stepfamilies.)

Length of marriage

The question of whether the time of pre-marital cohabitation can be taken into account has caused some legal controversy. It is likely to be taken into account if children were born during that period, or if one party had made a substantial financial contribution to the shared home before marriage. It is likely to be considered under the provision dealing with 'all the circumstances of the case' rather than the factor relating to length of the marriage.

After a short marriage and where there are no children, the court may be inclined not to order maintenance, or perhaps only for a limited period. The question as to what constitutes a short marriage is not clear: a marriage of three years has been held by the court not to have been a short marriage, whereas a marriage of five years was considered 'of short duration'. A short marriage between a young couple who are both working or able to do so is likely to be treated very differently from a short marriage between two people in, say, their mid-fifties where the woman had given up secure accommodation and/or a career and/or maintenance from a former spouse when she married, or if she is/was suffering from some kind of disability.

Secured payments

The court has power to order that periodical payments be 'secured' by a capital asset that the paying party possesses. A secured order is rare and is relevant only where there is a lot of available capital. It should not be contemplated without legal advice. A secured order can last for the life of the recipient because it survives the death of the payer; no other maintenance order does so.

Guidelines on maintenance levels

Maintenance for the children

Children covered by the Child Support Agency

The implementation of the Child Support Act 1991 in April 1993 has made the issue of how much maintenance should be paid paradoxically both more and less certain for parents with children. As long as the children come within the jurisdiction of the Child Support Agency (see page 81) the amount of child support that should be paid can be worked out in most cases relatively precisely. If the necessary information is available to make the calculation, a 'right' answer can be arrived at, which leaves only the question of how much spousal maintenance should be paid.

The figures to include in the calculation may not be easily available – say if one spouse plans eventually to leave the home but has not yet moved out, his (or her) future housing costs will not yet be known so a vital element of the calculation is missing. Even so, it should be possible to guess how much rent will be paid approximately and thus make a good stab at the eventual figure. This will provide a starting point for working out how much maintenance should be paid for the wife (or, where the wife is comparatively wealthy and the husband has no income, for the husband). See Chapter 5 for further information.

Children not covered by the Child Support Agency
Some children of the family are not covered by the Child Support Agency's powers, and so an application must be made to court for their maintenance. Those *not* covered by the Agency include:

- stepchildren
- children where one or both parents (or the child) are habitually resident abroad
- children whose parents made a pre-existing agreement for maintenance.

Where a parent with care had made an application for child maintenance before 5 April 1994 which has not yet been decided by the courts, she (or he) will have the option of either going ahead with the court application or withdrawing that application and instead making an application to the Agency. In most cases it will usually be cheaper to apply to the Agency but the main drawback of this may be a delay caused by the backlog of claims under consideration (although maintenance can be backdated to the date of the application).

If an application is made to the court for children's maintenance, the court should not only look at the factors it would have applied in the past to work out the amount of child support, but it may also look at how much child support would be if it were worked out under the new formula. In other words, the Child Support Act 1991 may influence the courts to increase the old levels of maintenance in line with the formula. On the other hand, the courts have more flexibility than the CSA and will be able to take other outgoings – like travel, childcare costs and debts – into account before deciding how much should be paid. Unfortunately at this stage it is difficult to judge exactly what will happen in individual cases until the court issues some guidelines following implementation of the Agency.

Having worked out child support the court will then address the question of spousal maintenance.

Spousal maintenance

.There are no set guidelines on how much should be paid for spouses. The old rule was that wives might expect to receive something like one third of the overall gross incomes. Nowadays that way of dividing up incomes is out of date: families often have two incomes and most of the tax advantages that used to exist in paying maintenance have been abolished. The court has instead adopted a more realistic approach, often dubbed the 'needs and resources' approach. It looks at how much each partner needs and then what the overall resources are to meet those needs. Producing a budget of how much each spouse needs to live on will be helpful.

The court's approach nowadays will usually have to be tailored to the introduction of the child support formula. So first the court should work out child support, then spousal maintenance. Its primary concern is to see that the needs of the parent looking after the children and those of the children are met. Where these are not met by the income of the parent looking after the children, the court will where possible set a level of spousal maintenance to top up that income. If not enough money is available to do this, the court will merely order the absent parent to pay what he (or she) can reasonably afford (if anything). Welfare benefits may be available to top-up maintenance levels.

The court's overall task is to evaluate all the various factors, balance them one against each other, giving what weight is considered appropriate to each factor and then trying to arrive at an order which is fair and reasonable. Capital and income are looked at together. It may be appropriate for a wife to receive more capital and less maintenance even if there is not to be a clean break.

The Finance Act 1988 changed the tax treatment of maintenance orders on divorce. Before then, parties had been able to maximise the tax effectiveness of maintenance orders by utilising each child's single person's tax free allowance through orders for maintenance payments to the children, to reduce the burden of tax upon the payer.

The changes in tax law meant that it is now easier to calculate the tax burden on the family; no skilful manipulation of maintenance figures can result in a decrease of the tax burden on the family after divorce. Divorcing families thus have to translate into reality a problematic equation: the division of one income (very often) to support two households.

Maintenance payments and welfare benefits

For a recipient, maintenance payments have a direct effect on all means-tested welfare benefits, for example income support. The basic rule is that all the maintenance paid is taken into account when the amount of benefit is calculated by the DSS, so for each pound of maintenance paid income support goes down by a pound.

This does not, however, apply to family credit, community charge, disability working allowance or housing benefit, where the first £15 of maintenance is disregarded: it is in effect an extra sum of income for the family on top of these welfare benefits.

Maintenance payments will not affect non-means-tested benefits, for example child benefit, disability benefits, unemployment, sickness and maternity benefits or a retirement pension.

If in doubt about the impact of a claim for maintenance on your benefit claim, you should consult your solicitor or Citizens Advice Bureau. Further information on maintenance payments via the Child Support Agency can be found in Chapter 5.

The clean break

The court has the explicit obligation, when making an order for financial relief, to consider whether it would be appropriate to make an order which would lead to each spouse becoming financially independent of the other 'as soon after the grant of the decree as the court considers just and reasonable'. It can make a clean break even in the face of adamant opposition from a wife (although this is rare).

The ability of the husband to finance a clean break may, however, have been adversely affected by paying higher levels of child support under the Agency formula. Child support levels will usually have to be worked out first, and only then can the husband's ability to make a clean break be assessed. Remember that clean breaks can apply only in respect of spousal maintenance, never for maintenance for the children.

Where an order for periodical payments is to be made to a spouse and a clean break might be appropriate, the court should consider whether the payments should be for a specific period only and then cease. The specified period should be what, in the opinion of the court, would be sufficient to enable the recipient to adjust without undue hardship to the ending of his or her financial dependance on the other spouse. In practice, courts are reluctant to look more than two or three years into the future and only if the future is pretty clearly foreseeable will a limited term order be appropriate. Time-limited periodical payments are much less likely to be appropriate where there are dependent children than, say, where there has been a short childless marriage and what the wife requires is just one or two years of financial assistance while she re-establishes herself.

A clean break settlement is sometimes fair and reasonable not on the basis of time-limited maintenance but by one spouse 'buying out' the other's maintenance claims with an additional capital payment. The availability of funds (or more usually their non-availability) is critical. The court will look at all the circumstances, including the wife's prospect of remarriage and any future earning capacity.

A wealthy wife may be ordered to pay a lump sum to her husband, perhaps to enable him to buy a house, just as a wealthy husband can be ordered to pay a lump sum to his wife.

Advantages and disadvantages
The advantages of a clean break order are certainty, both in terms of the husband knowing that his maintenance obligations to his ex-wife will end and the wife knowing that she will receive a specific sum of money. It can also encourage both parties to create

independent lives after the divorce. However, following the implementation of the Child Support Act 1991, remember that even if a clean break and lower levels of child maintenance are agreed now, the Agency is likely to have the right to review child support in the future and can raise the levels in line with the formula.

Another disadvantage for the recipient is that the capital awarded is unlikely to produce as high an annual income if invested at standard rates as the maintenance provision that there might otherwise have been. Moreover, the lump sum cannot later be increased to keep pace with inflation or a husband's financial fortune. If something unexpected happens, such as the wife falling ill and being unable to work, she will not be able to look to her ex-husband for support. Another point to bear in mind is that the husband might well feel indignant if his ex-wife remarries a short while later.

Even if there is no capital other than the net equity of the family home, a couple may prefer the wife to receive all or a disproportionate part of the net equity and to have her maintenance claims dismissed. But this is not always a realistic solution and must be considered very carefully. The court will be unwilling to provide for a clean break in circumstances where the wife's only means of support is income support. Where the marriage has been long-standing and the wife is in, say, her mid-fifties without ever having worked during the marriage and without reasonable prospects of working in the future, it is highly unlikely that the court will willingly grant a clean break order.

The court's power and duty under the 1984 Act

Before the 1984 Act, the courts had effectively been able to order what amounted to clean break settlements by refusing to order more than nominal periodical payments if circumstances so warranted, but a claim for maintenance could not finally be dismissed without the applicant's consent. The 1984 Act gave the courts more muscle: where a clean break approach is appropriate, a spouse's maintenance claim can be dismissed either at once or by an order for maintenance for only a specific period.

A 'clean break' order should include a provision to prevent one spouse from having a claim on the estate of the other spouse after death under the Inheritance (Provision for Family and Dependants) Act 1975.

The courts have a duty to investigate whether it is realistic to expect a husband and wife to be moving towards financial independence, but where there are dependent children, this may very well not be in their interests and the courts have a specific duty to give first consideration to the welfare of children. It cannot be over emphasised that the clean break approach can extend only to the parties to the marriage, not to provision for children.

The district judge's decision

Once all the evidence and all the arguments have been heard, the district judge can give judgement there and then. In a more complex case, he or she may reserve judgement until a later day.

If the district judge dismisses an application for periodical payments, it cannot later be revived. The applicant may have agreed to this in return for some other financial provision, such as a larger lump sum or transfer of the home.

If there is presently no scope for a lump sum order but there is a real possibility of capital arising in the foreseeable future, the application for a lump sum can be adjourned with 'liberty to apply' later.

Make a written note of the district judge's judgement in case there is an appeal. It may also be useful to have a note of the district judge's basis for arriving at the payments ordered – for example, the reasons for a low maintenance payment because the wife receives a larger share in the family home. This may be taken into account on any subsequent application to vary a periodical payments order.

Costs

An order for payment of costs can be asked for at this stage, as soon as the district judge has given his or her decision. You will have to explain why you think an order for costs should be made (or why there should be no order) and produce the relevant figures of overall costs incurred. The district judge will ask whether any Calderbank offers have been made and whether the

---

THE STEPS IN FINANCIAL PROCEEDINGS

1. Include financial claims in 'prayer' of petition (or answer)
2. If divorce is based on two-year or five-year separation, the respondent can file 'section 10' application
3. Form M11 or form M13 (plus affidavit of means) has to be lodged in duplicate plus fee of £20 and you have to serve a copy ('sealed' by the court) of the form and the affidavit on the other spouse (keep photocopies for yourself)
4. If property adjustment order is sought, it is wise to register a 'pending action' against the property in question at the Land Registry/Land Charges Department
5. Apply for directions hearing (the function of this hearing will be to ensure that all documents and information are ready for the hearing); some courts fix a date for the directions hearing automatically, some courts give directions automatically
6. At the first directions hearing the district judge can order:
   • further affidavits; • 'discovery' by exchange of lists of documents or 'rule 2.63'; • questionnaires; • valuations; • each party to attend final hearing to give evidence
   The district judge can also make an MPS (maintenance pending suit) order
7. Consider now (or earlier) making – or accepting – Calderbank offer
8. Exchange 'evidence' about means via lists of relevant documents and/or questionnaires (and replies) under rule 2.63
9. If spouse is uncooperative about supplying information, ask for penal notice to be endorsed on directions order and serve on your spouse
10. You can go back to the court at any stage to apply for further directions that something should be done or supplied by your spouse
11. When both parties are ready, they apply to the court for a hearing date by lodging 'certificates of readiness for trial and time estimates'; hearing date is fixed by the court (likely to be at least three months ahead)
12. Each party (or solicitor) prepares 'bundles of documents' including rule 2.63 questionnaires and replies
13. Before the hearing, prepare brief schedule of financial position and cost estimates and update valuations, if necessary
14. The hearing: arrange in advance for witnesses where appropriate; speak up
15. District judge considers all evidence and gives judgement and makes appropriate orders (but can 'reserve' i.e. postpone judgement to a later date)

NB: If you wish to claim child support, this will usually be dealt with by the Child Support Agency, not the courts.

terms of the order coincide with, or approximate to, the terms of the offer. This is also the time to raise the question of any costs 'reserved' on a previous interim application which deferred the decision on the amount of costs until the final financial order.

The court can order costs against either party on two bases only: 'standard' and 'indemnity'. If you have been legally represented, the standard basis will only cover a proportionate amount of your costs – probably about 60 per cent. An order for indemnity costs (that is, total costs) is made only in exceptional circumstances where one party appears to have been at fault, leading to an unnecessary increase in legal costs.

Attachment of earnings
You can apply for an attachment of earnings order at the same time that a spousal maintenance order is made under the Enforcement of Maintenance Act 1991. Under the same Act, the court can order that the payer sets up a standing order from a bank account. Both of these measures can be useful in reducing the risks of arrears building up.

The orders
After the hearing, the court office prepares the order(s) and sends a copy to both parties. Check the wording and figures carefully, in case there is a clerical error, and keep the documents in a safe place.

If any orders affect your tax position, a copy of the order should be sent to your inspector of taxes promptly.

Appeal
An appeal against an order or decision of the district judge can be made to a judge by filing a notice of appeal within five working days. The notice setting out the grounds is best prepared by a solicitor. From a judge's decision, an appeal lies to the Court of Appeal and thereafter to the House of Lords, although it is very rare for a case to get this far.

Tax and maintenance payments

It is most likely that your order will be governed by the changes in taxation of maintenance payments brought in by the Finance

Act 1988. The Act was a watershed for the tax treatment of maintenance orders made on divorce. Since the passing of the 1988 Finance Act, the only tax relief available to a divorced husband is, effectively, the retention of the married couple's allowance (as against a single person's tax-free allowance) to set off against his income. The married couple's allowance can be retained only if payments are made to a spouse under a court order or enforceable separation agreement and is available only whilst the marriage continues (i.e. up to decree absolute).

This relief is also available for child support maintenance but only where the payments are made through the Child Support Agency where the parents were married or are still married. The absent parent will make the payment gross and then claim tax relief up to the level of the married couple's allowance, which (in the 1994/5 financial year) is frozen at £1,720 per annum. The amount of maintenance due in the tax year is then deducted from the absent parent's taxable income. Child maintenance is not taxable income in the hands of the payee.

There are, however, certain circumstances where an old order will still be governed by rules under the old (pre-1988 Act) regime. You will need to determine whether your position falls outside or within the Finance Act 1988.

Under the old rules

Maintenance payments to which the old rules apply are described in the Finance Act 1988 as 'existing obligations' and it is this term that will be used throughout the next few pages. Payments by one party to another or to the children meet the definition of an existing obligation if made:

- under a court order made before 30 June 1988 subsequent to an application made in proceedings begun on or before 15 March 1988; *or*
- under an executed deed or written agreement made before 15 March 1988 and received by an inspector of taxes before the end of June 1988; *or*
- under an oral agreement made before 15 March 1988, written particulars of which were received by the inspector of taxes before the end of June 1988; *or*

● under an order made by a court or under a written
  agreement made after 15 March 1988, where the order or
  agreement replaces, varies or supplements an order or
  agreement that meets the definition of an existing
  obligation.

In any such case, the payer will be able to set against his (or her)
taxable income in the tax year 1988/9 and future tax years,
payments to a spouse and/or a child under an 'existing obligation'
up to the limit of the amount due and paid in the tax year 1988/9.
Similarly, the recipient of payments due under an 'existing
obligation' will be taxed on payments on this and future tax years
up to the same 1988/9 limit.

EXAMPLE

A couple separate in December 1987 and in January 1988 obtain
an order under section 6 of the Domestic Proceedings and
Magistrates' Courts Act 1978 that the husband should pay
maintenance to the wife of £5,000 per annum and maintenance to
each of the two children of the family of £2,000 per annum each.
The husband's income is £22,000 per annum. The husband and
wife eventually decide to get divorced in February 1989, and in
July 1989 the court makes an order, by consent, that the husband
should pay to the wife £6,000 per annum but confirms the
existing maintenance payments to each of the children.

In the tax year 1989/90 the husband is only able to offset against
his own income for tax purposes the amount that was fixed in the
tax year 1988/9, namely the £5,000 paid to his wife and £4,000
total maintenance paid to the children. The extra £1,000 remains
taxable in his hands.

Subject to her other income and allowances, the wife is only
taxed on £5,000 in 1988/9 and the subsequent tax year, and the
extra £1,000 is tax-free in her hands. The children will pay no tax
on the maintenance allocated to them because the amounts were
and are below the single person's tax free personal allowance
(£2,605 per annum in 1988/9 and £3,445 in 1993/4).

The benefits of this arrangement from the husband's viewpoint
are that he is able to utilise the children's single person's tax-free

allowance, and allocate part of his income to his former wife, taking him out of the (then) higher rate of tax bands. (The higher rate [40%] tax band in 1993/4 starts at £23,700.)

Under the current rules

The current rules have applied to all payments made following separation/divorce that were not made under an 'existing obligation'. Effectively, in all new divorce proceedings where no previous magistrates' court orders have been made, the current rules will apply.

All payments in these circumstances will not be part of the payee's taxable income. The payer will be able to deduct only the married couple's allowance (in the tax year 1994/5 £1,720) or the amount of maintenance paid, if less, in calculating his (or her) taxable income.

From the tax year 1994/5, this limited form of relief can be set off against tax only at the lowest band of 20 per cent instead of tax paid at the higher rate of 25 per cent or 40 per cent. You can get a leaflet explaining these changes from your local tax office: Leaflet FS1 *Factsheet on tax allowance restriction.* Another useful leaflet, *Separation, divorce and maintenance payments* (IR93), is also available free from tax offices.

Switch from the old to the current rules

Under certain transitional arrangements, it has been possible to choose to switch from being treated under the old rules to being treated under the current rules. You should check whether the rules under the Finance Act 1988 provide any real benefit to you, but in most circumstances it will be far better to continue your tax treatment under the old rules.

Additional relief for single parents

Whichever parent retains primary responsibility for the children will also be entitled to an additional personal allowance (£1,720 in the tax year 1994/5). The additional personal allowance is allowable in full from the date of divorce or separation to the following 5 April, and for every tax year thereafter while the primary carer is looking after a child under 16 years (or, if older, in full-time education), at the beginning of the year of assessment.

If it is the father who looks after the child(ren), he is not entitled to the additional personal allowance on top of his married couple's allowance in the year of divorce or separation. If he does not remarry, he will receive it in addition to the single person's allowance in the following tax years while he cares for the child(ren).

Advising the Inland Revenue of the date of separation

You and your spouse should endeavour to agree the date on which you separated, for tax purposes. It is open to you to choose a date between the date of your separation and decree absolute for the date of final separation. Although following on from the Finance Act 1988 this is unlikely to have much effect on your maintenance position, it may affect your position with regard to Capital Gains Tax.

Enforcement of payments

Actually receiving maintenance following a court order or Child Support Agency assessment often depends on the continuing ability of the ex-spouse to make the payments.

Should the payer (usually the ex-husband) fall into arrears with maintenance payments, there are several channels for enforcement, none entirely satisfactory. If child support is paid through the CSA, you can ask the Agency to use its collection and enforcement service. (The Agency has now taken over effectively from the DSS's liable relative proceedings.) If you are on benefit, no fee should be payable but otherwise a fee of £44 will be demanded (unless you are exempt – see page 84).

The main advantage of this service is that it is likely to be a lot cheaper than going to court. The Agency also has extra powers to trace a disappearing ex-husband, through access to Inland Revenue and DSS records, for example. It is still too early to judge how effective the service offered will prove to be. The CSA can make a deduction of earnings order, like an attachment of earnings order, which takes the maintenance due (plus a small administration fee) directly from the payer's salary. It can also apply for all of the enforcement procedures set out below: the ultimate sanction is committal to prison (although this is likely to be used only rarely). From April 1996 the CSA will also be able to collect and enforce spousal maintenance.

The sooner steps are taken to enforce the arrears, the better. If arrears are allowed to accumulate, they may well prove impossible to recover: courts will not enforce arrears that are more than a year old.

Enforcing a debt

A defaulting spouse getting away with not paying has traditionally been part of the wider problem of trying to enforce civil debts in general: your chances of success may not be particularly high.

An application for enforcement has to be made to the divorce court that made the order (unless the order has been registered at a magistrates' court). The divorce court will not automatically chase arrears and will make an order for enforcement only if asked to. But you can apply to the Family Proceedings Panel to register an order in the magistrates' court. The burden is then on the court to chase the arrears.

Enforcement in the county court

The main methods of enforcement are:

- a warrant of execution
- an attachment of earnings order
- a judgement summons for committal to prison.

Warrant of execution

A warrant of execution is an order issued by the county court for the district where the defaulting payer lives, for the court bailiff to seize sufficient of the person's goods as will, on sale by auction, discharge the debt shown on the warrant.

Secondhand goods seized and sold at auction rarely produce much money. It is only worthwhile getting a warrant of execution if the goods are in good condition – but merely the threat of seizure and sale may produce payment.

To get a warrant issued, you must swear an affidavit showing the amount of the arrears, provide a copy of the order, complete the appropriate county court forms and pay the fee (at present the fee is 15p per £ of the amount of the warrant; minimum fee £5, maximum £38, which is not returnable if there are no saleable goods).

Attachment of earnings order

Provided that the ex-husband is in regular employment, an attachment of earnings order may be a more effective way of collecting arrears. (Since the Maintenance Enforcement Act 1991, it can be applied for even before arrears build up, at the time the maintenance order is made). It requires the employers to deduct regular weekly or monthly amounts from his wages and to send the money to the court who will then pay it to the woman. The amount of deductions can include not only a regular sum off the arrears until they are discharged, but also the ongoing maintenance. (The employers can deduct £1 in addition each time for their pains.) The procedure is no use where the man is unemployed or self-employed.

The application usually has to be to the divorce county court which made the maintenance order. The appropriate application form (in duplicate), with a copy of the maintenance order, must be supported by an affidavit giving details of the arrears and, if possible, the name of the employers. The court fee for an application is 10p per £ of the amount claimed (minimum fee £5, maximum £40).

A notice of the application is served on the ex-husband, together with a form asking for details of his income and financial commitments. The court can ask the employers to supply information about the man's earnings over the past few weeks. The applicant should attend the hearing to give up-to-date evidence about the arrears.

Protected earnings

Any order the district judge makes will be on the basis that it must not reduce the man's net income below the protected earnings rate. This is the amount which would be allowed for him and his dependants for income support together with the amount of his rent (or mortgage payments) and rates and other essential and reasonably long-term commitments, such as other court orders or a hire purchase agreement.

When making an attachment order, therefore, the court may well take the opportunity – after an adjournment, if needed, for a formal application to be made – to adjust the maintenance order to take account of the realities of the situation as disclosed at the time of an enforcement proceedings.

Committal to prison
A judgment summons can be issued for maintenance arrears if it can be shown that the ex-husband has the means to pay mainten-ance and has failed to do; in theory, he can be sent to prison. A judgment summons is a potentially effective means of enforcing payment of arrears where a man has capital or is self-employed and cannot be touched by an attachment of earnings order.

A request for a judgment summons can be made to any county court convenient to the applicant. Legal aid is not available for a judgment summons in the county court but is in the High Court. (If the applicant would be financially eligible, the solicitor should consider whether it will be possible to have the case transferred to the High Court.)

The woman, or her solicitor, should attend the hearing of the judgment summons in order to question the ex-husband in an endeavour to prove that he could have paid the maintenance but neglected to do so. If it is proved that he had the means, an order committing him to prison can be made. It is essential that if you are applying for the ex-husband's committal to prison your application is drafted accurately. This is because the courts view committal as a remedy to be used only in extreme circumstances, so the documents that are drafted must be prepared correctly.

Sending him to prison is unlikely to produce the money that the ex-wife needs – although the threat of imprisonment may do so. The order can be suspended if he undertakes to pay regular amounts off the arrears together with current maintenance; it can be reinstated if he fails to keep up the payments.

The court is likely to order the ex-husband to pay the costs of the application.

Disappearing ex-husband
If the woman does not know her ex-husband's address, it may be possible to get the DSS to disclose it to the court because his up-

to-date address may be known to them through his National Insurance record. A form can be obtained from the court on which the ex-wife should give as much information as she can about his last known address and employer, his date of birth and National Insurance number. The Child Support Agency has powers to trace too for child support purposes but it cannot reveal a parent's whereabouts unless he or she authorises the Agency to do so.

Enforcement of lump sum or property transfer order

An unpaid lump sum may be enforced either by bankruptcy proceedings (unwise, save as a powerful threat) or by a court order that any property belonging to the person ordered to pay be sold to raise the sum. An order for such a sale (for example, a house or stocks and shares) can be made when the lump sum is ordered. If it is not made then, the usual procedure is to apply for a charging order and then for an order for sale of the asset.

If the transfer of property order is not complied with, the district judge at the court can execute the relevant conveyance in place of the person who is refusing to do so. Application has to be made to the court with the relevant documents prepared for the district judge and an affidavit in support.

It is advisable to have a solicitor's help in such enforcement proceedings.

Order registered in magistrates' court

If an order made in the divorce court is registered in the Family Proceedings Panel (magistrates' court), the magistrates' court staff will summons the payer to appear in court if he or she defaults. The procedure is quicker and simpler than in the county court.

If the payer is in arrears, the magistrates can order that a disclosure of means be made, and can make one of the following orders:

- attachment of earnings
- distraint on goods (seizure and sale)
- committal to prison (for not more than six weeks).

Changes in circumstances: variations

Variations and the Child Support Agency

One potentially useful feature of child support worked out by the Child Support Agency's formula is that there is an automatic inbuilt annual review of the amount paid every year on the anniversary of the assessment. Fourteen days before the anniversary is due, the Agency will send out further forms asking the parents about any changes in circumstances. Once the forms are returned, the Agency will recalculate the amount of maintenance. Further fees will be payable unless the parents are exempt.

As the formula is based on income support rates, which go up every year, there is an element of inflation-proofing built into the system, although usually the amount of child support actually paid will only increase where the paying parent's income has gone up too. In the tax year 1994/5, with most employees facing tax and National Insurance contributions increases, the amount an absent parent pays may well go down.

As well as the automatic annual review, parents can ask the Agency for a review during the year if circumstances change. There is no definition of a change in circumstances, so potentially any life or monetary change will be covered. One parent may, for example, gain or lose a job or go on to part-time working or have a baby. The Child Support Officer will review the case once a review has been asked for (either parent can request one) but the amount paid will change only if certain trigger points are reached. These are met where the changes result in a difference (up or down) of:

- in most cases, at least £10 per week, or
- in cases where the absent parent comes under the protection of the protected income formula, at least £1 per week

Variations and the courts

With a periodical payments order, even if a spouse had merely a nominal order of, say 5p per year, which has not expired because of either remarriage or time limit, it is possible to apply to the court to have the order varied – that is, for the amount payable to be increased or decreased, or even for the order to be brought to an end – if it can be shown that there has been a material change in the financial circumstances of either party. You can apply on your own behalf and/or on behalf of your children, but remember that if you are thinking about applying for a variation of child maintenance, the Child Support Agency will be taking on old cases from April 1996 onwards or earlier if the payee receives welfare benefits like income support.

An application for a variation can be made at any time after the decree nisi, even many years later, provided that the recipient has not remarried. There is no limit on the number of variations that can be applied for.

The court can also vary any agreement that the couple made between themselves, even though they may have agreed not to refer the agreement to the court. In law, any term in an agreement that precludes one party from seeking the assistance of the courts is void.

What cannot be varied
A lump sum order or a property adjustment order cannot be varied, nor can you go back to court to obtain another one, nor ask for one later if not included in the original application. Although a lump sum order cannot be varied, if the lump sum is being paid in instalments, the size and frequency of instalments can be varied, but not so as to alter the total of the lump sum originally awarded.

An order which was expressed to be 'final' cannot be varied, and a separation agreement so expressed is likely to be upheld.

If an application for maintenance made previously was formally dismissed by the court, the application cannot be revived later.

Applying for a variation
An application can be made at the divorce court where the order you want to vary was made. If that original court is now inconvenient or if that court has not been designated a Family Hearing Centre, you should ask for the case to be transferred to a Family Hearing Centre more convenient for you. (If the order was registered in a magistrates' court you must apply to the

Family Proceedings Panel there, not to the court which originally made the order.)

The application should be made on the standard form of notice of application, available from the court office. If circumstances have changed, lodge the application as soon as possible so that any variation of periodical payments can be backdated to the date of the application. You do not have to accompany the application with an affidavit but you may need to file an affidavit in order to spur your ex-spouse into responding to the application. He or she then has to file an affidavit in reply within 28 days. Your affidavit should give up-to-date details of your financial position and why you feel a variation is (or is not) appropriate. The court fee is £15 (there is no fee payable if applying for variation by consent).

Reasons for an application

Major factors that are likely to affect financial orders made in the divorce court are:

- a change in financial circumstances of the payer or payee, including retirement
- remarriage of the payee (periodical payments order ends)
- cohabitation of the payee
- remarriage or cohabitation of the payer
- death of either
- either becoming disabled
- children having got older
- length of time elapsed since the making of the last order.

If the court rejects the application for a variation, this does not preclude an application for a variation being made at some later stage if circumstances change again.

Variations made after the Finance Act 1988

If your former spouse pays maintenance under a court order made before 15 March 1988 or an order otherwise qualifying as an 'existing obligation', your spouse will continue to receive tax relief by offsetting against his or her taxable income the maintenance payment. The maximum amount of relief that will be given, however, is the limit of the amount due and paid by means of maintenance payments in the 1988/9 tax year.

Remember that for increases over and above this amount, the payer will have to pay any extra maintenance out of the taxed income and will be ineligible for tax relief.

The court's approach

The court must consider all the circumstances of the case anew, as well as any change in circumstances, giving first consideration to the welfare of any child of the family under 18. Where child maintenance is concerned, there are likely to be arguments that the amounts paid should increase to similar levels produced by the child support formula. The court must also consider whether in all the circumstances it would now be appropriate to vary an order for periodical payments so that the payments are only for such a further period as would be sufficient to enable the recipient to adjust without undue hardship to the termination of the payments, or to terminate the payments altogether – a clean break.

Marriage of ex-spouse

If she marries again, a former wife's right to maintenance for herself ceases immediately and cannot be revived against that ex-husband even if she finds herself on her own again – divorced, separated or widowed.

There is no formal requirement to tell the previous husband that she has married again, but if she does not do so and he finds out, he can ask her to repay what he has paid her since her new marriage; if she does not pay up, he can sue her for the overpaid money as a debt.

Maintenance payments for children are not automatically affected by the mother's new marriage, but the remarriage of either parent may give rise to a situation in which a variation is justified.

An ex-wife's right to occupy what had been the matrimonial home may cease on remarriage. The terms of the court order may require the house or flat now to be sold and the proceeds divided in the specified proportions.

If you made a lump sum payment of, say, £20,000 to your ex-spouse and six months later you hear that she or he has remarried, you cannot usually apply for a variation. Where a lump sum has been ordered to be paid in instalments and the recipient ex-spouse marries again, instalments have to be continued until the full amount is paid. (In rare cases, an application to have the order set aside on the grounds of fraudulent non-disclosure of the intention to remarry may succeed.)

Cohabitation
When a man who is paying his ex-spouse maintenance and she cohabits with another man, he may have grounds to apply to the court for a variation of the order. The court will normally expect it to be proved that there is some permanence to the cohabitation and that it is reasonable to infer that there is financial contribution from the cohabitant. However, the courts are still less likely to allow a variation for cohabitation as they can be reluctant to 'absolve' a former husband of his obligations to his ex-wife.

If you are paying maintenance to your ex-spouse and children and you set up home with someone who already has children, which involves you in additional expenses, this does not mean that your obligations to your former spouse and children cease. If you apply for a variation, the court will take into account your new obligations even though you are not married, but these will normally be expected to take second place to your obligations to the children of your previous marriage.

Since the Child Support Act 1991 came into force, any assumed obligations to children who are not your own will specifically be overridden by your obligations to pay child support for your natural children (whether born within or outside marriage).

Retirement
In the case of either the recipient's or the payer's retirement, an application should be made to vary the order by the party who is feeling the pinch. Usually, the court will look at the actual needs and resources of the parties and will be concerned to try to share out the more limited finances fairly.

Variation of a magistrates' court order
Magistrates' court orders also can be varied, either upward or downward, where there has been a change in circumstances.

Applications will now be dealt with by the Family Proceedings Panel (FPP) of the magistrates' courts.

If the couple subsequently divorce, this will not necessarily bring a magistrates' court order to an end. An order made during the marriage will end automatically only if the divorce court substitutes its own order. If not, the magistrates' court order will continue, and also the right to apply for a variation. The order will cease automatically on the recipient's remarriage or death. If the payer remarries, this does not affect the order but may provide grounds for variation.

In the case of a lump sum, the position is different to that in divorce proceedings: there is apparently no restriction on when and how often a lump sum may be applied for (subject to the £1,000 limit each time).

Registered order

If a divorce court order has been registered in the magistrates' court, application for a variation has to be made to the FPP. The FPP cannot discharge a divorce court order but can vary the amount of the order on application. No affidavits are required and the magistrates will not have before them the information and calculations on which the district judge at the divorce court based the original order. So, unless they are provided with full up-to-date information about the parties' finances, they may reduce the order unrealistically. A 1990 survey by the DSS showed that magistrates' courts made, on average, weekly maintenance of £15, as opposed to £20 made by county courts.

When on income support

Maintenance paid by a husband counts in full as income for income support calculations. Unless the maintenance that the husband could pay is more than the total income support payable, there is little point in a woman seeking an increase in her maintenance because she will still only be topped up to the same 'needs' level by the DSS; if maintenance increases, therefore, income support decreases. Occasional presents to an ex-wife or children are not counted as income, so it would be better for the wife to concentrate on getting these, where possible. However, the first £15 of maintenance will be disregarded in calculating entitlement for family credit, housing benefit and community charge benefit.

Registration of a maintenance order in the FPP is useful when the amount of maintenance is equal to or less than the rate of any income support the recipient would be entitled to. When the order is registered, the payments due under the order can be assigned by the woman to the DSS who will then pay her the full amount of her income support entitlement, irrespective of whether any payments are made by the man or not. This saves anxiety and inconvenience if he does not pay up.

Where the amount of the order is greater than the income support entitlement, payments by the DSS will be limited to the amount of income support the woman is entitled to.

Death of a former spouse

When the recipient dies, the payer can immediately stop any maintenance payments. But any outstanding instalments of a lump sum become due to the deceased's estate, and an unfulfilled transfer of property order can be enforced by the estate.

If the person paying maintenance dies, the maintenance order comes to an end (unless the order was for secured payments). The former spouse may be able to apply to the court under the Inheritance (Provision for Family and Dependants) Act 1975 for financial provision out of the deceased's estate (unless the court has previously ordered that such a claim shall not be made). An application can also be made by or on behalf of a child. The application must be made within six months of probate being granted – to be safe, make sure the application is lodged as soon as possible.

Other payment on death

Employers' schemes normally provide a lump sum death benefit (of up to four times the member's pay) when the member of the scheme dies before retirement. After the divorce, it is likely that the ex-husband will have changed the name of the person he wishes to receive the money on his death, so that his ex-wife may not benefit. The decision whether to pay any sum to her would, however, ultimately rest with the trustees for the pension scheme.

CHAPTER 11

OTHER MONEY MATTERS

Marriage contracts

You may have made a marriage contract with your spouse. Will this affect divorce proceedings?

The term 'marriage contracts' actually covers two different types of agreement – **pre-nuptial agreements**, made before a couple marry; and **contracts made during marriage**, which can include arrangements for division of the property on separation or divorce.

The purpose behind both types is to clarify who will get what in the event of marriage breakdown (whether by separation, death or divorce), often by side-stepping or trying to override the courts' powers. The formats can be flexible enough to cover agreements about other areas of concern for a couple (for example, when they want to start trying to conceive).

The Family Law Committee of the Law Society (which is broadly in favour of marriage contracts) recommends that areas of agreement would include:

- ownership of income and assets acquired before the marriage and the possibility of making claims against that property whether on death or divorce
- ownership of income or assets acquired in contemplation of or since the marriage
- whether assets are to be owned as joint tenants or tenants in common and if so in what proportions
- whether assets below a certain value are to be excluded
- treatment of gifts or inheritance

- ownership of items of personal use, such as jewellery
- liability for tax and debts
- provisions relating to duration, variation, review
- which country's law will govern the agreement
- liabilities for costs and expenses in relation to drawing up the agreement and any ancillary documentation
- methods of resolution of any disputes arising from the document
- any other issues of importance to the individual couple.

(Extracted from *Maintenance on Capital Provision on Divorce: Recommendations for Reform of the Law and Procedure made by the Family Law Committee*, May 1991.)

In fact, despite their media popularity, marriage contracts (and even cohabitation contracts) are fairly rare: they tend to be entered into more often by the super-rich. It is still doubtful whether they will actually achieve their purpose of circumventing the courts if one separating spouse later on chooses to try to challenge a contract's validity. English courts are resistant to the notion that their powers can be overridden. The main case cited in support of the effectiveness of marriage contracts certainly does not give a surefire answer.

A husband and wife had, as is usual in Brazil, entered into a marriage contract. Could the wife obtain a divorce and claim for financial relief in England having already made a marriage contract? Held: yes, she could claim. The marriage contract would be included as one of the factors which the court would consider in accordance with section 25 of the Matrimonial Causes Act 1973. (Sabbagh v Sabbagh, 1975)

Whilst this case related to a Brazilian marriage, it will none the less have persuasive effect in the courts here. However, all it really says is that a divorce court is likely to look at the terms of any marriage contract but may not necessarily feel itself bound by them.

Other matters to consider

During the course of divorce proceedings, or once these are finally over, you need to consider protecting your overall financial position in the areas of insurance, pensions and wills.

Life insurance

Because maintenance payments will cease when the payer dies, it may be advisable, on divorce, for the spouse who is going to be dependent on payments from the other to take out a life insurance policy on the payer's life.

You have to have an insurable interest in the life of anybody on whose life you wish to take out an insurance. An individual has an unlimited insurable interest in his or her own life and also in the life of his or her spouse and can insure it for any amount he or she chooses. Apart from yourself and your spouse, you have an insurable interest in somebody only if his or her death would cause you financial loss. You can insure for the amount of money you would lose if he or she dies. This would apply to an ex-spouse who is paying maintenance.

The parent who is not looking after the children may want to take out an insurance policy on the life of the parent who is looking after the children, so that if that parent were to die while the children were still dependent, some money would become available towards the extra cost to the other parent of taking on responsibility for the children.

The policy can be a whole life policy whereby the sum assured is paid out on the death of the insured person. Alternatively, it can be a 'term' insurance which pays out a set sum on death within so many years, taken out for the period of likely dependence. Premiums for term policies are generally lower than for other types of insurance. There are some term insurance policies, called 'family income benefit' policies, where instead of one lump sum on the insured person's death, regular sums are paid (say, every quarter) for the balance of the insured period.

Other insurance

You should check that your insurance cover is adequate for the change in your personal circumstances. When your finances are tight, insurances are often first thought of as potential sacrifices in order to reduce outgoings. However, this may be a short-term benefit and a long-term loss.

Buildings insurance is insurance for the destruction or damage of your privately owned freehold property. If you have a mortgage on your home, buildings insurance will usually have been arranged by your mortgagee. If you own a leasehold property, your landlord will normally have arranged the insurance but you pay the proportional cost for your property by means of a service charge.

Contents insurance to protect for the loss of, theft of, or damage to your belongings may need to be adjusted after divorce if now you own much more (or much less) of household and other property than before.

Car insurance either 'third party, fire and theft' (the statutory minimum) or comprehensive (providing you with full cover in the event of an accident however it is caused) may have to be transferred from one spouse to the other, depending on who now has the family car.

National Insurance after a divorce
Divorce does not affect a man's National Insurance contribution position. Nor does it affect that of a woman who is paying self-employed (class 2 and class 4) contributions or the standard rate of employed (class 1) contributions at the time. After divorce, each continues to pay as before.

It is not so straightforward for an employed woman who, before the divorce, had still been paying the class 1 contributions at the married woman's reduced rate: she is treated as a single person from the date on which the decree is made absolute and therefore becomes liable to pay the full class 1 rate. She should get from her employer a 'certificate of reduced liability' or 'certificate of election' to send back to her local DSS office. The full class 1 contributions will be deducted from her wages from then on.

Anyone whose earnings are below a specified minimum a year (£3,200 for the 1994/5 tax year), or anyone who is not earning at all, does not have to pay National Insurance contributions, but can pay class 3 contributions voluntarily; these give a woman the right to claim retirement pension. DSS leaflet NI42 gives information about making voluntary contributions.

A woman over the age of 60 does not have to pay National Insurance contributions.

There are various free DSS leaflets explaining the position about contributions and benefits in specific circumstances: leaflet

NI95 is a guide for divorced women. If you are at all unsure of your position, get advice from your local social security office in writing (and keep it safe) or a Citizens Advice Bureau may be able to help to clear up any queries. Detailed information about contributory benefits under the National Insurance scheme is given in the Child Poverty Action Group's *Rights Guide to Non-Means-Tested Benefits* (see page 76).

Woman's retirement pension

The payment of the basic state retirement pension to a divorced woman depends on her age when she got divorced and on whether it is based on her own or her former husband's National Insurance record (or a combination of both).

A woman divorced under the state pension age can have her former husband's contribution record added to her own record if that helps her qualify for a retirement pension when the time comes, or gains her a larger pension. She has a choice of formulae to calculate her state retirement pension. Either her former husband's contribution years replace *all* her years up to the time of divorce or the ex-husband's contribution years replace hers only for the years of the marriage. If, however, she marries again before she reaches the state pension age, she cannot make use of her previous husband's record: she has to rely on her new husband's record or on contributions she had made herself.

If a woman who is approaching the state pension age can time the decree absolute to follow closely on her reaching that age, she may qualify for a retirement pension immediately, without having to have contributed at all herself. If, however, the decree is made absolute before that birthday, she may have to pay contributions for the intervening period in order to be eligible for a full pension.

A woman divorcing over the state pension age may qualify for a retirement pension immediately the divorce is made absolute, even if her former husband has not yet retired. Where she was already receiving the named woman's lower rate of pension, she may be entitled to have her pension increased to the full rate. The amount of pension she gets depends on his contribution record: it is the amount she would have received had he died on the date of the decree absolute.

If a divorced woman marries again after the state pension age, any pension based on her previous husband's National Insurance contributions continues to be paid, despite her second marriage. But if her new husband's record would give her a higher pension, that may be used instead.

The current (1994) state pension age for women is 60; however, that age is due to be increased for women reaching 60 after 2010.

DSS leaflet NP32A deals with retirement pensions for women who are widowed or divorced, but the rules are complex so ask for help from the Benefits Agency.

Valuing pension rights may be outside the scope of your solicitor, so if you are getting divorced and your husband (or you) have pension rights, you should seek advice from a pensions specialist (for example, a member of the Society of Pension Consultants, Ludgate House, Ludgate Circus, London EC4A 2AB; tel: 071-353 1688) or the Association of Consulting Actuaries (1 Wardrobe Place, London EC4 5AH; tel: 071-248 3163).

You will have to pay for this advice, but it will be money well spent if it avoids financial hardship (and perhaps protracted argument) in the long run.

Wills

A will made by either a husband or wife is not automatically revoked on divorce but the will is interpreted as if the ex-spouse had died on the day before the divorce: any gift left to him or her goes to whoever is entitled to the residue of the estate. Where the terms of the will give the residue to the former spouse, this will be dealt with in accordance with the intestacy rules (rules which apply to cover the distribution of the estate of someone who had died without leaving a will). If the ex-spouse is named as executor, that appointment will be of no effect.

If there is no will and a divorced person's estate has to be dealt with under the intestacy rules, the former husband or wife will not be taken into account in the distribution of the estate. But any children remain eligible for their share of an inheritance.

Green form advice for making a will has recently been severely limited. You can now only ask for advice under the green form scheme for preparing your will (subject to financial eligibility) if you are aged 70-plus or disabled, deaf, dumb or blind (or if you have child who is so handicapped). A single parent looking after a child who wants to appoint a guardian for her or his child to act after death is also eligible. But you no longer need to appoint a guardian for your child after your death via a will as this can be done by deed or in writing. Make sure you check with the person you wish to act as a guardian that he or she is willing to take on this important responsibility first.

CHAPTER 12

DOMESTIC VIOLENCE

DOMESTIC violence most commonly occurs within the confines of the home, behind closed doors, with no outsider witnessing the event. That is not to say that it is rare. A campaign to challenge the acceptance of violence against women, Zero Tolerance (launched in February 1994), reported that domestic violence accounts for 1 in 4 of all reported crimes. Domestic violence cuts across all classes of society, although it is more likely to occur where a pattern of violence has already been formed, either in the relationship itself between the man and the woman or even having its roots in the childhood of either one. Frequently, violence is linked to substance abuse of some kind, whether of alcohol or drugs. The crisis of a separation or divorce can, in some few cases, be itself sufficient to spark off an incident of violence. In the great majority of cases, violence is inflicted by men upon women (although in a tiny minority, men are the victims), so the violent partner is here referred to as 'he' and the victim as 'she'.

If you are the subject of violence, you need to take steps quickly to protect yourself. If you are behaving violently towards your partner, you also need to take fast preventive action, for example by leaving the home or seeking help (for example, in contacting **Alcoholics Anonymous**, tel: (0904) 644026).

You can get legal advice about domestic violence matters under the green form scheme, if you are financially eligible. Legal aid is available (subject to financial eligibility) for applications for an injunction and emergency certificates can be issued on the same day in extreme cases. If you are not eligible for legal aid, the cost of obtaining an injunction is likely to be some hundreds of pounds. Your solicitor may be willing to agree to monthly repayments.

Contacting the police
In the past, the police gained a reputation for failing to treat seriously incidents of domestic violence. Nowadays the attitude is changing. In London, the Metropolitan Police have instructions to investigate and record every incident of domestic violence (which can provide useful corroborative evidence later in any proceedings). It is wise to contact the police if violence is threatened. They can lower the heat of the situation by talking separately to each partner, or in certain circumstances will remove the threatening spouse out of the home. If an assault has actually occurred, the police should consider whether criminal charges should be brought. They will usually only do so if the woman is prepared to give evidence. Some police forces are increasingly taking tougher action by, for example, charging the attacker with assault. Studies abroad have shown that levels of violence can drop if police take a consistently strong line.

Leaving the home
In principle, and generally, it is tactically better to remain in the matrimonial home until either an agreement is reached or court proceedings have been finalised. But in an extreme emergency you may have no choice but to leave home.

If your physical and mental welfare are severely threatened, it may be safer to leave the home for a temporary period – but get legal advice as soon as possible about your rights in the situation. Take your children with you if at all possible. You may want to contact **Women's Aid** (telephone in London 071-251 6537) for advice. The Women's Aid national helpline is (0272) 633542.

Finding somewhere to stay
As long as you have not made yourself 'intentionally homeless', your local authority is under an obligation to provide accommodation for someone with priority needs (for example, if you have young children to look after), if you have nowhere else to stay.

Contact – by telephone, or go there if you can – the housing department of your local authority or the social services department. The accommodation they are most likely to offer will be basic bed and breakfast.

There are a number of women's refuges across the country which provide a roof to sleep under for female victims of domestic violence and their children. Women's Aid (see above) can advise you about where to go.

Changing the locks

If you jointly own or rent the home with your partner, you have no instant right to lock him out. Until divorce proceedings have been concluded, both spouses have a legal right to continue to occupy the matrimonial home. If you do change the locks, your partner may be able to get a court order restoring him to the home. If your partner has been violent, you can apply to the court for an injunction to force him out of the house. After he has been ordered to leave, you are in a position to change the locks.

Children and violence

In some cases where a spouse is behaving violently towards his partner, the children suffer violence as well. It is extremely important for you to protect your children's interests if they are being physically attacked by your spouse. If you have to leave home, take them with you if at all possible. If you have to leave them, get immediate legal advice on what action to take to get them back with you.

Domestic violence and injunctions

There are basically two types of court order which you can obtain; both are often termed 'injunction'. An injunction is an order by the court telling someone what he or she must or must not do; the penalty for disobedience can be imprisonment. The two types are:

- a non-molestation injunction or personal protection order
- an ouster order or exclusion order.

A non-molestation injunction orders the spouse not to assault, molest or otherwise interfere with you. Non-molestation orders can be obtained also for the protection of children. Molestation can include pestering such as repeated telephone calls or other form of harassment.

An ouster injunction can require a spouse to leave the home and/or not come within a specified area around it (for example, 100 yards around the home). Occasionally, the court may make an order confining one spouse to a defined part of the home, but this is rarely practicable.

Before divorce proceedings have started
If you have not yet started off divorce proceedings and are not yet ready to do so, the magistrates' court can be asked for a personal protection order to restrain a spouse who has used or threatened violence towards the other spouse and/or children. Where there is imminent danger of physical injury, an expedited order can be made; most courts will arrange an emergency hearing the same day as the application. A personal protection order is similar to a non-molestation order in the divorce courts.

Where violence has been used or threatened towards the other spouse or a child, or used towards any other person, the magistrates' court can be asked for an exclusion order (similar to an ouster order in the divorce courts). This orders the violent spouse to leave the home or, if he or she has already left, not to return.

Where a person is receiving legal advice under the green form scheme, an application can be made to the legal aid area office for approval of extending the green form to 'assistance by way of representation' (known as ABWOR). If granted, this covers a solicitor's representation of his or her client in the magistrates' court for an application for an exclusion order or for a protection order. In some cases, the solicitor will instruct a barrister to appear instead.

Obtaining an injunction in divorce proceedings
Where divorce proceedings have already been started or where you wish to commence divorce proceedings immediately, an application for an injunction may be made to the divorce court. If divorce proceedings have not already been filed, you will have to lodge the divorce papers when making the application or give an undertaking to the court that you will do so within 24 hours.

Alternatively, it is possible to make an application to the county court without starting off divorce proceedings under the Domestic Violence Act 1976. However, it might be cheaper (avoiding extra court fees, etc.) and simpler not to duplicate proceedings and to apply in the divorce court for an injunction and divorce together if you are contemplating divorce proceedings.

Ex parte or on notice

In the case of a real emergency, it is possible to apply for an injunction 'ex parte', which means that the other spouse is not told of the hearing before it has taken place. Courts are more ready to listen to an ex parte application and grant an injunction if the application is for a non-molestation injunction. For ouster orders, the situation needs to be fairly desperate before a court will order a spouse out of the home without his having been given the opportunity of presenting his case to the court. If you do obtain an order ex parte, this will usually be limited to a temporary period of a week and your spouse has to be told of the resumed hearing, usually one week later, and be given the opportunity to put his case before the court. By this time he will have had the chance of obtaining legal advice after he has received the papers from the court.

In all other cases, when you apply for an injunction this application will be 'on notice', that is your spouse will be told in advance of the hearing date. Your application with accompanying papers must be served on your spouse at least two clear working days before the hearing date.

The documents that you will need to file at court to start off the application are:

- an application, in duplicate, together with the court fees
- an affidavit in support, giving particulars of any children, of the accommodation and alternative accommodation available to each party, and of the conduct complained of and why an injunction is necessary.

In turn, your spouse should produce an affidavit dealing with the allegations and can suggest solutions, such as alternative accommodation or explaining the possibility of remaining living in the same house.

If you have been injured, or even just bruised, you should go and see your doctor or the casualty department of your local hospital and make sure that a physical examination is carried out and your injuries noted on medical records. Medical records can provide useful evidence in court proceedings and your solicitor may ask the doctor concerned to prepare a report, for which a fee of about £40 will be charged. If anyone other than you and your spouse has witnessed the violence, ask if he or she would be willing to come forward to attend court, if need be, as a witness.

An application 'on notice' for an injunction is usually heard very quickly – normally within a few days. In ex parte proceedings, the procedure can be short-circuited by the applicant appearing before the judge to give oral evidence, without the necessity of filing an affidavit. Before making an ouster injunction, the judge will want to be satisfied both that the circumstances warrant such an order and that there is no satisfactory alternative in the light of the spouse's conduct, the children's needs and the available accommodation. In one case in 1993, an ouster order was granted because of very serious dissension caused by the husband's 'jealous, argumentative and unyielding nature': the wife found it impossible to live with him. However, this case is very rare: usually the courts require evidence of fairly severe violence before an ouster order will be granted.

Injunctions can be limited to a specific period, for example three months, or in more severe cases they may have no time limit. If the parties are reconciled and resume cohabitation, the injunction automatically lapses.

Power of arrest
In cases of actual physical injury to the applicant or a child, the court can attach a power of arrest to the order. This means that if, once the offending spouse has been served with the order, he breaches it, the police can be called to arrest the offender straightaway without a warrant and bring him before a magistrate. If a power of arrest is given, it is wise to take a copy of the order to your local police station straight after the court hearing, to put the police on notice.

A power of arrest normally lasts for a fixed period of three months. It is in practice the most effective preventive action that can be taken to curb future violent attacks. It cannot, however, be attached to an undertaking not to be violent in the future, if this is offered by the man. So a woman should think carefully before accepting and undertaking rather than asking the court for a formal court injunction.

A note of warning
Injunction proceedings should be considered carefully before being commenced.

Bear in mind the consequences of seeking and obtaining an ouster injunction in terms of your future relationship. If that is the way your divorce proceedings begin, the prospect of negotiating reasonably and reaching a sensible agreement recedes dramatically. If, however, you have no alternative, you must take the best steps to protect your and your family's safety.

What to do if you have been served with an injunction
If you know that you are at risk of being violent towards your spouse, whether because you have been violent in the past or because you feel the tension in the house is becoming unbearable, you need to take steps to minimise the risk. Take responsible action, such as leaving the house for a cooling-off period.

If you are served with an injunction or injunction application, read it carefully, together with any other documents given to you, for example the affidavit. See a solicitor as soon as possible and make an appointment with him or her as much in advance of the hearing date as you can. If you are financially eligible, you can get advice under the green form scheme.

A few solicitors will not act for violent men, so check this in advance. The solicitor will take a statement from you and make this into an affidavit to be lodged at the court. As an alternative to having an order made against you, you can offer the court an undertaking not to molest your partner. Breaking the terms of an undertaking can invoke just as serious a penalty as breaking the terms of a court order.

Unless you have real grounds to contest your partner's claim for a non-molestation order, you are unlikely to be able to obtain legal aid to be represented in court, even if you would otherwise qualify on financial grounds.

CHAPTER 13

CHILD ABDUCTION

CHILD abduction is one of the most fraught areas of separation and divorce. It actually happens only rarely but when it does so it splits the family apart as one parent faces the prospect of never seeing his or her child again.

Prevention is by far the most effective form of action. Many countries (including the UK) are signatories to the International Hague Convention, under which they undertake to enforce other countries' custody orders about children (this will apply to the new residence orders, too) and to return any abducted child to the country he or she was snatched from. However, many countries have failed to sign, so there the Convention could provide no remedy. Even if a child has been taken to one of the signatory states, the procedures for enforcement are at best time-consuming and at worst unsuccessful.

There are two areas of law which have a bearing on child abduction. The first is the criminal law: the Child Abduction Act 1984 made kidnapping a child a crime. Under that Act, a parent who takes a child out of the country without the prior written consent of the other, or permission of the court, may be committing a criminal offence.

Secondly, there are civil laws which prevent children from being abducted, but the position nowadays is different from that before the Children Act 1989 was brought into force on 14 October 1991.

Before 14 October 1991
Whenever there were children of the family in divorce proceedings, the court not only made an order for custody and care and

control, but also an extra order that the children should not be taken out of the country without the consent of the other parent or the court. If such an order has been made, it will remain effective and enforceable after 14 October 1991.

After 14 October 1991
After that date, in the majority of divorces involving children no court orders will be made, so there will usually be no civil order stopping the other parent from removing the child abroad. (An abducting parent may, however, still be committing a criminal offence under the Child Abduction Act.) If a residence order is made, it prevents the other parent from removing the child without consent, but the parent in whose favour it was made is allowed to take the child abroad for periods of up to one month at a time.

The purpose behind these changes was to emphasise that it is the parents' responsibility to agree on arrangements for the children wherever possible and to allow the parent with whom the child lives to take him or her abroad for a holiday. Obviously, if there are real grounds for suspecting that the other parent intends to take the child abroad permanently and not just for a holiday, then the circumstances are different and court action can and should be taken fast.

Worries about abduction
If you have fears that your child may be abducted by the other parent (if, for example, the other parent is a foreign national and there are grounds for believing that he or she plans to return to his or her home country), you could ask the court to make a **prohibited steps order** to state that the other parent could not take the child abroad without your prior consent or the court's permission. Alternatively, it might be in the child's best interests for a **residence order** to be made either on decree nisi or later on: this will automatically include an order that the child may not be removed abroad without the consent of the other parent or the court. Talk to your solicitor about the best course of action.

If your child is abducted
If you believe that your child is about to be abducted by the other parent you need to take action fast.

Contact your solicitor immediately, who can act to obtain an emergency court order preventing the child from being taken abroad, either via a residence order and/or a prohibited steps order, or by using the old remedy of making a child a ward of court (whereby the court becomes in law the parent of the child and no step affecting the child can be taken without the court's consent). The courts can make such orders even outside court hours: a duty judge should always be available. The order should be served on the potential abductor if his or her whereabouts are known.

Emergency legal aid and advice under the green form are available, subject to financial eligibility.

In addition to taking legal action, either you or your solicitor should contact the police and ask for a port alert to be carried out. Under this, if there is a real and imminent danger of the child being abducted ('real and imminent' means within the next 24 hours), the police are obliged to notify all airports and seaports of the danger of the child being taken out of the country.

In practice, it is often difficult for officials to recognise and intercept children at ports where there is heavy traffic and the effectiveness of this action has been lessened since the reduction of border controls between European Union countries in 1993. To maximise the usefulness of a port alert, provide as many details as you can of the potential abductor and the child, such as full names, addresses and dates of birth, personal descriptions, photographs, and (best of all) details of the flight or sailing if you have them.

After your child has been abducted, your remedies are fewer and harder to enforce, but you should still not give up hope. If the child has been taken to a country which is a signatory of the International Hague Convention, you should be able to get the appropriate authority to act to get the child returned to you. Even if the child has been taken elsewhere, it may be possible to ask the court here to sequester the abducting parent's property if he or she has broken a court order – this can act as a lever to force the abducting parent to return the child (as in the 1993 Peter Malkin case). Ask your solicitor for more information.

Support for parents and families

For support and information for parents and families about child abduction, contact the parents' self-help group, Reunite (The National Council for Abducted Children) at PO Box 4, London WC1X 3DX (advice line: 071–404 8356; Mon, Wed, Fri 10–1; Tue, Thur 2–5).

A free booklet called *Child abduction* is available from the Child Abduction Unit, Official Solicitor's Department, 4th Floor, 81 Chancery Lane, London WC2A 1DD (tel: 071–911 7047/7094).

CHAPTER 14

STEPFAMILIES

STEPFATHERS and stepmothers often occupy a distinctive place within a new family having taken on the burdens (and joys!) of an actual parent but without being recognised by the law as such. However, the greater flexibility of the courts' new powers under section 8 of the Children Act 1989 can be helpful for stepfamilies.

Stepfamilies and children

Stepparents do not automatically have parental responsibility during a marriage (nor after divorce) for their stepchildren (for a further explanation of 'parental responsibility' see page 135). Parental responsibility belongs automatically to both the father and mother of a child (if the parents were married at the time of the birth or later married each other) or to the mother alone if the parents were unmarried.

An unmarried father can acquire parental responsibility either by making a special formal agreement with the mother and registering it at the Principal Registry of the Family Division or by successfully applying to court for a parental responsibility order or a residence order. If a residence order is granted to an unmarried natural father of a child, the court will also automatically order him to have parental responsibility too under section 4 of the Children Act.

Stepparents cannot apply for a parental responsibility order on its own, although they can apply for a residence order (see below). A natural parent cannot agree to share parental responsibility with a stepparent by making a formal agreement. The only ways that a stepparent can acquire parental responsibility is by successful application for a residence order (or by being appointed a guardian). So stepparents cannot in law make decisions about a stepchild's upbringing themselves, although they will usually be involved in decision-making via their partner.

To change this and to become recognised by the law as having the role of a parent, stepparents can apply for a residence order under section 8 of the Children Act jointly with their new partner if the children are living with them. This indirectly gives them parental responsibility and puts them on an equal footing with anyone else who has parental responsibility – usually the parents. In this case parental responsibility for the stepparent lasts only as long as the residence order lasts, rather than lasting until the child reaches 18.

As long as the stepparent is married to the parent of the child, he or she will not need the court's permission to make an application. Other people who can apply to the court as of right are those:

- with whom the child has lived for at least three years, *or*
- who have the permission of everyone who has a residence order in their favour, *or*
- who have the consent of everyone with parental responsibility for the child, *or*
- if the child is in care, who have the consent of the local authority.

Anyone else can apply too, but the court will first have to give its permission before giving the application the go-ahead. The factors the court then considers are the type of application being made, the connection between the applicant and the child and any risk the application might have of harmfully disrupting the child's life.

When the court considers an application for a residence order, it will have to consider whether making an order is better for the child than making no order at all. Very often this 'no-order' principle means that in practice courts are reluctant to make a residence order. The court's first and paramount consideration is the welfare of the child (see page 143 for a more detailed explanation of the welfare principle). The court may grant such an application in the joint favour of the parent and a concerned and involved stepparent, particularly if more certainty would benefit the new family and if the absent natural parent takes little or no interest in the child. The court would want to be satisfied that the new family arrangement is stable.

Another option would be for the stepparent to apply jointly with his or her new spouse for an adoption order. However, the courts are unlikely to grant this as they are unwilling to terminate all links with natural parents which an adoption order necessarily does.

Stepfamilies and money

One situation which can generate considerable strain and even resentment on a new stepparent's part is the possibility of the former spouse 'getting their hands on' their own assets. Second wives or husbands can find it especially galling to feel that their own paypackets are being used to fund maintenance payments for a former spouse and family.

If a stepparent or parent pays child support via the Child Support Agency, when calculating the amount that he (or she) should pay, the formula ignores in its initial stages the extra costs of looking after the children of the second family. However, lower earners should find themselves and their second families being cushioned from the harsher effects of the formula by the Protected Income formula, designed to ensure that their income does not sink below income support rates. The Child Support Agency will need to know the amount of a new partner's income to work out the level of protected income (see further Chapter 5).

The court on the other hand will not approach the question of dividing up the family's assets by seeking to get its hands on the new partner's money. It will not formally take the individual income and assets of a new partner into account, but will look at them to the extent that the new partner's income and property frees up the ex-spouse's ability to meet any financial order that may be made against him or her. So, if a man remarries and moves into his new wife's home, the bills for which are met out of her own earnings, the court will take into account the fact that his housing needs have been met without any great outlay, so he could possibly afford to make greater maintenance payments.

A new partner can refuse to disclose details of his or her income and assets. However, he or she can be forced by a witness summons (or subpoena) to attend court to give verbal evidence. The court will not necessarily require to know what a new partner earns, but will want to know the extent to which she or he relieves the ex-spouse from having to provide for living accommodation, for example.

The courts draw a distinction between a woman cohabiting and remarrying. On remarriage, her former husband's financial obligations to maintain her (although not the children) end. If she instead chooses to live with a new partner, whilst the ex-husband can indeed apply for a reduction in her maintenance payments if his ex-wife's own financial position has improved, the court will not transfer the ex-husband's duty to maintain her to her new live-in partner.

As a general rule, it is best to try to conclude arguments over money before remarriage (or even before permanent cohabitation) to ensure that problems of the earlier marriage do not become enmeshed in the creation of a new family relationship.

If the parent/partner dies

On the death of his or her partner, the stepparent has no automatic rights vis-à-vis the stepchildren. If the parents were married at the time of the birth, then the other parent (not the stepparent) should automatically take over responsibility for looking after the children and the stepparent would have no automatic legal rights. However, the other parent may be unwilling to give access in the future to the stepparent: if there is any conflict the stepparent could apply for a contact order under section 8 of the Children Act (see further page 141). If the stepparent wanted to continue looking after the children, then again he or she would have to apply for a residence order.

To protect against a legal shutting out of the stepparent, especially where the absent parent was uninterested in the children, the parent/partner could make a will or deed appointing the stepparent as a guardian of the child on his or her death. This would suffice if the mother of the children had not been married to the father at the time of the birth or had later married him. Otherwise, to make the position watertight, the stepparent and parent should apply jointly to the court for a residence order too as otherwise the appointment as a guardian would not take effect until the death of the surviving natural parent (which defeats the object of an appointment).

Another problem that can arise on death (or even if the remarriage breaks up) is that of securing a family home for the children. If a parent following divorce purchases a property jointly with a new partner, perhaps with the aid of a capital sum paid via the divorce courts, he or she should be careful how the joint ownership of the new home is expressed.

If the new partners buy as joint tenants, the share of one would pass automatically to the surviving partner whatever the owning partner's will might state. This could mean that if there were later relationship problems between the stepparent and the children, the stepparent would be within his or her legal rights to ask the children to leave the home and they might have no financial security. If, however, a new property were purchased expressly under a tenancy in common, both partners' property interests would be clearly defined and the parent could ensure that his or her share passed to the children by will.

A tenancy in common will be assumed to divide the ownership equally between the partners unless any other proportionate division is stated. So if the parent has provided most of the capital for the purchase and wants to ensure that the children are securely provided for in the event of death, the tenancy in common could be stated to be divided as to 75 per cent to the parent, 25 per cent to the stepparent. The parent should also execute a will leaving his or her share of the property to the children in trust until they reach the age of 18 (or some other later date). A deed of trust for the ownership of the property can also set out clearly what will happen if certain events occur: for example, if the parties split up, the agreements for one buying out the other.

A solicitor can advise further about ownership of the property, making a deed of trust and a will. Some of the costs may be offset by the green form, if you are financially eligible, although there are now restrictions on green form advice about wills (see further page 224). Otherwise, if you are paying privately the extra costs of preparing a deed of trust are likely to be around £200 + VAT upwards.

Making a will

Remarriage (as with any marriage) automatically revokes any earlier will unless that will was specifically made in comtemplation of the marriage. In any event making a will after a remarriage if there are children should be a priority. Otherwise, the rules of intestacy will automatically operate after your death, which may not accord with what you actually want to happen. Although these rules differ depending on the circumstances, what they achieve in broad terms is to give an ex-spouse the first £125,000 following death if there are children, the first £200,000 where there are no children. Any remaining balance will be divided amongst the children (or amongst other relatives if there are no children).

If your priority is to ensure that the children are cared for after your death, by making a will you will be certain that your wishes will be carried out. You can also appoint a guardian to care for your children after your death: the appointment will be effective immediately after your death if you have a residence order in your favour; otherwise the appointment is not effective until your surviving ex-spouse has died too.

Stepfamilies and divorce

If the stepfamily itself breaks up, broadly the advice contained within this book will apply. However, the question also arises of whether a stepparent (more commonly the stepfather) may face claims about the children by his or her ex-partner.

If the children have been treated as 'children of the family' (this term generally covers any child who has been brought up in the same household), then their details must be included on the statement of arrangements form and in the divorce petition itself. The divorce court will consider the arrangements made for them as well as for any natural children of the parties. If the stepparent wants to look after the children in the future, he or she will probably have to make an application for a residence order even if this proposal is agreed to by the natural parent. Without such an order, the stepparent's responsibilities will not be recognised in law. Usually, however, the court will be predisposed to the natural parent continuing to care for the children.

Following a marriage, as the stepchildren would be 'children of the family', applications for maintenance (which could be secured), lump sums, transfers of settlement and transfers of property could be made against the stepparent (although if the parties had never married and if the stepparent had not otherwise legally assumed financial responsibilities for the stepchildren then no such claims could be made). Applications will usually be limited to children aged up to 17, although they can be allowed after that age if the children are continuing in full-time education or training. Child support applications cannot be made against a stepparent via the Child Support Agency unless he or she had legally adopted the child(ren).

The Child Support Agency seeks to trace the natural (or adoptive) parents for them to pay maintenance for their children: financial duties to one's own natural (or adopted) children will specifically override assumed obligations for the previous children of a new partner.

The courts will also expect the natural parents to fulfil their financial obligations towards their children first, so before a financial order was made against a stepparent, the court would want to ensure that exhaustive steps had been taken to track down the absent parent to make an order against him (or her) for the children.

WHICH COURT? (ENGLAND AND WALES)

Before divorce

Applying for spousal maintenance or for maintenance for any children not covered by the Child Support Agency

Applying for a Children Act order

Make application to:
1. Family Proceedings Panel of local magistrates' court (FPP),
or
2. Family Hearing Centre (FHC) (county court), or
3. If case is especially complex, the High Court

Applying for domestic violence injunction

Make application to:
1. FPP
2. County court or FHC

Starting divorce proceedings

Make application to divorce county court (DCC) or FHC. DCC will deal with administrative paperwork of divorce only; contested applications (e.g. for finance, about the children) will be transferred to FHC.

If divorce becomes defended or is especially complex, DCC or FHC will transfer case to the High Court.

Once divorce underway

Applying for ancillary (financial) relief and/or

Applying for a Children Act order and/or

Applying for domestic violence injunction

Make application to court dealing with divorce. If this is only a DCC, case will be transferred to FHC (see above).

CHAPTER 15

DIVORCE IN SCOTLAND

SCOTTISH family and divorce law is significantly different from that in England and Wales. You can bring divorce proceedings in Scotland if you or your spouse are domiciled in Scotland or if either of you were habitually resident in Scotland for at least a year immediately before starting proceedings.

Citizens Advice Scotland and the Scottish Council of Voluntary Organisations have published *Splitting Up*, by David Nichols, a guide to separation and divorce in Scotland (£4.95).

Grounds for divorce

There is no minimum period you have to wait after marriage before you can bring divorce proceedings. The grounds for divorce are much the same as those in England and Wales:

- adultery
- unreasonable behaviour
- desertion
- non-cohabitation for two or more years and your spouse consents to the divorce
- non-cohabitation for five or more years.

If your spouse has committed adultery you do not have to show you find it intolerable to live with him or her. You cannot base your case on adultery which you have condoned or connived at. Condonation means that you forgave your spouse by resuming married life for more than three months after you knew about the adultery. Connivance means active encouragement, such as wife swapping or sex parties.

Non-cohabitation means not living together as any normal married couple would. You and your spouse may have to continue sharing the home after your marriage breaks down because neither of you can get anywhere else to live. You would have to have been living separate lives to get a divorce on grounds of non-cohabitation.

Most divorces are dealt with in the sheriff courts. These are local courts situated in most towns throughout Scotland. You can bring proceedings in the court for the area in which you or your spouse have been living for the past 40 days; you would usually choose your own local court. Divorces are also heard in the Court of Session in Edinburgh. Legal aid is not available for a Court of Session divorce, unless the case is unusually complex or difficult.

There are no decrees nisi or absolute in Scotland. The court grants a single decree of divorce which is immediately effective, although a certain period (14 days in the sheriff court, 21 days in the Court of Session) is allowed for an appeal.

Divorce procedure

There are two types of procedure: the simplified procedure (usually called a d-i-y divorce), and the ordinary procedure. D-i-y divorce can be used where the ground for divorce is non-cohabitation for two or five years. In addition, there must be no children of the marriage under 16 years of age, no financial claims by you or your spouse, no other legal proceedings affecting your marriage waiting to be heard, the divorce must be uncontested, and you and your spouse must not be suffering from any mental disorder. As the name implies, you do not need a solicitor for a d-i-y divorce. Nevertheless, you should consider seeking legal advice before you start in order to make sure that you are fully aware of the consequences and are not giving up rights in ignorance.

Printed forms for the d-i-y procedure are available from the courts or Citizens Advice Bureaux. In a two-year non-cohabitation divorce, you fill out part 1 of the form, and send it to your spouse for completion of part 2 (the other's consent to the divorce). On its return, you complete the affidavit in part 3, swearing it before a notary public or a justice of the peace. Most solicitors in Scotland are' notaries public but they will charge for affidavits. Your local council has a list of justices of the peace whose services are free. In a five-year non-cohabitation divorce, your spouse's consent is unnecessary. Part 2 of this form is the affidavit which is sworn as before.

You send the completed form (parts 1, 2 and 3 or parts 1 and 2) to the court with your marriage certificate (the original or an official copy, but not a photocopy) and the court dues (currently £55). If you are on income support or seeing a solicitor under the legal advice and assistance scheme (pink form) you will not have to pay these dues. The court takes all remaining steps and will tell you and your spouse when the divorce has been granted. This usually takes about two months.

If you cannot get a d-i-y divorce, you will have to use the 'ordinary procedure'. This is more complex and you are strongly advised to get a Scottish solicitor to act for you. Most divorces are heard in the sheriff courts so only that procedure will be described here. Court of Session procedure is slightly different.

Your friends may be able to recommend a solicitor if you do not already have one. Alternatively, your library or Citizens Advice Bureau should have lists showing which local solicitors undertake divorce work and whether they will act for clients on legal aid (most do). The Law Society of Scotland, 26 Drumsheugh Gardens, Edinburgh EH3 7YR (tel: 031-226 7411) will also help you find a solicitor.

Divorce expenses and legal aid

In d-i-y divorces the pursuer (the spouse seeking the divorce) pays his or her own expenses (£55 plus a little more for service costs). The defender (the other spouse) usually has no expenses since the proceedings must be undefended and have no associated financial and other claims.

Ordinary divorce procedure is not cheap. The expenses of an ordinary undefended divorce with financial and other claims will amount to about £700. Defended proceedings are much more expensive. It is sensible for couples to keep disputes and litigation to an absolute minimum. Your respective solicitors should be able to help you negotiate a fair settlement without having to fight it out in court. The more that goes in legal fees, the less there is for both you and the children.

The question of liability for expenses is decided by the court at the end of the proceedings. The rule usually followed is that the husband is liable for his wife's expenses as well as his own, whether he wins or loses, unless:

- the divorce is based on five years' non-cohabitation (each pays his or her expenses)
- the divorce is based on two years' non-cohabitation and the husband agrees to consent to his wife's divorce only on condition that he is not liable for her expenses (such a condition is common)
- the wife has substantial income or savings of her own (she will have to pay her own expenses).

For proceedings other than divorce proceedings the normal rule is that the loser pays the winner's expenses as well as his or her own.

Although these are the usual rules the court may decide to deal with the expenses some other way in view of a spouse's conduct of the proceedings. For example, a wife who makes groundless claims or is uncooperative, forcing her husband to establish every fact, could find herself paying her own expenses or even those of her husband as well. When the husband is legally aided he is usually asked to pay only such a proportion of his wife's expenses as he can reasonably afford. Even if your spouse pays your expenses you will almost certainly be out of pocket. You will have to pay for bills for consultations with your solicitor and other extras which your spouse is not required to pay.

Legal advice and assistance (the 'pink form' scheme) is available to help you with preliminary advice and to find out whether grounds for divorce exist. It does not cover representation in court. Assistance by way of representation (ABWOR) is not available for family litigation in Scotland. Legal aid is available for court proceedings: divorce, financial claims and matters concerning the children or housing, whether with the divorce proceedings or separately. Your solicitor will help you apply for legal advice and assistance or legal aid. The Scottish Legal Aid Board runs both schemes. Eligibility depends on your own income and savings (your spouse's income and savings are not considered together with yours where you are opponents or living apart). For legal aid the Board has also to be satisfied that you have a reasonable case. The financial limits are the same as in England and Wales.

Legal aid does not mean you can indulge in expensive litigation without fear of the financial consequences. The Scottish Legal Aid Board deducts the amount of your expenses from money the court awards you, or property that the court orders to be transferred to you, if they cannot recover the sum in full from your contributions and your opponent. However, no deduction is made from any aliment (maintenance) or periodical allowance or the first £2,500 of any capital sum or transfer of property awarded.

First steps

Proceedings start with your solicitor lodging the initial writ in court. This document sets out briefly the facts of your case and details the orders you are asking the court to make. A copy of this writ is then served on your spouse. You are called the pursuer and he or she is the defender. A copy also has to be served on any person (a co-defender) with whom you aver your spouse has committed adultery. In a divorce action based on either two or five years' non-cohabitation, your spouse is also sent a notice warning of the possible financial consequences of divorce (loss of pension or inheritance rights, for example). The notice alerts your spouse to the financial and other applications he or she may make to the court.

In your initial writ you can apply for various interim orders, or you can add them on later. Interim orders last until the divorce is granted, when the position is reviewed and fresh orders made. Typical interim orders are:

- interim aliment for you. The Child Support Agency deals with maintenance for the children

- interim custody and access
- an interim interdict (prohibition) against violent behaviour or disposal of assets
- an interdict against taking the children out of Scotland. Your application for this need not be intimated to your spouse so that he or she may get no warning at all)
- an exclusion order excluding your spouse from the family home.

You can also apply for these remedies separately; they are not only available in divorce proceedings. If you cannot apply for a divorce as soon as you and your spouse split up, you may need to use separate proceedings.

Many couples agree between themselves on custody, access, aliment, occupation of the family home and the other issues arising out of splitting up. Written legally binding agreements (often called separation agreements) are sometimes prepared with solicitors' help. Remember that you cannot prevent your spouse from applying to the Child Support Agency for the children's maintenance to be fixed. The amount fixed could make it difficult or unfair for you to fulfil the other terms of the agreement which you may not be able to alter.

Defences

A notice of intention to defend must be lodged within 21 days (42 if the defender is abroad). The court will then specify the date defences have to be lodged by and the date of the options hearing. In your defences you can oppose your spouse's claims and/or make claims against your spouse. Each of you can then adjust your case to meet the other's. You and your spouse and your respective solicitors must attend the options hearing where the court will clarify the issues in dispute and decide how to proceed. Failure to attend may result in your action or defences being dismissed.

It is unusual for the divorce itself to be defended. More commonly your spouse will defend your application for financial orders or apply for similar orders. Where the divorce is defended, the case is heard in court with each side and their witnesses giving evidence. But where only financial and custody aspects are at issue, the divorce is generally disposed of on the basis of sworn statements (affidavits).

Affidavits

An affidavit is accepted by the court as evidence of the facts contained in it. Unless the divorce itself is defended, you, your spouse and others can give evidence by affidavits instead of attending court. Your solicitor will prepare your affidavit from the information you give, and you will then swear it before a notary public (who may be your own solicitor). The information must be up-to-date, complete and accurate; otherwise further affidavits or oral evidence will be called for. Deliberately concealing facts or making false statements is regarded as a very serious offence for which you could well be imprisoned.

Reconciliation

You and your spouse can still try to save your marriage even though divorce proceedings have started. The court will, if asked, stop proceedings for a reconciliation. If this does not work, you can ask the court to let the proceedings continue from where they were stopped.

The children

You have to show that satisfactory arrangements have been made for any children of the marriage who are under 16, before the court will grant your divorce. Most couples reach agreement about who is to look after the children. Your or your spouse's affidavit will state who is going to look after the children, how they are going to be looked after, and what accommodation will be available for them. In addition, the court requires an affidavit from a relative or a person (such as a neighbour) who knows the children well. If these affidavits are satisfactory, the court will accept the arrangements without interviewing the couple or the children.

If you and your spouse cannot agree about the future arrangements for the children, the court will order a much more thorough investigation to be carried out. Conciliation services are available to help couples reach agreement.

Mediation

Mediation services are available in most parts of Scotland. At present they help couples resolve disputes relating to the children and do not attempt to negotiate agreements about financial and housing matters. Information about local services in your area can be obtained from a Citizens Advice Bureau or from Family Mediation Scotland (see page 267). Mediation by a service affiliated to Family Mediation Scotland is free.

You and your spouse can agree to go to mediation at any time: before, during or after divorce. You can either contact the service directly or ask your solicitor to make the arrangements. When you and your spouse are engaged in legal proceedings relating to the children the court may refer you to mediation if it thinks that that could help resolve the dispute. The sheriff court can refer a couple without their consent, but in the Court of Session they have to agree. Courts refer to a local service affiliated to Family Mediation Scotland.

What you and your spouse say during mediation can probably be used in evidence in court, but judges discourage the use of such evidence.

Joint minute

If you and your spouse can agree on the financial aspects and future arrangements for the children before proceedings start, you can simply ask the court to make the appropriate orders and your spouse need not defend. In many cases, however, agreement is reached after proceedings have started as a result of negotiation or mediation. You and your spouse will then arrange for your respective solicitors to submit a joint minute to the court. This minute sets out the orders that you and your spouse request the court to grant or it may request the court to make no orders since the matters are to be covered by a written agreement. The terms of the joint minute should be checked very carefully. Once it has been lodged in court is is normally impossible to change your mind and ask the court to do something different.

Where the proceedings are undefended or a joint minute is submitted, the court will normally grant the orders sought without further enquiry. The court may, however, demand further information in matters affecting the children.

An important element in some agreements is a renunciation by a spouse (usually the wife) of any right to claim periodical allowance on divorce or afterwards. This will be strictly enforced even if the decision turns out to have been unwise.

Defended proceedings

If you and your spouse cannot reach an agreement about the financial orders, the court will require full information about your respective needs and resources. The affidavits will detail the income and capital of each of you and your requirements (living expenses, accommodation, and so on). It is rare for witnesses to be called to give evidence in court about financial matters.

Where there is a dispute about future arrangements for the children, the court asks for a report from an independent person. The reporter is usually an advocate but sometimes a social worker is used. After looking at the report and hearing your comments and any further evidence either of you wishes to present, the court decides what to do on the basis of what would be in the children's best interests.

Decree

A decree is the formal document containing the orders made by the court. The financial orders are usually granted at the same time as the divorce, although it is possible to have these left over for a later hearing if disagreement is holding up the divorce.

The court will notify you that decree has been granted and will also notify your spouse if his or her address is known. There is a 14–day period allowed for appeal (21 days in the Court of Session). After that, an extract (certified copy) of the decree can be obtained from the court which details the orders the court made. You will need an extract to show that you are divorced if you plan to marry again and to enforce the orders if your spouse refuses to pay.

The home

Before divorce

Most couples now own their home together as co–owners. This means that both of them are equally entitled to live there and occupy it and both equally liable for the outgoings. Both have to consent to any sale or other disposal, although the court will order a sale against the wishes of one co-owner unless a sale is undesirable. A sale will not be ordered while the divorce proceedings are pending if a transfer of the home on divorce is sought. On sale, the proceeds of sale are divided equally between the couple unless the title deeds specify a different proportion. Each co-owner's share of the proceeds increases his or her capital which the court can reallocate on divorce.

The Matrimonial Homes (Family Protection) (Scotland) Act 1981 gives you certain rights if you do not own the home and your spouse is the sole owner. You are entitled to continue to occupy and live in the home. Moreover, your consent is required for any sale or other disposal, although the court can dispense with your consent if it is being withheld unreasonably. These rights are automatic: you do not have to register them in the Land Register for Scotland or the Register of Sasines (public registers of property and its owners).

Married co-tenants and spouses of sole tenants have similar protection against the tenancy of the home being given up.

You can renounce your occupancy rights but it is seldom in your interest to do so. A renunciation must be in writing and signed and declared before a notary public.

Exclusion orders
You can apply to the court for an order excluding your spouse from the family home and immediate vicinity if he or she behaves violently towards you or the children. This order is called an exclusion order and even a sole owner or tenant can be excluded. You can apply separately or as part of your divorce proceedings. The court has to be satisfied, first, that the exclusion order is necessary to protect you and/or the children from your spouse's violent behaviour or threats and, secondly, that it is reasonable for him or her to be excluded. Your spouse must be sent a copy of your application for an exclusion order and given an opportunity to oppose it. You will have to back up your claim with as much evidence as you can, such as affidavits from your doctor or neighbours about your health and past incidents of violence,

reports by the police if they have been involved, and evidence of your need for the home and the unsuitable nature of your present temporary accommodation if you have been forced to leave home.

An exclusion order has no time limit: it lasts until the court recalls it or you and your spouse are divorced. On divorce, the whole issue of the home is reviewed by the court; for this reason the order is often called an interim exclusion order.

Interdicts

Another way of protecting yourself from violence or molestation by your husband or wife is to apply for a court order (called an interdict) prohibiting such conduct. Interdicts can be obtained extremely quickly, within a day if necessary. You can apply separately or as part of your divorce proceedings. Interdicts last until the court recalls them. Behaviour contrary to the interdict (a breach of interdict) is regarded as contempt of court. Your spouse can be fined or imprisoned, but is usually given a warning for the first breach. It is possible to have a power of arrest added to your interdict. The advantage of this is that once you have sent a copy of the interdict and power of arrest to the police you can ask the police to arrest your spouse for breaching the interdict. Also, the police will generally respond more quickly to your call for assistance if you have a power of arrest. The drawback is that your spouse has to be given notice of your application for the interdict and an opportunity to oppose it if you want a power of arrest added. Courts usually require one or more past violent incidents before a power of arrest is added.

On divorce

Orders regarding the home are part of the overall financial settlement (see page 258). The court on granting divorce may:

- make no order and allow the home to be sold; the proceeds will have been taken into account in any lump sum award made
- transfer the ownership (or tenancy) of the home or a share of it from one spouse to the other. The date of transfer can be deferred, but delays of more than a few months to allow time for the legal documents to be prepared are not common

- regulate who is to occupy the home after divorce (this power is exercised infrequently). It might be used to allow a wife and children to continue to occupy the home owned by her husband until she can get a job and afford somewhere else. An express exclusion of her husband from the home might be necessary if he was likely to interfere with her occupation. The wife's occupancy rights prevent the home being sold without her consent.

The children

You and your spouse have to decide what is to happen to the children after divorce. Talk things over with them, explain what is going on and what is going to happen to them, and if they are old enough, take account of their views as well as your own. You and your spouse should make every effort to reach agreement over the children. A mediation service is available to help divorcing couples resolve their disputes about the children. You can either contact the service directly or ask your solicitor to refer you (see page 267).

The Children Act 1989 does not apply to Scotland. In Scotland custody means the right to have the children living with you, take day-to-day care of them, and make day-to-day decisions about them. Guardianship is normally concerned with representing the children in legal proceedings and holding property for them, but the views of a guardian on the child's long-term education or upbringing must be taken into account. Access is the right of the parent without custody or other relative (such as a grandparent) to see the children or have them to stay for a while.

Custody, guardianship and access applications are not restricted to parents. Anyone (including the children concerned) can apply. Custody and guardianship cease when children reach 16. They can then live where they like, look after their own money and generally make their own decisions. A child under 16 can consent to medical treatment if the doctor thinks that he or she can understand what the proposed treatment involves.

Before divorce, parents are joint guardians and have joint custody of their children. It is extremely uncommon for guardianship to be altered on divorce. As far as custody is concerned, either the parent looking after the children can be awarded sole custody or both parents can retain joint custody. Sole custody is the norm, but joint custody is an option if both parents can co-operate and if the absent parent does not interfere with the other's day-to-day care. A person wanting sole custody has to apply to the court for this; if nothing is done the parents retain joint custody. Arrangements for access are best worked out on the basis of what is mutually acceptable. The parent with the children should allow the other reasonable access and, indeed, encourage the children to keep up links. If these informal arrangements break down, the court will regulate access – for example, allowing the other parent to see the children for a certain number of hours every weekend or having them to stay for part of the school holidays. The court will refuse a parent who has been involved with the children access only in exceptional circumstances.

You may want to change your children's surname to that of your new husband. Think carefully about this because their father (and perhaps the children too) may resent a change. In theory the court could be asked to prohibit any change but few applications are made.

Child abduction

The Scottish provisions of the Child Abduction Act 1984 are different from those for England and Wales. A parent commits a criminal offence by taking a child out of the United Kingdom only if the other parent (or someone else) has sole custody and has not agreed to the child's removal or the court has interdicted removal. If your spouse is likely to take the children abroad you should apply for custody or an interdict at once. You can apply without applying for divorce but if you have started divorce proceedings the application has to be made in the context of those proceedings. Children cannot be made wards of court in Scotland. In an emergency you can obtain an interdict at any hour of the day or night. Once you have an interdict or sole custody you can ask the police and sheriff officers to trace the children and prevent their removal from the country.

If your child is abducted abroad see your solicitor immediately. Most European and Commonwealth countries and the United

States are in the Hague Convention which obliges the foreign country to trace the children and secure their return.

Financial orders

The main financial orders the court can make on divorce are:

- ordering one spouse to pay a lump sum (a 'capital' sum) to the other; *and/or*
- ordering one spouse to pay the other a periodical allowance – a regular sum each week or month; *and/or*
- ordering a spouse to pay aliment for the children of the marriage but only if the Child Support Agency cannot assess maintenance (see page 260); *and/or*
- transferring the ownership of property from one spouse to the other.

It is possible, but unusual, for the court to grant a divorce and postpone the financial orders to a later date if disagreement is holding up the divorce.

The court can also order the house to be sold immediately or at a later date and/or say who is to occupy it and to have use of the contents. Where the house is rented, the court can transfer the tenancy from one spouse to the other.

Either the pursuer or the defender can apply for financial orders. You have to state in your initial writ or defences exactly what orders you seek from the court and give evidence of your and your spouse's needs and resources to demonstrate that they are reasonable claims. Making exaggerated claims is bad tactics as it merely gets your spouse's back up. Almost inevitably a couple's living standards drop after divorce. A fair settlement should result in this drop being shared between the spouses.

A claim for a lump sum or transfer of property must be made before the divorce is granted. You can claim periodical allowance afterwards but you are very unlikely to get it then, because the principles required to justify an award (Principles 3 to 5 below) generally speaking apply to your situation at the time of divorce. You cannot claim periodical allowance later if you and your spouse at the time of divorce made a formal agreement that you would not claim.

The Family Law (Scotland) Act 1985 sets out a series of principles to guide the court in making financial orders, as follows.

1. Sharing family assets

The home, its contents, savings, investments and other assets which you or your spouse own and which were acquired between the date of marriage and the date of final separation are family assets. The home and contents are also counted as family assets if they were acquired before marriage as a family home for the couple. Assets given to you or inherited by you are not regarded as family assets. Family assets are to be shared equally unless there is a good reason for unequal division. Unequal division might be ordered where your parents helped you buy the home or where you run a business that cannot be divided. An important family asset, especially for older couples, is the lump sum and pension payable on retirement under a superannuation scheme. This cannot be divided between the spouses, but its value is taken into account in calculating each spouse's share.

2. Balancing economic advantages and disadvantages

The court has to take account of your financial and non-financial contributions to your spouse's wealth – and the other way round. Examples include helping with the running costs of the home, sacrificing a career to look after the children or working in your spouse's business at an artificially low wage. In practice this principle is seldom utilised..

3. Sharing child-care

Child-care costs are to be shared. These include your loss of earnings while looking after the children and the expense of keeping up a larger and more expensive house than you would need if you were living on your own. If maintenance for the children is assessed by the Child Support Agency it includes an amount for your child care costs. The court will therefore not usually take account of this principle.

4. Financial dependency

Under this principle you are entitled to support for up to three years to enable you to become self-supporting if you were financially dependent upon your spouse during the marriage.

5. *Severe financial hardship*
If you are unlikely to become self-supporting (too old or ill, for example), you may need support for many years (the rest of your life, perhaps) to avoid severe financial hardship.

Court orders
Principles 1 and 2 can be satisfied only by the award of a lump sum and/or a transfer of property. The lump sum may be payable all at once, shortly after divorce or at a specified later date, or by instalments. Principles 3 to 5 should be satisfied by a lump sum or transfer of property if possible, otherwise by a periodical allowance. Wives who are looking after young children ought to get a periodical allowance under Principle 3 as compensation for loss of earnings or the child-care costs if they work. Wives tend not to ask for a periodical allowance as they do not wish to have continued financial links with their husbands.

If a periodical allowance at the time of divorce cannot be justified by either Principle 3, 4 or 5 you will not be awarded one. The court will not award a nominal periodical allowance on divorce with the intention that it could be increased later if your financial circumstances got worse.

What has just been said applies if you and your spouse cannot agree so that the court has to resolve the dispute. If your claim is undefended or a joint minute is presented most courts will grant whatever is asked for, but any periodical allowance must be justified by reference to the appropriate principles. However, your and your spouse's negotiations will obviously be influenced by what the court would do if you cannot agree.

Aliment for the children
The Child Support Agency now assesses maintenance for children up to and including 18 years of age who are still in secondary education. The courts have no power to deal with claims for aliment made for these children.

Certain categories of children are not within the Agency's remit and can still be awarded aliment by the courts. Aliment is money to be paid periodically for a person's support. The most important categories are:

1. Children aged 19 to 24 who are undergoing further educational training at a university, college, apprenticeship or so on. Children have to look after themselves once they reach 25 as the parental obligation of aliment ceases then.

2. A child who has been accepted by you or your spouse as a child of the family. The accepting spouse will have an obligation of aliment. The usual example is the stepfather accepting his wife's children by her former marriage. The Child Support Agency will assess the children's father for payment, but if this is not feasible (father dead, untraceable or no money) aliment can be claimed via the courts against the stepfather.

3. Where the parent due to pay aliment is abroad.

The amount of aliment awarded depends on what the person paying it can afford and what the child needs. The previous level of support the child enjoyed is also important.

A child over 11 can apply to the Child Support Agency for an assessment of his or her own maintenance. Children over 18 who wish aliment via the courts must claim themselves. Below that age a parent may claim on their behalf.

Change in circumstances

After divorce your or your ex-spouse's financial circumstances may change. You may be able to go back to court to get your orders changed, depending on the type of order involved.

Lump sum order

You cannot apply for a lump sum order after divorce. If you were awarded a lump sum on divorce the court cannot generally change the amount payable. There are two rare exceptions. First, if the true facts were concealed from the court or lies were told to obtain the original order, the court will make a new order; secondly, if your ex-spouse became bankrupt within five years and the order resulted in his or her debts exceeding assets. In this case the court can order you to repay all or part of the lump sum. Apart from these two exceptional cases, all the court can do is to alter the way in which the lump sum is paid, perhaps by ordering payment by instalments or giving more time to pay.

Property transfer orders
You cannot apply for a transfer of property order after divorce. If you were awarded a transfer on divorce the court cannot alter the property to be transferred except in the two rare cases mentioned above. All it can do is to alter the date set for transfer.

Periodical allowance
You can apply for a periodical allowance after divorce but one would be awarded only in unusual circumstances. You cannot apply if you agreed not to do so as part of the divorce settlement.

You or your ex-spouse can apply to the court for the amount to be increased, decreased, terminated or made payable only for a certain number of years more. For example, if you lose your job or now work part-time your allowance could be increased. If your ex-spouse's business is not doing so well, your allowance could be decreased or even terminated. Your allowance, which was awarded on grounds of severe financial hardship, could have a time limit put on it if you were offered a re-training course with a job at the end.

You cannot expect your allowance to be increased simply because of inflation. Inflation may be affecting your ex-spouse just as much as you.

Your remarriage terminates your allowance automatically. A woman's allowance is usually terminated by the court if she lives with another man even if he is not supporting her, but not all courts take this attitude. Your ex-spouse's remarriage will result in your allowance being reduced or terminated if the court thinks his or her commitments have increased. Your allowance should not be reduced if your ex-spouse lives with another partner. But if they have children the court will take these new liabilities into account.

If you die, your allowance comes to an end automatically. But the death of your ex-spouse does not mean that your allowance comes to an end automatically. The executors have to apply to the court for it to be terminated. Occasionally the court will then order payment at a reduced rate or set a time limit on the allowance, rather than terminate it.

Any variation the court awards can be back-dated to the date of the application, or to the date when the circumstances changed, as long as there was a good reason for the delay in applying for the variation.

Another variation the court can be asked to make is to substitute a lump sum (payable by instalments perhaps) for a periodical allowance. You and your ex-spouse should weigh up the advantages and disadvantages carefully because once the substitution order is made it cannot be reversed.

Old orders

There are some special rules for periodical allowance awarded in divorce proceedings started before 1 September 1986 (when the Family Law (Scotland) Act 1985 came into force). First, the court cannot substitute a lump sum for your allowance. You or your ex-spouse could, of course, agree to do this without going to court. Secondly, the court cannot back-date a variation of the allowance.

Aliment

The Child Support Agency now deals with the assessment of most children's maintenance. The assessed amount depends on the financial circumstances of each parent and also on the age of the child. Application may be made to the Agency for variation of the assessment.

In exceptional cases (see pages 260–1) the court may still award aliment and can vary the amount awarded subsequently. Apart from these cases, if aliment is payable under a court order which was made in proceedings commenced before April 1993 then the court retains power to vary the amount. A variation of aliment can be applied for if the circumstances of the child or the paying parent change. The amount of aliment is not reduced merely because the paying parent or the parent looking after the children remarries or cohabits. Aliment ceases automatically if either the paying parent or the child dies.

Enforcing maintenance

A great number of people who have a court order for their own periodical allowance or aliment for the children never get paid regularly. The longer the time the arrears have built up, the less likely it is that you will be paid.

If informal demands for regular payments do not produce the required results, you will have to use legal enforcement methods (called diligence). You do not have to go back to the court but you will need a solicitor's help. The legal aid certificate for your divorce covers the cost of diligence for up to 12 months later. After a year, or if you are applying for your ex-spouse to be imprisoned for failure to pay, you will have to apply for legal aid or legal advice and assistance.

Where your ex-spouse is employed, the best diligence to use is a *current maintenance arrestment*. You (or your solicitor) send a copy of the court order to your ex-spouse, and if, not less than four weeks later, three or more instalments are in arrears, a current maintenance arrestment can be served by a sheriff officer on your ex-spouse's employer. The employer thereafter automatically deducts every pay-day the maintenance due to you for the period since the last pay-day and sends it to you or your solicitor. A current maintenance arrestment does not enforce arrears but you can use an earnings arrestment or another diligence at the same time to recover the arrears.

The following diligences enforce arrears only, although the threat of repeating them may make your ex-spouse keep up regular payments in future:

- *Earnings arrestment*: a sheriff officer serves a notice on your ex-spouse's employer who deducts every pay-day an amount which varies with the earnings payable then. The deductions are sent to you or your solicitor and stop when the arrears are paid off.
- *Arrestment of a bank or building society account*: a sheriff officer serves a notice which freezes the money in the account. You then have to apply to the court for an order requiring the bank or building society to pay you, unless your ex-spouse agrees to release the money.

- *Poinding and sale of goods*: a sheriff officer goes to your ex-spouse's home or business premises and makes a list of his or her goods and their value. The court can then order these 'poinded' goods to be auctioned to pay the arrears.

- *Imprisonment*: if the court is satisfied that your ex-spouse's failure to pay was wilful, he or she can be imprisoned for up to six weeks. Only a handful of people are actually sent to prison each year, but the threat usually works wonders. Imprisonment is only available for failure to pay aliment. You cannot use it to enforce your periodical allowance.

The Child Support Agency will collect and if necessary enforce child maintenance on request and will always do so if the parent looking after the children is on benefit. If your ex-spouse is employed the CSA will use a deduction from earnings order (very like an earnings arrestment). If not it will have to go to court to get a liability order for the arrears and then use the diligences of bank arrestment, poinding or imprisonment.

Effect of divorce on your inheritance rights

After divorce, you have no rights to your ex-spouse's estate if he or she dies without a will or leaves you nothing. The Inheritance (Provision for Family and Dependants) Act 1975 does not apply to Scotland.

Legacies or other provisions for you in your ex-spouse's will are not cancelled by divorce after the date of the will. Generally speaking, you are entitled to take them unless the will makes it clear that you are not. Your ex-spouse's will is not cancelled by his or her subsequent remarriage.

After divorce, you and your ex-spouse should review any existing will. You will probably want to cancel any bequest to your ex-spouse, but other changes may also be desirable. Most married couples who own their home together have in the title deeds that the property will go to the survivor if one of them dies. This is another thing that ought to be changed after divorce. A solicitor's help will be needed to change the title deeds.

Judicial separation

Instead of a divorce, you can apply for a judicial separation. The grounds are the same as for divorce. The court granting a judicial separation has no power to award a capital sum or order a transfer of property: it can only award aliment for you and the children. You and your spouse remain married to each other so neither of you can remarry. Judicial separations are uncommon nowadays.

A husband does not inherit any of the property the wife acquired after separation if she dies without having made a will. There is no equivalent rule disinheriting a separated wife.

Stepfamilies

A stepparent has, by virtue of marriage to the child's parent, few legal rights and responsibilities towards the child. A stepparent is not a guardian of, and does not have custody of, the child in the absence of a court order. A stepparent cannot appoint a guardian for the child by will, even after he or she has been appointed a guardian by the court.

The Children Act 1989 does not apply in Scotland. A stepparent can obtain all the rights of a parent by adopting the child jointly with his or her spouse (the child's parent). The child then becomes the legal child of the adopting parents and the legal relationship between the child and his or her other parent is cut off. Adoption by a stepparent is becoming less common. Alternatively, the stepparent can apply for custody and guardianship jointly with his or her spouse. The court can award custody in an application for adoption if it thinks custody would be a more appropriate solution. In a custody or guardianship application the welfare of the child is the paramount consideration and the court will not grant the application unless satisfied that to do so would be in the interests of the child.

A stepparent becomes liable to aliment a stepchild if he or she accepts the child as a child of his or her family. This liability can be enforced by an application to the court by, or on behalf of, the child either in connection with the divorce proceedings between the stepparent and the child's parent or in separate proceedings. While the child's father is alive and able to afford aliment he is regarded as primarily liable to pay. The Child Support Agency will make a maintenance assessment against the child's absent father. The CSA will not deal with aliment due by stepparents.

On the breakdown of the marriage between a child's step-parent and parent the court hearing the divorce must be satisfied that the future arrangements for the children of both the parties' first and second marriages are suitable.

A person's will is not revoked by his or her subsequent marriage or divorce. If the stepparent is not mentioned in his or her spouse's will a claim for legal rights could be made. Legal rights amount to one half or one third of the spouse's property other than land or buildings. The higher fraction applies if the spouse leaves no surviving children. The Inheritance (Provision for Family and Dependents) Act 1975 does not apply to Scotland.

The title to the 'stepfamily home' may be taken simply in the name of the spouse and the stepparent. Each person then owns an equal share (unless the title deeds specify a different proportion) and on his or her death that share is dealt with by his or her will (or the rules of intestacy). Where the title is taken in the name of the spouse, the stepparent and the survivor of them, the home will belong entirely to the survivor. If you are remarrying you should think carefully about your will and whether to use a survivorship title.

The child's parent may appoint the stepparent to be the child's guardian by will. The stepparent will share guardianship with the other parent if he or she is still alive. Any disputes between them as guardians have to be resolved by the court.

Useful addresses

The Scottish Council for Single Parents
13 Gayfield Square, Edinburgh EH1 3NX
Tel: 031-556 3899
Helps all parents bringing up children alone by providing information, publishing leaflets and booklets, offering counselling and establishing local support groups and services.

Family Mediation Scotland
127 Rose Street, South Lane, Edinburgh EH2 4BB
Tel: 031-220 1610

Runs local mediation services to assist couples in reaching agreement about matters relating to breakdown of their relationship, especially concerning the children.

Marriage Counselling Scotland
105 Hanover Street, Edinburgh EH2 1DJ
Tel: 031-225 5006; helpline 031-220 1207

Catholic Marriage Advisory Council
13 North Bank Street, Edinburgh EH1 2LP
Tel: 041-204 1239

Scottish Women's Aid
11 St Colme Street, Edinburgh EH3 2JR
Tel: 031-221 0401
Runs refuges for abused women and their children. Also gives information and advice about legal rights and housing. Has network of local branches (see telephone directory).

Shelter Scottish Campaign for the Homeless
8 Hampton Terrace, Edinburgh EH12 5JD
Tel: 031-313 1550

CHAPTER 16

DIVORCE IN NORTHERN IRELAND

The jurisdiction and practice concerning divorce in Northern Ireland are similar to those operating in England and Wales. While the following list is not exhaustive we highlight some of the main points of difference below.

page 11
Although full civil aid is available, the green form scheme does not exist. Each divorce case has to have a full hearing in court with the petitioner giving oral evidence to support the petition.

page 14
All property dealt with by way of a property adjustment order under the Matrimonial Causes Order (Northern Ireland) 1978 is exempt from the statutory charge but not if the property is divided by way of partition proceedings under the Partition Acts (see below, page 271), which are deemed to be civil proceedings.

As yet there is no Legal Aid Board in Northern Ireland. The Law Society administers the legal aid scheme with very similar 'rules'.

page 26
Solicitors' costs: the hourly rate is £43; mark-ups tend to be more flexible than in England and Wales.

page 65
The Solicitors Family Law Association in Northern Ireland has adopted a similar code of practice to its counterpart in England. A

list of SFLA solicitors can be obtained from Oonagh Quinn at Trevor Smyth & Co. of Chester House, 13 Chichester Street, Belfast (tel: 0232) 320360.

page 68
Any complaint about a solicitor must be made in writing and sent to the Law Society of Northern Ireland, Law Society House, 98 Victoria Street, Belfast BT1 3GN; tel: (0232) 231614. The Lay Observer appointed under the Solicitors' (N.I.) Order 1976 investigates such complaints; tel: (0232) 242486.

page 70
In-court conciliation does not apply. In Northern Ireland, the petitioner lodges in court a statement as to the arrangements for the children. Together with a copy of the petition, this completed form is sent to the Health and Social Services Board who provide a report in every case, contested or uncontested, where children are involved. A social worker interviews both parents and completes a form provided by the court which gives details of income, living conditions and proposed arrangements for the children. This is completed and sent to the court. On occasions the Master will ask the social worker to provide further details but normally a standard report is completed and forwarded to the court, where it is read by the judge on the hearing of the divorce. He or she will read the report before making any order in relation to the children.

page 74
The Family Mediation Service (under the umbrella of RELATE) is the main organisation offering a conciliation service to couples who face divorce: 76 Dublin Road, Belfast BT2 7HP; tel: (0232) 322914.

page 107
Legislation has recently been introduced into Northern Ireland to allow the special procedure in the case of divorces where irretrievable breakdown is evidenced by two years' or five years' separation. However, it has not yet come into force as necessary changes in the Court Rules will probably be introduced at the

same time as the rules for the Children (Northern Ireland) Order 1992(3) – see below.

page 133

The Children Act does not apply in Northern Ireland and the principles of custody and access are still used, but the Children Order (see above), due to start being phased in from 1995, should be fully implemented by 1998.

page 155

In Northern Ireland two systems of registering co-exist: the Registry of Deeds (unregistered land) and the Land Registry (registered land). Your solicitor will need to find out where the title to your property is registered, by carrying out a search if necessary. It will then be possible for a matrimonial charge to be issued along the lines described for England and Wales. Because of the difficulty in registering an interest, the client would be wise to ask a solicitor to act on his or her behalf. The green form scheme would cover such a registration.

page 157

The land law in Northern Ireland is substantially different to that in England and Wales: a 'notice of severance' will probably be insufficient in Northern Ireland to sever a joint tenancy in order to create a tenancy in common. If there are no grounds for divorce, most solicitors in Northern Ireland will apply under the Partition Acts of 1868 and 1876, either to force a sale of the property and split the proceeds, or to force one party to buy out the other party's interest.

The statutory charge would apply in cases such as these where one or both parties have Legal Aid, as Partition proceedings are considered civil proceedings and do not form part of the matrimonial process.

page 228

Exclusion orders and personal protection orders (the equivalent of ouster orders) are speedily available through the Magistrates' Court for dealing with spouses who demonstrate or threaten violent behaviour. Note that these are available only if the parties are not divorced. If the parties are divorced and violence occurs after the date of the decree absolute, an application must be made to the County Court for an injunction to restrain the perpetrator, based on proceedings issued for damages for assault and trespass to the person; alternatively, particularly if there is no violence or if the behaviour is insufficient to satisfy the requirements for a protection and exclusion order, the applicant may apply for an ouster injunction as set out in Chapter 12.

Women threatened with domestic violence can contact Women's Aid, 129 University Street, Belfast BT7 1HP; tel: (0232) 249358.

GLOSSARY

Absent parent   A term laid down by the Child Support Act 1991 as meaning a parent not living in the same household with the [qualifying] child where the child has his or her home with the Parent with care

Access   See contact

Acknowledgement of service   Form sent by the court to the respondent (and co-respondent, if any) with the petition, with questions about his or her intentions and wishes in response to the petition; its return to the court establishes service of the petition

Adultery   Sexual intercourse by a husband or wife with a third party (of the opposite sex) at any time before a decree absolute of divorce

Affidavit   A statement in writing containing a person's evidence, on oath or by affirmation. The evidence in the affidavit need not be expressed in any formal way but should be set out in numbered paragraphs in the first person. If the person making the affidavit wishes to refer to any document, this document should be attached ('exhibited') to the affidavit

Ancillary relief   General term for the financial or property adjustment orders that the court can be asked to make 'ancillary' to a petition for divorce or judicial separation

Annuity   Money investment designed to produce regular fixed amounts of income, either for a fixed period or until death

Answer   The defence to a divorce petition, denying the allegations in the petition or cross-petition; strict time limits apply for filing an answer

Application A document giving details, in broad terms, of the order sought from the court. All applications within divorce proceedings are started by filing a notice of application. Standard forms are available at divorce court offices; they include a space for the place, date and time of the hearing of the application, to be completed by the court office

Calderbank letter Where a husband knows he will be ordered to make payment if the case goes to hearing, his solicitor writes a 'without prejudice' letter making an offer of settlement; if the wife rejects the offer and at the hearing is awarded less, the wife risks having to pay the husband's costs incurred after the date of the offer as well as her own; a wife can, similarly, make a Calderbank offer

Care and control An old order pre-dating the Children Act 1989: care and control orders are no longer made. The responsibility for looking after and making everyday decisions about a child and providing the child's main home base

In chambers When the district judge or judge considers an application in private rather than in open court; the proceedings tend to be less formal than normal court hearings and members of the public are not admitted

Charge (on property) Security entitling the holder of the charge to be paid out of the proceeds of sale when the house (or other property) is eventually sold

Child of the family Any child of both the parties and any child who has at any time been treated by both the parties as if a child of their own (but not foster-children); has to be listed in the petition irrespective of age

Clean break A once-and-for-all order that deals with all financial issues between spouses, provides for the dismissal of maintenance claims and is not capable of subsequent variations even if circumstances change

Conciliation A process of non-partisan mediation to help a couple reach agreement on issues such as the arrangements for children

Conflict of interests Where a solicitor cannot act for a potential client because he or she would be unable to discharge his or her duty to the client because of a pre-existing professional relationship to another client or a duty owed to another

Consent order   Order made by a court in terms agreed by both parties

Contact (formerly termed access)   An order under the Children Act for the child to visit or stay with the parent with whom the child is not living or exchange letters, cards or telephone calls; contact orders may also be made in favour of non-parents, e.g. grandparents (the obligation to provide contact is on the parent with whom the child lives)

Co-respondent   The person with whom the respondent has committed adultery

Counsel   Barrister

Cross-decrees   When a petitioner is granted a decree on the basis of the petition and the respondent on the basis of the answer

Cross-petition   When the respondent puts forward different reasons for the breakdown of the marriage from the petitioner's, and seeks a divorce on those facts

Custody   The right formerly granted by a court for one parent (or both) to make major decisions for a child, such as education and upbringing, change of religion (subject to the non-custodial parent's right to ask the court to review any such decision). An old order pre-dating the Children Act 1989: custody orders are no longer made

Decree absolute   The order dissolving the marriage

Decree nisi   Document issued once the court is satisfied that the grounds for divorce are established, allowing the petitioner to apply to have the decree made absolute after a further six weeks and one day. It does not end the marriage

Directions for trial   The stage of divorce proceedings when the district judge considers the petition and affidavit in support, and requests further information if required, before giving his or her certificate for a decree nisi to be pronounced by the judge; financial proceedings and applications about the children also have a directions for trial stage, when the district judge considers what further evidence will be required and makes orders accordingly

Disclosure   Full information about all matters relevant to any financial application; each spouse has a duty to give full and frank disclosure

Discovery Procedure by which each party supplies to the other a list of documents relevant to an application and permits the other to inspect them

District judge Judicial officer appointed by the Lord Chancellor; responsible for dealing with most applications to a divorce court (used to be called a registrar)

Divorce court Any county court designated by the Lord Chancellor as a court where divorce proceedings can be heard; the Divorce Registry in London serves as a divorce court. Divorce county courts not designated Family Hearing Centres (FHC) can deal only with the administrative process of divorces; any contested applications will be referred to an FHC

Domicile Legal concept, not necessarily related to residence: domicile of origin is normally determined by the place where a person was born and is retained unless a new domicile – a domicile of choice – is adopted by a conscious decision to take up permanent residence in, and actually moving to, another country

Equity (of a property) The net value of house or flat after mortgage debts are discharged and expenses of sale met

Exhibit Document referred to in, sworn with, and attached to an affidavit; usually identified by initials and number

Ex parte An application made directly to the court without prior notification to the party or parties

Family Hearing Centre A county court with the power to deal with the administrative process of divorce and any contested applications under the Children Act or for financial relief

Filing Leaving documents – petition and accompanying documents, affidavits, notices of application – with the court office for sealing, and subsequent service

Green form Popular term for legal aid scheme under which a limited amount of legal advice and assistance is given

Hearsay evidence A fact reported to a witness, as opposed to being known by the witness; second-hand knowledge; hearsay evidence can now be accepted by a court in family proceedings

Injunction Order by the court telling someone what he or she must do or must refrain from doing; the penalty for disobedience can be imprisonment

Intestacy Dying without a valid will

Legal aid   Government-funded scheme administered by the Legal Aid Board based on financial eligibility and merits of case. What you pay towards your solicitor's bill is:

● any contribution you are assessed to pay out of your disposable income and/or capital

● payment out of any money or property gained or preserved which is subject to the statutory charge.

Your being legally aided does not preclude your opponent being ordered to pay some or all of your costs. If costs are awarded against you, you personally have to pay (the Legal Aid Board will not) but your liability for your opponent's solicitor's bill will be limited to what the court considers reasonable

Liable relative proceedings   Proceedings taken by the DSS against person legally responsible for maintaining wife or husband and/or children who has failed to do so

Maintenance Application Form and Maintenance Enquiry Form   A standard form sent out by the Child Support Agency to parents with care and absent parents respectively asking them about their means and circumstances

Mediation   An alternative form of dispute resolution over issues arising in the wake of separation or divorce. Comprehensive mediation covers both problems over the children and finances; other mediation (or conciliation) services may deal with child-related disputes alone

Minutes of order   Draft terms of agreement placed before the court with a request that a consent order be made in those terms

Mortgagee   The building society, bank or other corporate lender, or individual lending money on the security of a house or flat

Mortgagor   The person who borrows money on mortgage usually to enable him or her to buy a house or flat

Nominal order   When recipient is entitled to maintenance but at the time of the order payment cannot be made or is not needed, an order for a nominal amount of maintenance (for example, 5p a year) is made so that if circumstances change, there is an order on the court's file which can be reviewed and increased

Non-molestation Order to prohibit one person from assaulting, harassing or interfering with another

Notice of application Form on which applications to the court are made, beginning with the words 'Take notice that . . .' and containing full details of what is applied for

Ouster Order excluding one spouse from the matrimonial home (or a part of it)

Parental responsibility The bundle of rights and duties that parents have towards their children; mothers and married fathers have parental responsibility automatically, while non-married fathers may acquire it by formal agreement or court order; others (e.g. guardians, a person with a residence order in his or her favour) can acquire parental responsibility too

Parent with care A term laid down by the Child Support Act 1991 to mean the parent with whom the child has his or her home and who usually provides day-to-day care for the child

Penal notice A warning endorsed on a court order, notifying the recipient that he or she is liable to committal to prison for breach of the order

Pending suit While the divorce is still continuing (i.e. before decree absolute)

Petitioner The person who initiates divorce proceedings by filing the petition

Pleadings Formal statements or documents containing a summary of the issues in a case

Prayer Formal request in the petition, or answer, for the court orders which the petitioner or respondent seeks; for example, dissolution of the marriage, orders under the Children Act, costs, ancillary relief

Prohibited steps order Court order under the Children Act restricting a person's exercise of parental responsibility (e.g. preventing a parent from removing a child from the country without the other parent's consent or court permission)

Qualifying child A term laid down by the Child Support Act 1991 to mean a child under 16 or under 19 and in full-time non-advanced education – one of his or her parents must be an 'absent parent' (see Absent parent)

Questionnaire List of questions delivered by one spouse to the other requiring further information and/or documentation about finances, in accordance with that person's duty of disclosure; also referred to as 'request under rule 2.63', the rule of court permitting such a questionnaire

Recovered or preserved ' Gained or retained (money or property) in the course of legal proceedings

Relevant child Child of the family under 16 years of age at the date of the decree nisi or between 16 and 18 years of age receiving instruction at an educational establishment or undergoing training for a trade, profession or vocation (or up to any age, if disabled and dependant)

Reply Document filed by the petitioner in response to an answer and/or a cross-petition from the respondent, containing the petitioner's defence

Reserved costs When decision on amount of costs to be awarded is deferred until later hearing

Residence order An order under the Children Act which settles the arrangements about where a child will live; residence orders can be split between parents (or others) or shared, e.g. in favour of a parent and stepparent

Respondent The spouse who is not the petitioner

Rule 2.63 The rule of court relating to the statement of information which has to be supplied to the court for a financial consent order to be made

Sealing by the court The court's stamping of a document when it is filed at the court office or for an order or decree when it is issued

Section 41 appointment Or 'children's appointment' – this was a short hearing before a judge for certificate of satisfaction in respect of arrangements for any relevant children before decree nisi could be pronounced. Section 41 appointments are no longer made since the Children Act came into force (except for divorces which were filed before 14 October 1991)

Secured provision When some income-producing asset of the payer is put under the control of trustees and, if necessary, the income diverted to the payee to provide the maintenance

Service The method by which the petition, notices of application, orders and decrees are supplied to the parties concerned; certain documents need to be served personally, others are served through the post, some by or on behalf of the person issuing them and some by the court

Special procedure In an undefended divorce, the decree can be issued without either petitioner or respondent having to appear (or be represented) at the court: the facts submitted by the petitioner in the petition and verified on affidavit are considered by the district judge. When he/she is satisfied that the facts in the petition are proved and that the ground for a divorce exists, he/she issues a certificate to that effect and fixes a date for the formal pronouncement of the decree nisi by the judge. A copy of the decree is sent through the post to both husband and wife by the court office

Specific issue order An order under the Children Act resolving some particular dispute (e.g. schooling) about the children's upbringing

Statement of arrangements Form which has to be filed with petition if there are relevant children of the family, setting out arrangements proposed for them in the future; this should be agreed with the respondent and countersigned if possible before the divorce is started

Statutory charge The amount payable by legally aided person out of any property or cash that was recovered or preserved in the proceedings, where contributions to legal aid fund not sufficient to meet the legal costs of the case (in matrimonial proceedings, maintenance and a lump sum of £2,500 are exempt)

Summons Demand issued by a court for a person against whom a claim or complaint has been made to appear at the court at a specified time

Undefended divorce Where the dissolution of the marriage and how it is to be achieved are not disputed (even if there is dispute about ancillary matters such as the children or finances)

Undertaking Promise to the court to do or not do something which is outside the court's powers to order but is incorporated within a court order so that it is enforceable; the court has no power to vary an undertaking

Without prejudice Phrase used to prevent communications in the negotiation process being made known to the court if those negotiations fail to produce agreement

INDEX